THE ITALIAN EXPERIENCE
IN THE UNITED STATES

A9.95R

THE ITALIAN EXPERIENCE IN THE UNITED STATES

edited by Silvano M. Tomasi
and Madeline H. Engel

New York
CENTER FOR MIGRATION STUDIES, INC.
197

LIBRARY
COLBY-SAWYER COLLEGE
NEW LONDON, NH 03257

E
184
.I8
T6
1977
c.1

#25186/93

The Center for Migration Studies is an educational, non-profit institute founded in New York in 1964 to encourage and facilitate the study of sociological, demographic, historical, legislative and pastoral aspects of human migration movements and ethnic group relations everywhere. The opinions expressed in this work are those of the author.

THE ITALIAN EXPERIENCE
IN THE UNITED STATES

Published 1970
Second Printing 1977

Copyright © 1970 by
The Center for Migration Studies of New York, Inc.
All rights reserved. No part of this book may be reproduced
without written permission from the publisher.

Center for Migration Studies
209 Flagg Place
Staten Island, New York 10304

ISBN 0-913256-01-3
Library of Congress Catalog Card Number: 76-131436
Printed in the United States of America

Preface

Questions of group identity, power and organization are being increasingly recognized as crucial for an understanding of the American scene. Although many writers have considered race and religion to be the most significant elements in group identity, ethnicity is hardly, as they suggest, unimportant to Americans. In fact, it would seem we are now witnessing a resurgence of ethnic influence on behavior, both among Blacks who have become "Afro" orientated and among third and later generation whites of Irish, Italian, Polish or other European backgrounds. If the attempt to establish themselves as an ethnic group with a proud heritage underlies, in part, current Black movements, then that same factor also underlies, in part, the retaliatory white ethnic reactions against the Blacks, including the social and political backlash which reaches its most intense forms in working class communities.

Given the importance of ethnicity, it is surprising that so many nationality groups have been ignored by both historians and sociologists. The Cornish and the Welsh, for example, have received little scholarly attention, perhaps because their groups were small and were perceived to be WASPS (white, Anglo-Saxon, Protestants). The Italians, too, have been slighted in social science literature, perhaps because of cultural and linguistic barriers to research on their adjustment in this society. Whatever its causes, the fact remains that there is great need, on both the theoretical and the practical levels, of detailed, scientific studies of all the ethnic groups in our country. This book is offered as a necessary step toward remedying the paucity of materials on Italo-Americans and some of the consequent lacunae in considerations of the American scene.

We have assembled ten articles on various aspects of the Italian experience in the United States. Certain of these first appeared in the special 1968 issue of The International Migra-

tion Review [1] *and others have not been previously published.
The articles are grouped into four sections.*

*Part I deals with facts and figures about Italian migra-
tion to the United States. The first article in this
section is concerned with the basic characteristics and
trends of the migration, especially as these have developed over the last twenty years. The second article
examines Italian migration to the United States in the
1960's emphasizing the role played by the 1965 Immigration Act with respect to the size and nature of the
movement.*

*Part II considers the overall impact of the Italian and
American society on each other. It deals, therefore,
with the distribution of Italians in the United States,
especially as that distribution was affected by the
padrone system. It is evident that the padroni were
extremely important in keeping the migrants in urban
areas, especially in the northeastern states. This gave
their relations with the larger society a distinctive
characteristic which is the subject of the next section.*

*Part III deals with selected illustrations of the ways
in which Italians related to American mores in economic, educational, political and religious institutions.
Five different views of Italo-American adjustment
emerge from the articles in this section, each suggest-
ing a process of interaction in which both the Italians
and the receiving society changed their orientation,
attitudes, beliefs and behavior patterns. They indicated
that Italian migrants, in ways both like and unlike those
of their white ethnic predecessors, such as the Irish,
adopted American cultural patterns (i.e., became acculturated or culturally assimilated) and in time were
accepted by other Americans, especially those in power
(i.e., became socially assimilated). This is not to imply*

---

[1] *International Migration Review*, vol. 1 (New Series), n. 3 (Summer
1967), pp. 95.

*that the migrants were without problems in the process
or that they have been victims of less than their share
of prejudice and discrimination. The assimilation
process always has its ups and downs, its joys and its
heartaches. Italians have found, and continue to find,
employers, landlords, educators and others who do not
welcome them or afford them a chance for upward
social mobility. Nevertheless, the vast majority of
Italians in the United States have begun to "make it,"
and have found a life in this society not unlike the one
dreamed of by their parents or grandparents. A few
Italians did not succeed and did not find happiness, or
they succeeded economically but found this was not
enough to satisfy their desires. For this small segment
of the Italo-American population, social and psychological fulfillment is to be found back in Italy, or so some
of the migrants think.*

*Part IV analyzes return migration to Italy, focusing
on its causes and effects, both for migrants and for
Italian society.*

Thus, Parts I through IV form a cycle in the study of
migration.

At this particular point in time, no one book can claim to
be the definitive work on a group as large and important as
the Italians in the United States. Each of the articles in this
book is, of necessity, limited in scope and orientation, and
none, or even the ten considered together, can claim to present
a complete picture of the Italian experience. Each section
includes a selected bibliography, prepared by the respective
authors, on a number of topics connected with the feelings
and actions of Italo-Americans as they assimilated to a new
way of life.

Listed are many easily accessible sources of further information which also provide additional bibliographical material.

The papers assembled here seek to answer questions about
Italo-Americans, but perhaps more significantly they seek to
pose questions, too. It is the hope of the authors, as well as
the editors, that these articles will furnish insights into the
Italian experience and fruitful hypotheses for future research

on this experience, its impact both on the Italians and the larger society, and its relevance for theories of assimilation.

The editors wish to gratefully acknowledge the encouragement and the financial assistance received from Mr. Louis Cenci of the Education Committee of the Italian Club of Staten Island, Inc., Mrs. Hedy Giusti-Lanham, Executive Director of the America-Italy Society, Inc. and Dr. Joseph Valletutti, Executive Director of the Italian Cultural Center, Inc., in the preparation of this reader.

MADELINE H. ENGEL
Herbert H. Lehman College
of the City University
of New York

SILVANO M. TOMASI
Center for Migration Studies
and Richmond College of the
City University of New York

January 1970.

Contents

FACTS AND FIGURES

Any discussion of Italian migration to the
United States must begin with an analysis of
the number of people involved in the movement. Who were they? What were some of
their more salient characteristics? Where
did they wish to go? Why? The two papers
in this section explore these and related
questions. The first deals with major trends
and patterns in migration; the second deals
with the effect of recent American legislation
on the migration.

Italian Emigration: Basic Characteristics and Trends with Special Reference to the Post-War Years

by Giuseppe Lucrezio Monticelli *

Italy's external migration constitutes the largest population movement from Europe in terms of numbers and length of residence abroad. It can be studied statistically from the time of the political unification of the country, even though some figures are uncertain. The 1861 census presents the first data regarding Italians abroad: about one hundred thousand on the American continent. Since then, no fewer than 26 million Italians emigrated. It is more difficult, however, to determine the number of returns, since in the first decades of the movement they were not regularly recorded. In any event, since 1900 more than 10 million Italians have left their country permanently. On the basis of the natural demographic increase, the median age and the distribution of emigrants, some have projected a total of 40 million persons as the number of descendants of Italian migrants. The projection, however, is based on personal estimates and theoretical considerations and is mentioned only to suggest the volume of the phenomenon.

According to estimates of competent Italian consular and diplomatic authorities, about five million Italian citizens are now permanently residing abroad: 45 percent of these are in Europe, 50 percent in the Americas, 3 percent in Oceania. The largest community of people retaining Italian citizenship — about 1,300,000 persons — is in Argentina, while there are 650,000 of them in both France and Switzerland; 350,000 in West Germany; 300,000 in Brazil; 250,000 in both Canada and the United States of America; fewer than 200,000 in Venezuela, and still fewer in other countries.

During the 19th century various demographers dealt with

---

* Dr. G. Lucrezio Monticelli, former Assistant of Statistics and Economics in the Universities of Bari and Rome, is on the Editorial Board of *Studi Emigrazione* and is Secretary of the Central Office for Italian Emigration, U.C.E.I.

3

Italian emigration. The phenomenon began early in that century and affected not only a few artists and a handful of merchants and adventurers, but also significant numbers of migrants in search of economic opportunity. From the *Annuario Statistico per gli anni 1857-58* by Cesare Correnti and from the *Histoire de l'émigration* by Jules Duval (Paris, 1862), we learn that before 1860 more than 115,000 Italians had settled abroad: 60,000 in Europe, mainly in France; 40,000 in the two Americas, of whom 30,000 were in Latin America; 15,000 in Algeria and some even in Australia. The 1861 census reported the existence of even larger communities abroad: 110,000 in Europe (77,000 in France; 14,000 in Germany and the same number in Switzerland; 5,000 in Great Britain); a few thousand in Africa (12,000 in Egypt; 6,000 in Tunis).

The first thorough and systematic statistical survey of Italian emigration, however, dates from 1876 and was prepared by what was then called the General Office of Statistics. From 1869 to 1876 statistical research was carried out for the Ministries of Foreign Affairs and of the Interior by Leone Carpi, who was also the author of valuable publications in this field. The criteria and the methods used were substantially different from those used in the previous surveys and they differ again from those in use later. It is well to remember, therefore, in this brief survey of the Italian migratory movement from the unification of Italy in 1860 to 1967, that the statistics available are not completely homogeneous and comparable.

In any event, Italian emigration made up at least half of the total intra-European population movement. Then, from the beginning of the twentieth century, it formed the largest group in the flow of European emigration overseas, with the occasional exception of British emigration.

In the first period of Italian emigration, up to the year 1900, the gross total was about 7 million persons. It was a movement mostly of individuals, two-thirds of whom came from Northern Italy and three-fifths of whom emigrated to other European countries.

In the second period, from the beginning of the century to the outbreak of World War I in 1915, there was a total of about 9 million migrants. Three characteristics distinguished this period from the first: a) Emigration was now regulated by the State. At the beginning of 1901 an emigration law was enacted, *Legge 31 1901, n. 23*; and the *Commissariato Generale della Emigrazione* was established; b) Emigration from South-

Italian Migratory Movement, 1861-1967
(yearly average in thousands)

Years	Emigrants			Returns			Net Emigration		
	Europe & Mediterranean Countries	Overseas	Total	Europe & Mediterranean Countries	Overseas	Total	Europe & Mediterranean Countries	Overseas	Total
1861-1870	99	22	121	—	—	—	—	—	—
1871-1880	91	27	118	—	—	82	—	—	36
1881-1890	93	95	188	—	—	—	—	—	—
1891-1900	129	155	284	—	—	—	—	—	—
Average 1861-1900	103	75	178	—	—	—	—	—	—
1901-1910	251	351	602	—	172	—	—	180	—
1911-1914	285	365	650	—	202	—	—	163	—
Average 1901-1914	261	355	616	—	180	—	—	175	—
1915-1918	51	40	91	—	58	—	—	18	—
1919-1920	176	258	434	—	84	—	—	174	—
1921-1930	148	110	258	77	61	138	71	49	120
Average 1915-1930	127	111	238	—	63	—	—	48	—
1931-1940	46	24	70	40	19	59	6	5	11
1946-1951*	131	106	237	58	21	79	73	85	158
1952-1957	160	129	289	93	31	124	67	98	165
1958-1962	261	71	332	158	27	185	103	44	147
1963-1967	214	55	269	186	11	197	28	44	72
Average 1946-1967	187	93	280	119	23	142	68	70	138

* Since this time, countries of the Mediterranean Basin are included in those overseas.
Sources: From official data published by the Istituto Centrale Di Statistica, Rome (ISTAT).
N.B. The dash (—) means that statistical data are not available.

TABLE 2
Italian Migratory Movement, 1946-1967
(in thousands)

Countries of Immigration	Emigrants		Returns		Net Emigration	
	Total	Annual Average	Total	Annual Average	Total	Annual Average
European Countries						
1946-1951	788	131	351	58	437	73
1952-1957	957	160	554	93	403	67
1958-1962	1,306	261	790	158	516	103
1963-1967	1,070	214	932	186	138	28
Total 1946-1967	4,121	187	2,627	119	1,494	68
Non-European Countries						
1946-1951	633	105	121	20	512	85
1952-1957	779	130	190	32	589	98
1958-1962	355	71	137	27	218	44
1963-1967	274	55	51	10	223	45
Total 1946-1967	2,041	93	499	23	1,542	70
Entire Movement						
1946-1951	1,421	237	472	79	949	158
1952-1957	1,736	289	744	124	992	165
1958-1962	1,661	332	927	185	734	147
1963-1967	1,344	269	983	197	361	42
Grand Total 1946-1967	6,162	280	3,126	142	3,036	138

Source: Data from the Istituto Centrale di Statistica (ISTAT). The same system of elaboration of data available from ISTAT (Rome) is used in the following tables.

TABLE 3
Components of the Italian Migratory Movement, 1946-1967
(percentage of the total)

Years	Emigrants		Returns		Net Emigration	
	Europe	Overseas	Europe	Overseas	Europe	Overseas
1946-1951	55	45	74	26	46	54
1952-1957	55	45	74	26	41	59
1958-1962	79	21	85	13	70	30
1963-1967	80	20	95	5	33	64
Average 1946-1967	67	33	84	12	49	51

ern Italy outnumbered that from the North; c) Emigration overseas outnumbered the movement to European countries. In 1913, 872,598 persons emigrated. This figure represents the peak of Italian emigration and, for this period, the greatest number of emigrants from any country, including Great Britain.

With Italy's entrance into World War I the average number of emigrants fell from 600,000 a year to below 100,000. About 60 percent of these emigrants went to European countries, and emigration from the North again outnumbered that from the South, as it had in the first period. After the War, from 1919 to 1927, the previous annual average was tripled reaching a total of 2,900,000 persons. The movement was directed in almost equal measure to European and overseas countries, and the net movement was less than half the total emigration.

In 1928 emigration was drastically reduced because of restrictive legislation enacted by the receiving countries and by Italy itself. From 1928 to 1940 the total movement numbered less than 1,300,000 persons, an annual average below the 100,000 average of the war years. The majority of emigrants were from the North, and two-thirds went to other European countries. There were 70 percent more returns than exits and the net emigration was less than 350,000 persons, less than 27,000 a year.

After World War II, during which economic emigration was almost non-existent and returns were far greater than exits, the emigration movement increased considerably, but with different characteristics. The totals for this period were not as high as those of the first years of the century. From 1946 to 1968, however, 6,400,000 persons emigrated from Italy, and about half of them returned. Two-thirds of the migrants, most of them from Central and Southern Italy, went to European countries. This figure, however, falls to 49 percent if we consider only net emigration. Thus, Italian emigration, after a period of considerable development in the last years of the nineteenth century and even greater development during the first years of the twentieth century, fell off sharply during World War I and did not resume — with the exception of the period 1919-1927 — until after World War II. At first, migrants came mainly from the North and moved overseas. Then, the trend changed. Today the opposite is true, the stream coming mainly from the South and being directed toward Europe.

Quantitative and Qualitative Aspects of the Movement in the Post-War Years.

Available statistical data show that Italian emigration, like most migratory movements, has fluctuated in cycles or pseudo-cycles of varying length and volume in different periods. The post-war period is no exception.

Although it may be somewhat arbitrary, it seems useful to divide this period into two parts, before and after 1958, when the latest system of data collection was adopted: the first, from 1946 to 1957 and the second, from 1958 to 1967. Each of the two parts could be subdivided as follows: 1946-1951 and 1952-1956; 1958-1962 and 1963-1967.

The subdivisions seem sufficiently indicative as far as the general movement and the movement toward European countries are concerned. The tables and the analysis of the general trends, therefore, will follow the above subdivisions.[1]

Tables 2 and 3 present a comprehensive view of the totals, annual averages and percentages of the total on the cycles mentioned above. Table 4 presents the index numbers and percentage variations for each period as compared to the one preceding it. In the years from 1946 to 1967 about 6,150,000 persons emigrated from Italy and 3,150,000 returned. Thus, 3,000,000 persons, an average of 145,000 a year, settled abroad permanently, and of these, 1,500,000 remained in Europe. These figures begin to suggest a constantly increasing European component. Furthermore, from the 1946-1951 period to the 1963-1967 period the over-all European movement increased from 55 percent to 80 percent of the emigrants and from 74 percent to 95 percent of the returnees, a net change from 46 percent to 38 percent.[2] In addition to the progressive intra-

---

[1] The first period ends in 1951, when the European Coal and Steel Community was constituted; the second, in 1957, when the Treaty of Rome was signed for the founding of the European Economic Community; the third and the fourth are linked with the cycles of the economic situation. The figures are given in the nearest round numbers and are, therefore, approximate.

[2] For more details: Lucrezio, G., Perotti, A., Falchi, N., *L'emigrazione italiana negli anni '70.* Roma, 1966, Prospettive CSER, n. 1, Ed. Centro Studi Emigrazione and Morcelliana.

TABLE 4

Index Numbers and Percentage Variations of the Italian Migratory Movement, 1946-1967
(yearly averages of each period)

Countries of Immigration	Index Numbers [1]			Percentage Variations [2]		
	Emigrants	Returns	Net Emigration	Emigrants	Returns	Net Emigration
Europe						
1946-1951	100	100	100			
1952-1957	122	158	92	22	+58	—8
1958-1962	199	271	142	64	71	+54
1963-1967	163	319	38	(-18)	18	-73
Overseas						
1946-1951	100	100	100			
1952-1957	123	157	115	+23	57	+15
1958-1962	67	135	51	45	-14	-56
1963-1967	52	51	52	-23	-62	2
Total Movement						
1946-1951	100	100	100			
1952-1957	122	158	104	+22	+58	+4
1958-1962	140	236	93	15	49	-11
1963-1967	114	250	46	-19	6	-51

[1] Base 1946-1951 = 100.
[2] With respect to the yearly average of the preceding period.

TABLE 5
Percentage of Returns over Exits, 1946-1967

Year	Europe	Overseas	Total
1946-1951	45	19	33
1952-1957	58	24	43
1958-1962	60	39	55
1963-1967	87	19	73
Average 1946-1967	64	24	51

European trend of the movement, we must note a continuing increase in its temporary nature. Emigration overseas, by its nature, tends to be permanent, at least in most cases. The decrease in the movement overseas — in 1958 it fell to half the annual average of the period 1946-1951 — is a factor in the increase general percentage of returns over exits.[3] In fact, Table 5 also reflects the fact that European emigration has assumed an even more temporary character, and the percentage of returns increased from 45 per cent (average 1946-1951) to 87 percent (average 1963-1967), not only because of the seasonal aspect of some of the movements, but because of a general tendency toward higher geographic mobility.

Italian Emigration in Europe.

The most important component of Italian migration abroad, which influenced the general trend, was the flow to European countries. In recent years this accounted for more than 80 percent of the exits and 95 percent of the returns. Furthermore, migration to countries within Europe constituted almost the entire movement in 1946-1947. Then the percentages decreased, except for some modest increases, until 1954, after which they progressively increased, as did the absolute number, until 1961-1962, when totals and percentages again decreased. In 1967 the European percentage of the total migration flow was about 73 percent. In addition, the returns from European countries have formed a larger part of the total movement

---

[3] The ratio of returns (R) and emigrations (E) may also be taken as an approximate measure of the temporary character of a specific migratory stream T = R.E.

than the exits. The percentage of returns increased constantly and reached 96 percent of all returns in 1967. For the net emigration, the situation is analogous to that of the exits, but obviously with smaller percentages and greater fluctuations.

Data relating to the European movement show great variability, usually greater than that of the general movement, but they evidence a general trend toward increase, although with the fluctuations and decreases noted.

The trend, which is very clear regarding exits and returns, persists in the net figures. These figures, in recent years, however, have undergone a far greater reduction than the emigrations. The Italian movement toward European countries presents, in turn, two fundamental subcomponents: emigration to the European Economic Community and to Switzerland. Analysis of Table 6 indicates that, if European emigration reflects the main direction of the general movement, emigration to the European Economic Community countries reflects today the direction of the European flow. Emigration to Switzerland, which represents a notable segment of the exit-return movement, is a smaller part of the net emigration because of its strong seasonal character. It is also to be noted that for the 1946-1951 period especially the trend is quite variable. In 1949 the number of returns far exceeded that of exits, a phenomenon not found before or after that year and which may be accounted for by the criteria for computing data at that time.

From 1946 to 1951 the movement toward the European Economic Community was directed almost exclusively to France and the Benelux nations, and from 1952 to 1958 France continued to absorb the strongest current. After 1958, however, migration to France tended to decrease while migration to Germany increased rapidly. The increasingly temporary character of the emigration movement is reflected in Table 7 in the percentage of returns as compared to the percentage of exits in the same years. This percentage progressively increased for all destinations with only a brief exception, for Switzerland and the Federal Republic of Germany in the period 1958-1962.

A more detailed analysis shows that emigration to European countries has increased continuously and rapidly: it doubled from 1958 (157,800) to 1961 (329,597); it decreased gradually to 1964 (216,498) and resumed in 1965 (232,421), obviously influenced, first, by the economic boom, and, then,

TABLE 5

Principal Components of Italian Emigration in European Countries

Countries of Immigration	Yearly Averages (in thousands)			Percentage of total		
	Emigrants	Returns	Net Emigration	Emigrants	Returns	Net Emigration
EEC						
1946-1951	63	16	47	48	27	64
1952-1957	81	35	46	50	37	69
1958-1962	141	77	64	54	49	62
1963-1967	100	89	11	47	48	40
Average 1946-1967	94	51	43	50	43	63
Switzerland						
1946-1951	63	42	21	48	71	29
1952-1957	68	56	12	43	61	18
1958-1962	111	79	32	43	50	31
1963-1967	106	93	13	49	50	46
Average 1946-1967	85	66	19	45	55	28
Other Countries						
1946-1951	5	—	5	4	2	7
1952-1957	11	2	9	7	2	13
1958-1962	9	2	7	3	1	7
1963-1967	8	4	4	4	2	14
Average 1946-1967	8	2	6	5	2	9
Total Europe						
1946-1951	131	58	73	100	100	100
1952-1957	160	93	67	100	100	100
1958-1962	261	158	103	100	100	100
1963-1967	214	186	28	100	100	100
Average 1946-1967	187	119	68	100	100	100

TABLE 7

Percentage Comparisons of Returns with Emigrations in some European Countries

Countries	1946-51	1952-57	1958-62	1963-67	Total 1946-67
Benelux Nations	34	28	57	80	40
France	19	45	64	85	48
Federal Rep. of Germany .	—	66	47	91	69
Total for EEC	25	43	54	89	55
Switzerland	66	82	71	88	78
Total for Europe	44	58	61	87	64

by the recession, phenomena which have a delayed effect on migratory movements. Later, with improvement in the Italian economy, recession in other countries, especially Germany, and the restrictive measures adopted in Switzerland, the flow diminished again to 219,353 persons in 1966 and 167,000 in 1967. It seems that in 1968 a slight increase took place (175,000 persons).

The number of returns increased continuously up to 1962 (210,575) and has fluctuated since then, in relation partly to the number of exits. The returns decreased in 1963-64, rose in the three following years (200,913 persons in 1966), and decreased again in 1967.

The pattern of net emigration is similar to that of emigration, but with a clearer trend. The percentage of returns, after a marked decrease in 1960, has continuously increased, except in 1964 and 1965, and in 1967 it was over 97 percent.

It is to be noted that on the basis of data available in 1964, a little less than a fourth of the returnees in the three previous years had sojourned abroad less than six months; over half had lived abroad from six months to a year; less than a tenth, from one year to two years, and slightly more over two years. For more than 75 percent of the returnees residence abroad lasted less than a year because of the seasonal character of many work contracts. Italian emigration in Europe in this 1964-1967 period flowed mainly as mentioned above, toward the European Economic Community countries and Switzerland. In the same period, the relative population dynamics underwent several changes. Emigration to and from the European Economic Community countries has always constituted the main trend, but has gradually diminished in relation to the total European flow. It accounted for almost 60 percent of the emigrants in Europe in 1958 and less that 42 percent in 1967 while in 1968 the percentage reached 47 percent. Similar situations obtain for the returns: 56 percent in 1958 and 47 percent in 1967. The decrease is more significant for net emigration, from 65 percent to 17 percent in 1966 with negative figures for 1967. Such results are brought about by the marked decrease in emigration to France and Germany. The causes differ for the two countries and are probably of a more temporary character in the case of Germany, as seems to be evidenced in the resumption of the flow in 1968 with 65,000 persons estimated against 47,000 registered in 1967. There is also a remarkable incidence of returns from Germany which brings the net emigration to negative figures.

All in all, however, Switzerland is the European country that received the largest number of Italians, almost all *de jure* and *de facto* seasonal workers. The number increased from 57,000 in 1958 to 143,000 in 1962 and then decreased continuously, falling in the last two years to less than 100,000.

By the end of 1967 almost 2,200,000 Italian citizens were residing in European countries, in addition to those who had asked for and obtained new citizenship, as in France, where they exceed a half million. Three fifths of these are in European Economic Community countries — 29 percent in France, 17 percent in Germany, and 11 percent in Belgium — 29 percent in Switzerland, 8 percent in Great Britain and the rest in other countries. The movement is composed primarily of emigrants from southern and island regions of Italy, about two-thirds of the total. However, since 1964 the percentage from these regions has been markedly reduced as compared to that of 1960. There was, instead, an increase of the net emigration movement from the northern regions, due, presumably, to the numerous workers who had migrated there and during the economic recession had moved abroad for new jobs.

Overseas Emigration

The Italian migratory flow to non-European countries (Table 8) reflects a totally different trend. The number of overseas emigrants increased from only a few thousand in 1946 to almost 160,000 in 1949, and then gradually decreased to 113,000 in 1953. There was a short increase through the two

TABLE 8

Italian Migratory Movement Toward Extra-European Countries Yearly Averages for Each Period
(in thousands - rounded figures)

Countries of Immigration	1946-48	1949-54	1955-60	1961-66	1967-68	Total 1946-68
Emigrants						
Canada & USA . . .	16	29	47	34	41	37
Latin America	41	87	36	5	2	43
America	57	116	83	39	43	80
Oceania	1	16	19	13	14	15
Africa & Asia . . .	3	7	4	1	2	4
Total	61	139	106	53	59	99
Returns						
Canada & USA . . .	3	3	5	—	—	3
Latin America . . .	4	19	18	6	3	13
America	7	22	23	6	3	16
Oceania	—	1	2	1	1	1
Africa & Asia . . .	2	7	7	7	3	6
Total	9	30	32	14	7	23
Net Emigration						
Canada & USA . .	13	25	42	34	41	34
Latin America . . .	37	69	18	-1	-1	30
America	50	94	60	33	40	64
Oceania	1	15	17	12	13	14
Africa & Asia . . .	1	—	-3	-6	-1	-2
Total	52	109	74	39	52	76

following years (148,000 in 1955), and then a continued decrease to about 42,000 in 1964. In 1965, the number went up to about 50,000 and to almost 77,000 in 1966. It began to decrease again in 1967 to 62,500 and in 1968 to 57,000.

The number of returns almost always increased until 1958 (41,000), when it decreased steadily and at a more rapid rate than that of emigration. In 1966 the number of returns was slightly above 5,500. It increased to 7,000 in 1967 and 7,700 in 1968. The net figure, therefore, followed the emigration trend, but with decreases, in general, less accentuated and with clearer resumptions (about 42,000 in 1965; 72,000 in 1966; 55,000 in 1967 and 49,300 in 1968). Just as the general trend of Italian emigration in the post-war period appears clearly related to that toward European countries, the overseas movement is related to the flow toward American countries, which accounts for more than 80 percent of emigrations, 75 percent of returns and more than 85 percent of the net emigration. Of the other destinations, the most important is Oceania toward which the movement, which for all practical purposes began with some consistency in 1949, fluctuated with an average of 15,000 emigrants and 1,000 returns yearly. From 1946 to 1968 about 300,000 Italians definitively settled in Oceania.

Returns clearly marked the movement with respect to African and Asian countries. Since 1946 the number of returns surpassed by 70,000 the number of emigrations. These trends are confirmed in Table 9. The percentage progressively decreased to insignificance for Canada and the United States; it remained constant, with some moderate fluctuations, for Oceania; it has progressively increased to more than 100 percent for Latin American countries. The increase was even greater for African and Asian countries. In addition, Italian overseas emigration is composed primarily of emigrants from southern and island regions more than three-fourths of the total, though this has fallen off slightly in the last four years.

TABLE 9

Percentage of Return Compared to Emigration Overseas

	1946-48	1949-54	1955-60	1961-66	1967-68	1946-68
Canada & US	18	12	11	—	3	8
Latin America	10	21	49	127	97	30
America	12	19	28	17	11	20
Oceania	14	6	12	6	5	7
Africa & Asia	67	102	186	600	133	175
Total	15	22	30	28	12	24

Emigration to American Countries.

Italian emigration to the Americas affected two groups of countries: 1) Canada and the United States and 2) Latin America. Since 1946, in fact, 1,365,000 Italians definitively settled in the Americas: 725,000 or 53 percent, in Canada and the United States, and 640,000 or 47 percent in Latin America.

1 - Italian emigration to Canada and the United States is characterized by a low percentage of returns, the number of which was almost insignificant in recent years. The number of prospective emigrants seeking family reunion and work is larger than any admission quota, especially in the United States so that every provision of liberalization greatly influences the trend in question. These two countries have participated equally in the global movement since 1946. Exits (54 percent) to, and returns (87 percent) from, the United States are higher, while net emigration (52 percent) is higher in the case of Canada. The population of the United States includes the highest number, among all countries, of persons of Italian origin: about five million born in Italy or of Italian parentage, while the entire Italo-American ethnic group numbers at least 10 million persons.[4] Italians holding Italian passports number about 250,000. After World War II, the flow to the United States resumed quickly and in 1947 numbered more than 23,000 emigrants. The figures decreased until 1953, when the annual quota assigned to Italy was less than 6,000 and very few exceptions were made for admission beyond the quota after the departure of most of the refugees who could take advantage of special legislation. The Refugee Relief Act of 1953 allowed a new significant increase until 1956, when the highest quota (36,000) was reached. This and other special Acts of Congress kept figures consistent (more than 25,000) until 1958 and allowed a further increase between 1960-1962, after which emigration decreased until 1964. Finally, a new law passed in 1965 again permitted an increase (21,600 in 1967). Returns averaged 3,600 a year from 1946 to 1958, reaching a maximum

---

[4] It is not easy to ascertain the number of Italo-Americans, and different figures are given according to different criteria of calculation. For example *Il Popolo Italiano*, a Philadelphia newspaper, and *Fra Noi*, a Chicago newspaper, seem to have estimated in 1963 and 1969 that, if one included the generations after the second (with which official statistics stop) there would be 21 and a half million persons of Italian descent, half of whom are living on the Eastern Coast (New York, New Jersey, Pennsylvania, Connecticut and Massachusetts). However, according to an interesting demographic study by Massimo Livi-Bacci, *L'immigrazione e l'assimilazione degli italiani negli Stati Uniti secondo le statistiche demografiche americane*, Milano 1961, Ed. Giuffrè, in 1950, there were in the United States no fewer than 7 million people, belonging to three generations, who have at least one Italian grandparent. No doubt, closer to the truth seems the figure of 15 to 16 million Americans who consider themselves to be Italian Americans.

of 6,000 in 1957. Since then the number has sharply decreased to only a few hundred in the last four years, during which the percentage of returns fell from a previous average of 24 percent to 3 percent. In conclusion, 300,000 Italians have settled in the United States since 1946 and tens of thousands of them are already American citizens.

In Canada there are about 800,000 persons of Italian origin in addition to more than 230,000 holding Italian passports. Since 1947 the difference between exits and returns has been about 350,000. Approximately 100,000 have asked for and obtained Canadian citizenship. The movement began in 1947 and grew rapidly, with significant fluctuations, and reached 28,500 in 1958. It decreased steadily until 1962 (12,500), increased again to 28,500 emigrants in 1966, and decreased to 16,600 emigrants in 1968. The number of returns was never too significant: a few hundred until 1953 with an increase until 1958 (a maximum of almost 3,000), after which there followed a rapid decrease so that in 1968 they numbered just over 400. The percentage of returns in the entire period as compared with emigrations was 4 percent and in recent years this fell to 1 percent. It is, therefore, a continuing emigration of significant size.

2 - Emigration to Latin America reached a peak in 1949 (127,000) and has decreased ever since (2,100 in 1968), except for a slight increase in 1954. Returns, although subject to fluctuations, have steadily increased until 1968, and their decrease since 1959, even if remarkable, was less significant than the decrease in the flow to that continent. The curve of net emigrations was marked by a very rapid decline and reached negative values from 1961 to 1965, when returns outnumbered emigrations by 8,500 in 1966. In 1967 returns again outnumbered exits by 400. The total net emigration is positive, however. From 1946 to 1968 about 640,000 Italians settled permanently in Latin America, especially in Argentina, Brazil and Venezuela.

In Argentina there are about six million persons of Italian descent and 1,300,000 with Italian passports, while in the years under study 380,000 other Italians have settled there. Emigration from Italy began immediately after World War II and grew rapidly until 1949, when it reached its peak (98,000); then it decreased rapidly, with some small exceptions, to just a few hundred. Net emigration follows the same curve and becomes negative from 1960 to date with more returns than emigrations.

The population of Brazil has about 4,500,000 persons of Italian origin, with about 300,000 holding Italian passports and almost 80,000 new Italian settlers. Even in the case of Brazil there was a gradual increase at the beginning, but the numbers were less and the increase more gradual than for Argentina. The peak was reached in 1952 with 17,000 emigrants and a net emigration of almost 16,000. After this date there has been a continuous decline. In recent years emigrants have numbered fewer than 300 a year and net emigration has been negative since 1962.

Venezuela hosts far fewer Italians: about 185,000 persons with Italian passports and a small number of persons of Italian background. Most of these person arrived after 1946, since in the post-war years there were more than 240,000 emigrants from Italy to this destination and more than 100,000 returns with a net emigration of 140,000. The general trends are the same as for other countries, but less marked and with some fluctuation: a rapid emigration growth until 1955 (almost 30,000 emigrants and 18,000 net emigrants) and then a progressive decrease. However, the number of emigrants did not fall below 2,000 until 1955 (900 in 1968), and net emigration was negative only in 1958, in 1961 and in 1968. Return figures increased until 1958 (17,000, with the highest negative net emigration of 4,000) and then fell to less than 1,000 since 1965.

It must not be forgotten that the movement toward Latin American countries received a strong impulse, especially between 1953 and 1958, from the plans of assisted emigration organized by the Intergovernemental Committee for Eureopean Migration (ICEM) and, in particular, from those aiming at reunion of families. When this goal was achieved the volume of emigration rapidly declined.

Sex Composition of Italian Emigration

Lack of data limits the analysis of sex composition to the years following 1958. We will examine only the female component, since by noting the differences one can obviously deduce patterns within the male component.

Italian female emigration had a pattern similar to the general one, but with fewer fluctuations. It increased from 1958 to 1960, decreased up to 1963, and then began to increase again in a more significant way than the general pattern of emigration, particularly to European countries, where it has assumed an increasingly seasonal character.

TABLE 10
Yearly Percentage of Women in the Total Migratory Movement

	Workers	Exits Family Members	Total	Returns	Net Emigration
Europe					
1958	16	69	22	17	29
1959	15	75	20	16	29
1960	13	75	16	16	17
1961	12	75	15	14	17
1962	11	79	14	13	17
1963	12	78	14	13	22
1964	11	77	18	15	29
1965	11	78	20	18	29
1966	15	71	22	19	58
1967	18	70	25	23	114
Overseas					
1958	3	68	49	30	63
1959	1	69	49	37	54
1960	8	65	46	43	47
1961	18	71	51	43	58
1962	18	70	52	46	55
1963	14	68	51	46	53
1964	14	68	48	46	54
1965	17	64	47	47	48
1966	13	59	46	45	47
1967	12	62	46	45	46
Total Movement					
1958	14	68	32	21	45
1959	14	71	28	19	40
1960	13	67	22	19	25
1961	13	73	21	18	24
1962	11	72	19	15	25
1963	12	70	20	15	37
1964	11	72	23	18	39
1965	11	72	25	19	38
1966	14	64	28	19	49
1967	18	65	31	24	51

"L'emigrazione dei minori", in *Notizie, fatti problemi dell'emigrazione*. Ed. ANFE, X, 67 (June-July 1965) pp. 163-82. Lucrezio, G., "L'emigrazione femminile italiana negli anni '60", in *Notizie, fatti, problemi dell'emigrazione*, Ed. ANFE, 68, nn. 7-8 (July-August 1968).

3

Above all, in recent years, female emigration has been an emigration of women leaving Italy to join their families. The percentage of these women increased for all destinations, including European countries, whereto, previously, the prevailing motive for emigration had been economic. The increase, however, is not yet sufficient to reduce noticeably the number of separated families.

The largest number is comprised of young women aged 14-30, but their percentage importance tends to diminish for emigration and immigration. However, in terms of net migration they constitute 60 percent of the European bound emigrants; for overseas countries, their percentage decreases. The percentage incidence of adult women, 30-50 years of age, tends to increase moderately especially among people going overseas. A clear increase occurs in the incidence of very young girls, under 14 years of age, who consistently represent 20 percent of the female migrants to European countries and 27 per cent of those migrating overseas. An increase also seemed to be evident in returns from extra-European countries by women over 50 years of age.

Some Conclusions

Briefly, we may conclude by recalling that Italian emigration has been characterized in the post-war period mainly by the movement toward European countries. Emigration to overseas countries, although significant in the beginning, progressively lost its impact because of the decreasing flow toward its main destination, Latin America. There was no substantial change in the movements toward Canada, the United States and Australia. Among the European nations, those of the European Economic Community and Switzerland absorbed the greatest number of Italians and did so in an ever increasing flow. Among the European Economic Community countries, however, there has been, in a certain sense, an exchange of position between France and Germany. The latter, since 1958, the most significant period among those analyzed, has received an increasing number of Italians, while the stream toward France has greatly diminished.[5]

[5] Cf. also: Lucrezio, G., *I movimenti migratori Italiani. Note Statistiche*, Roma, 1965, Ed. UCEI, Lucrezio, G., "Emigrazione fenomeno giovanile", in *Iniziativa Giovanile*, ACLI. IV, 3, pp. 22-57. Lucrezio, G.,

Italian Immigrants in the United States in the Sixties *

by Joseph Velikonja **

The immigration of Italians to the United States reached a significant threshold in 1965. A new chapter of immigration history was opened by the new Immigration Act, which after a transitional period between December 1, 1965, and July 1, 1968, has replaced the national origin quota system with a new set of criteria, based primarily upon family relations and technical skills.

The restrictions and national origin preferences which regulated the migration during the period between 1924 and 1965 affected thoroughly the numerical magnitude of the migratory flow and regional distribution of the Italians. The trickling of small groups in this period, conditioned also by the social and political climate of Italy, did not add very many new immigrants to the groups which arrived in the 1880-1915 period, but it nevertheless kept the selected clusters of *italianità* alive.

Some previous studies [1] indicate that the mass migration at the turn of the century established the basic regional distribution of the Italian immigrants; the post-1924 flows followed the already established channels of communication and movement. The history of migration in general is known; so is its

---

[1] Bibliography of numerous studies is found in: G. Dore, *La democrazia italiana e l'emigrazione in America*. (Brescia: Morcelliana, 1964), pp. 389-493.

Joseph Velikonja, *Italians in the United States* (Bibliography), Occasional Papers No. 1, Department of Geography, Southern Illinois University, Carbondale, 1963, 90 pp.

---

* The study is a revised and up-dated version of a report published originally in *The International Migration Review*, vol. 1 (N.S.), No. 3 (Summer, 1967), 25-37.
** Joseph Velikonja is Associate Professor of Geography at the University of Washington in Seattle.

numerical consistency. What, however, remains to be investigated is the regional direction of flows and the changes which
have been occurring in their intensity and orientation. After
additional probing, we hope to ascertain with some confidence
what factors contributed to the movement of the Italians to
specific areas in the United States.

The general theories of migration flows emphasize economic motivation as the base of the gross migration. This might
be true also for the Italian migration. The theory, however,
does not provide an adequate answer to the question as to
why some areas of the country were greatly preferred over
others, often in contrast to regional economic opportunities.
The objective existence of opportunities does not determine
specific orientations of the flows; it seems rather obvious that
other factors as well contributed to the selection of destinations
of the migrants. The move from the local community in Italy
to the unknown world across the ocean was more than could
be visualized before the actual move was made. The mobility,
which seems to be great after the decision is made to leave
home, vanishes soon after arrival in the United States. For the
majority of Italians, the New York area becomes the goal, the
refuge, and the only part of America with which they become
acquainted. The self-perpetuation of flows to selected areas in
the United States is generated through the avoidance of other
potential opportunities, and produces a concentration seldom
encountered by another national group.

The Italian migration in the United States and its numerical consistency are open to speculation since there is no
reliable information which could provide an adequate answer
to the general question: How many Italians are there in the
United States? [2]

The reason for the inadequacy is the type of information
provided by official sources in the United States, primarily by
the Census of Population and the annual reports issued by
the U.S. Immigration and Naturalization Service.[3] The sets

---

[2] The U.S. Immigration and Naturalization *Annual Report* for 1967
gives the figure of 5,096,204 Italians admitted in the period between
1820-1967 (Table 13). The figure includes the repeated admittance of the
same immigrant and does not take into account the repatriates.

[3] U.S. Bureau of the Census, *U.S. Census of Population: 1960. Vol. 1.
Characteristics of the Population.* Washington, D.C. U.S. Government
Printing Office, 1962-64. 57 parts. U.S. Immigration and Naturalization,
Annual Report 1953-67 (annual).

of information consist of the actual count of residents of the United States who were born in Italy (first generation) and their children born in the United States (second generation); the additional set of information is given by the Immigration and Naturalization Service, indicating the number of entering immigrants from Italy, without adequate evidence of how many of them returned. This apparently exact set of information would provide the basic data for ascertaining the numerical consistency of the group. Although the reliability of information concerning the Italian-born is high, the number of American-born persons of Italian parents is considered undercounted, primarily in the areas of dispersal. In addition, the third generation is not counted at all since by that time the "melting pot" is supposed to accomplish the merging of nationalities in the American nation. As some studies document, this does not happen in reality in all cases.[4]

The inter-war migration was regulated by the provisions of the Immigration and Nationality Act of 1924, amended in 1940, and revised in 1952 by the Walter-McCarran Act, Public Law 414 of the 82nd Congress. The thorough revision in the early 1960's led to the complete overhaul of the immigration legislation and was finally completed with the approval on October 3, 1965, of the new Act, Public Law 89-236, which sets new classes of preferences for relatives of citizens and permanent residents of the United States (first, second, fourth and fifth preference) as well as for specialized professionals (third and sixth preference). The interim period between December 1, 1965, and June 30, 1968, has seen a gradual transition from the nationality quota system to the new preferences. As of July 1st, 1968, the new law is being fully enforced.

The general restrictions on migration during the 1924-65 period strongly affected the Italian immigrants. The annual quota of 5,666 in the 1952-65 period was used completely. Frequent special laws admitted more than twice as many non-quota immigrants. In the 1953-65 period, under the Walter-McCarran Act, a total of 254,088 Italians entered the country, the highest number of 21,442 in 1962 (judicial year July 1, 1961-June 30, 1962) and the lowest, 10,821 in 1965 (Table 1). The pressure of prospective immigrants is evident in the fact

---

[4] Herbert Gans, *The Urban Villagers* (Glencoe, Ill.: The Free Press 1962). Nathan Glazer and Daniel Patrick Moynihan, *Beyond the Melting Pot.* (Cambridge, Mass.: The M.I.T. Press, 1963).

that in 1962 no less than 266,184 prospective immigrants were registered on the quota list, which means that the quota was filled for almost a half century in advance. Another indication of the pressure is that 19,225 Italian immigrants were admitted during the first seven months under the 1965 law, between December 1, 1965, and June 30, 1966, bringing the total for 1965-66 to 25,154. Similarly large numbers of Italians have been admitted in the following years of the transitional period: 26,565 in 1966-67 and 23,593 in 1967-68. In addition, during the three years of the transitional period the total of 1,560 (1965-66), 2,626 (1966-67) and 2,990 (1967-68) Italians who entered the United States as non-immigrants changed their status under the provision of the new law to that of permanent residents and are included in the total count of new immigrants.

The new legal provisions reduced considerably the backlog of prospective immigrants, although in the case of Italy, did not exhaust it. The primary consequence is that after July

TABLE 1

Year	Entering Immigrants	Others *	Naturalized	Resident Aliens
1960	14,933	1,034	14,560	257,477
1961	20,652	1,068	18,362	248,733
1962	21,442	1,468	17,449	234,229
1963	16,588	1,342	12,171	228,766
1964	13,245	1,291	12,323	225,320
1965	10,821	1,283	10,742	214,618
1966	25,154	1,560	10,981	210,649
1967	26,565	2,626	10,572	223,357
1968	23,593	2,990	9,379	226,595
1960-68	172,993	14,662	116,539	

* Italian born aliens who entered the United States as non-immigrants and adjusted their status to permanent residents, i.e. immigrants with intention to stay.

Source: U.S. Immigration and Naturalization. Annual Report, 1953-1967. Immigration and Naturalization Reporter, Vol. 17, No. 1, p. 14 (July 1969).

TABLE 2
Structure of U.S. Population (1960)

	Total	Urban	Rural Non-Farm	Rural Farm
Total population . . .	179,323,175	69.9	22.6	7.5
Foreign stock	34,050,406	83.7	12.6	3.7
Italian stock	4,543,935	91.8	7.4	.8
Foreign-born of Italian mother tongue . . .	1,226,141	93.4	5.7	.9

1, 1968, the number of immigrants was again reduced to the possible maximum of 20,000 allowed for any single country for any single fiscal year (from July 1st to June 30th of the following year). The prospects for the future are, therefore, not so favorable. After the exhaustion of priorities, the labor restrictions will keep out of the country most of the immigrants who expect to come but are not sufficiently skilled.

The studies of assimilation and adjustments in selected areas and cities of the United States provide an excellent in-

TABLE 3
Regional Distribution of the Italians

	Italian born (I. generation)		Native-born of Italian parentage (II. generation)		Italian stock I. and II. generation		Italian aliens	
	1960 Total	%	1960 Total	%	1960 Total	%	1968 Total	%
Northeast	883,074	70.3	2,273,235	69.2	3,156,309	69.5	164,336	72.5
North Central	190,686	15.2	486,982	14.8	677,668	14.9	34,905	15.4
South	58,239	4.6	208,059	6.3	266,298	5.8	9,544	4.2
West	125,000	9.9	318,660	9.7	443,660	9.8	17,615	7.8
Total	1,256,999	100.0	3,286,936	100.0	4,543,935	100.0	226,595	100.0
Per cent of total population		0.7		1.8		2.5		0.1

Source: U.S. Census of Population, 1960, Summary Volume.
U.S. Immigration and Naturalization Reporter, Vol. 17, No. 1, July 1968, p. 14.

ventory of case studies from which some general trends can be identified. This study, however, presents only the regional distributional pattern of the Italians in the United States in the 1960's, ascertains the high degree of concentration in selected regions, and attempts to offer some explanatory suggestions.

The Italians form only a small fraction of the total population of the United States: 0.7 percent of the American population in 1960 was born in Italy; the Italian stock, including the first and second generation, accounted for 4,543,935 people, or 2.53 percent of the total population, a relative decline from 3.05 percent reported in the 1950 census; in the period 1960-68, the total of 172,993 Italians entered as immigrants which would add about 15 percent increase to the first generation Italians — taking into account also the departures — not quite enough to alter considerably their proportion of the U. S. population.

The urban concentration of the Italian stock is evident: 91.8 percent of all Italians reside in urban areas, while the relative figure for the total U. S. population was 69.9 percent.

The preference for urban living is not uniquely characteristic of the Italians, although the level of urban preferences is higher than for most groups. Since the vast majority of Italians in the United States lives in urban areas, valid inferences can be drawn from the examination of the urban centers alone. The rural areas, furthermore, have received only a trifle of new immigrants in recent decades. The rural clusters of Italian peasants, as a consequence of this development, slid slowly down from the official statistics which do not identify ethnic origin beyond the second generation. The micro-examination of the Italian communities, especially rural settlements, is possible through historical research and field investigation which can uncover untold stories of the accomplishments of pioneering settlers in many areas of the United States. Sunnyside and Tontitown in Arkansas, Rosati in Missouri, centers in Johnsboro and Herrin in Illinois, Bryan in Texas, Roseto in Pennsylvania, Independence and Hammond in Louisiana, are but a few examples of these scattered settlements, not noticeable in the generalized population statistics.

The central city preference, however, is not in line with the general trend of the American cities. The move from the central city to the suburbs, on one hand, and the reduced growth on the Atlantic seaboard, on the other, characterize the general population growth pattern of the United States; the Italian immigrants nevertheless persist in the central cities particularly on the Atlantic seaboard. The principal disrupting events which affected the "Little Italies" in major cities are the urban renewal projects: Boston, New York, Philadelphia, New Haven, Chicago and St. Louis, are but a few examples.

The urban agglomeration of Italians is particularly strong in Megalopolis, loosely defined by Jean Gottmann as the urbanized area extending from North of Boston to south of Norfolk, Virginia.[5] This area contains 39 million people, or

---

[5] Jean Gottmann, *Megalopolis* (New York: Twentieth Century Fund, 1961). For an analysis of the population in the area, see Irene B. Taeuber and Conrad Taeuber, "The Great Concentration: SMSA's from Boston to Washington", *Population Index* ,Vol. 30, (January 1964), pp. 3-29.

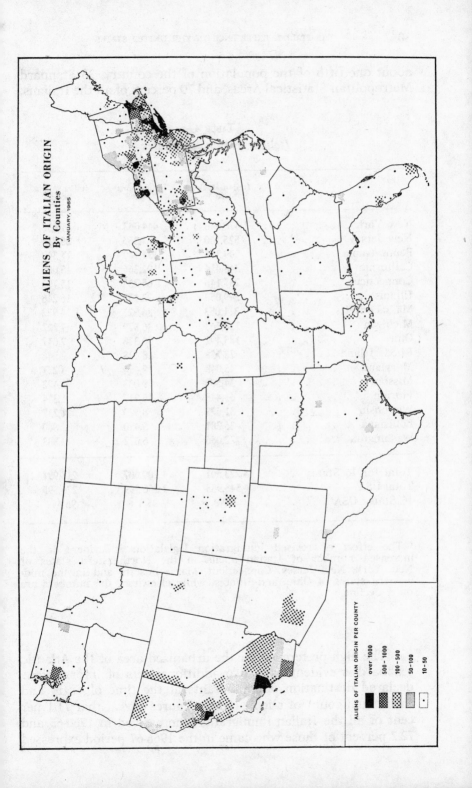

ALIENS OF ITALIAN ORIGIN
By Counties

JANUARY, 1965

ALIENS OF ITALIAN ORIGIN PER COUNTY

over 1000
500 - 1000
100 - 500
50 - 100
10 - 50

about one fifth of the population of the country, 33 Standard Metropolitan Statistical Areas, and 70 percent of all the Italians.

TABLE 4

Italians in Principal States

	Italian stock 1960	Italian-born 1960	Italian Aliens 1968 *
New York	1,476,946	444,063	87,658
New Jersey	525,100	137,356	25,715
Pennsylvania	509,314	131,149	17,349
California	348,414	102,366	15,000
Connecticut	237,146	65,233	15,703
Illinois	249,053	72,139	16,246
Massachusetts	311,053	86,921	14,922
Michigan	120,363	36,879	7,222
Ohio	185,492	50,338	7,617
Rhode Island	78,758	18,438	2,546
Maryland	45,048	18,454	3,227
Missouri	34,509	9,033	1,422
Florida	61,445	16,217	1,354
Wisconsin	31,673	8,479	1,237
Louisiana	36,281	5,470	880
Washington	22,086	6,072	883
Total for 16 States . . .	4,273,501	1,200,607	218,991
Total USA	4,543,935	1,256,999	226,595
16 States USA	94%	95.5%	96.6%

* The effect of revised immigration legislation is evident in the increased number of Italian aliens in the Northeastern states of New York, New Jersey, Connecticut, Massachusetts and in the mid-western states of Ohio, and Illinois, while elsewhere the numbers are on a decline.

The high preference for the urbanized area of the Atlantic seaboard is evident from two additional sets of information: declared destination of immigrants at the time of entry and the annual count of aliens. Gross figures reveal that 71.1 per cent of all the Italian immigrants who arrived in 1960-65 and 72.2 percent of those who came in the 1966-67 period expressed their preference for the Northeast. The total of 72.5 percent of all the resident Italian aliens in January 1968 were registered in the Northeast [6] and the percentage has not changed during the last few years in spite of the sizeable increase of immigration. One of the reasons for this concentration is the legislative provision for quota and non-quota immigrants which requires the sponsorship or the documentation of parentage for admission to the United States. The legislative restrictions, therefore, which originally aimed to prevent the establishment of national clusters through national quota restrictions, instead reinforce these same concentrations.

As a consequence, the regional pattern which was established in its basic outline at the turn of the century is being reinforced by new migration although this has hardly been the intention of the legislators.

The urban preference is further evident in the fact that 88.2 percent of all Italians reside in Standard Metropolitan Areas, and 3.6 percent in smaller cities.

The degree of concentration is generally related to the size of the metropolitan area and its distance from New York. A brief examination of major metropolitan areas reveals that only a small number of them has large numbers of Italians. In 1960, 23 Standard Metropolitan Statistical Areas (Table V) accounted for more than 25,000 people of Italian stock each, including primarily the cities of the Megalopolis: Boston, Providence, Hartford, New Haven, Waterbury, Philadelphia, Baltimore and Washington, D. C.; other cities in this category are: Albany-Schenectady-Troy, Utica-Rome, Syracuse, Rochester, Buffalo, Pittsburgh, Youngstown-Warren, Cleveland, Detroit, Chicago and St. Louis. The only western cities with more than 25,000 Italians are Los Angeles, San Francisco-Oakland, and San Jose. The number of Italians in these cities alone permits the establishment of many Italian cultural and social services, and contributes to the survival of the Italian cultural character even in cases where the relative position of the Italian group is not very strong. The Italians form only 1.0 percent of the total population in Chicago, 1.3 percent in St. Louis and Washington, D. C., 1.7 percent in Baltimore, and 1.8 percent in Los Angeles.

---

[6] *U. S. Immigration and Naturalization Service Reporter*, Vol. 17, (July, 1968), p. 14.

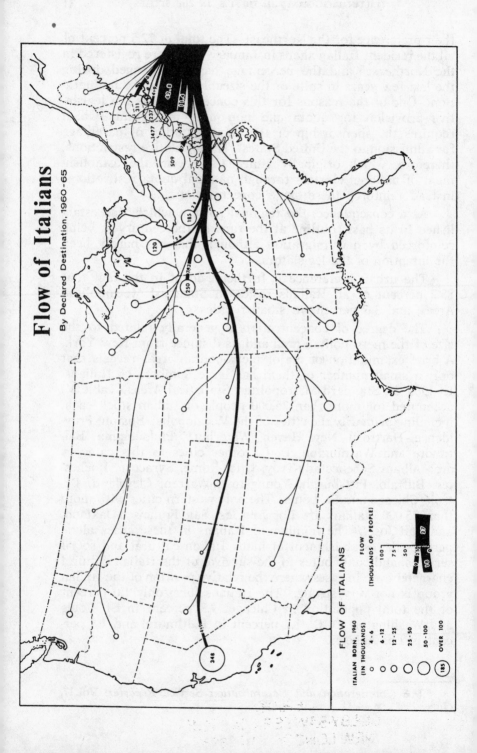

Flow of Italians
By Declared Destination, 1960-65

FLOW OF ITALIANS

ITALIAN BORN, 1960
(IN THOUSANDS)

- ∘ 4-6
- ○ 6-12
- ◯ 12-25
- ◯ 25-50
- ◯ 50-100
- 185 OVER 100

FLOW
(THOUSANDS OF PEOPLE)

100
75
50
25
0

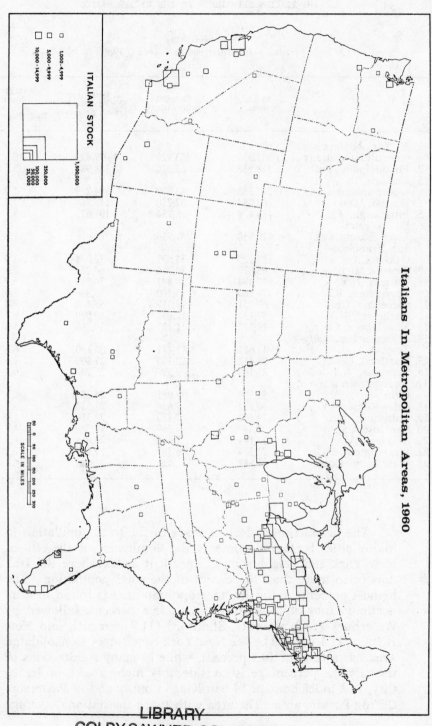

Italians In Metropolitan Areas, 1960

ITALIAN STOCK

1,000-4,999
5,000-9,999
10,000-14,999

1,500,000

250,000
100,000
50,000
25,000

SCALE IN MILES

60 0   50   100   150   200   250   300

LIBRARY
COLBY-SAWYER COLLEGE
NEW LONDON, NH 03257

TABLE 5
Italians in Metropolitan Areas, 1960

Rank	Italian Stock	I. Generation (Italian-born)	II. Generation (Native-born of Italian parents)	Italian Stock as % of Total Population
1. N. York-N. Jersey (consolidated area) .	1,531,352	453,929	1,077,423	10.3
2. Philadelphia, Pa. .	248,558	63,570	184,988	5.7
3. Chicago, Ill. (consolidated area) .	217,788	63,509	154,279	1.0
4. Boston, Mass. . . .	202,987	57,718	145,269	7.8
5. Pittsburgh, Pa. . .	138,429	36,754	101,675	5.7
6. Los Angeles-Long Beach, Cal. .	120,950	31,934	89,016	1.8
7. San Francisco-Oakland, Cal. . . .	106,125	34,051	72,074	3.8
8. Detroit, Mich. . . .	95,077	30,794	64,283	2.5
9. Buffalo, N.Y. . . .	77,434	20,441	56,993	5.9
10. Providence, R.I. . .	76,580	18,200	58,380	9.4
11. Cleveland, Ohio . .	67,721	19,317	58,404	3.8
12. Rochester, N.Y. . .	57,134	17,047	40,089	9.7
13. New Haven, Conn. .	49,172	11,727	37,395	15.8
14. Albany-Schenectady-Troy, N.Y.	41,611	11,471	30,140	6.3
15. Hartford, Conn. . .	39,812	12,303	27,509	7.6
16. Syracuse, N.Y. . .	35,165	9,398	25,767	6.2
17. Youngstown-Warren, Ohio	33,300	9,081	24,220	6.5
18. Utica-Rome, N.Y.. .	30,192	7,659	22,533	9.1
19. Baltimore, Md. . .	29,692	7,373	22,319	1.7
20. San Jose, Cal. . . .	27,449	8,069	19,380	4.2
21. St. Louis, Mo. . . .	27,144	7,086	20,058	1.3
22. Washington, D.C. .	26,374	6,397	19,977	1.3
23. Waterbury, Conn. .	25,987	n.a.	n.a.	14.3

The proportion of Italian stock in the total population in major cities further documents the dominance of the city of New York and neighboring Connecticut areas where the Italians form more than 10 percent of the total population. The highest percentage for any metropolitan area is found in Connecticut cities of New Haven, with 15.8 percent, followed by Waterbury (14.3 percent), Stamford (11.7 percent), and New Britain (11.1 percent). The New York-New Jersey Consolidated Area has a total of 10.3 percent, while in many subdivisions of the city the percentage is considerably higher: 13.6 in Jersey City, 14.8 in Richmond, 14.1 in Kings County and in Patterson-Clifton-Passaic area. The area with twice the national average

COLBY-SAWYER COLLEGE
NEW LONDON, NH 03257

of the Italians includes also the major cities in Massachusetts, Providence in Rhode Island, and extends southwards to include Trenton, Philadelphia and Atlantic City. Eastward, the string of major cities: Albany, Utica-Rome, Syracuse, Rochester, and Buffalo, each has more than 5 percent. The only other major cities with high percentages are Scranton, Pennsylvania (9.0); Youngstown-Warren, Ohio (6.5); Steubenville with Weirton,

TABLE 6

Declared Destination of Immigrants, 1960-65, 66-68

	Total 1960-65	Per Cent	Total 1966-68	Per Cent
New York	30,951	28.9	22,117	29.4
Chicago	6,452	6.0	5,019	6.7
Newark	3,699	3,4	1,479	1.9
Philadelphia	3,075	2.9	2,210	2.9
Rochester	2,053	1.9	1,343	1.8
Boston-Cambridge . .	1,896	1.8	1,848	2.4
Detroit	1,532	1.4	1,198	1.6
Cleveland	1,255	1.2	922	1.2
Pittsburgh	1,052	1.0	631	0.8
San Francisco-Oakland .	986	.9	564	0.7
Hartford	939	.9	851	1.1
Los Angeles	936	.9	306	0.4
Total for 12 cities . . .	54,826	51.2	39,488	52.4
Total for U.S.	107,184	100%	75,312	100%

Source: U.S. Immigration and Naturalization. *Annual Report* 1960, 1967, Table 12B.

Ohio; West Virginia (6.7); Kenosha, Wisconsin (5.5); and Stockton, California (6.3).

Values higher than the national average of 2.53 percent are further encountered in major cities in Pennsylvania; Cleveland and Canton in Ohio; Detroit, Michigan; Rockford, Illinois; Pueblo, Colorado; San Francisco and San Jose in California; New Orleans, Louisiana; and Fort Lauderdale in Florida. A real dispersal is, therefore, minimal. Only selected centers outside the quadrangle Boston-Washington-Milwaukee-St. Louis have significant clustering of Italians, primarily in California, as is evident from the distribution map.

The registration of aliens every year provides an additional source of information about the scatter of the Italians, primarily recent arrivals, throughout the United States. The 1965 count was used [7] to derive some additional conclusions, primarily to indicate the persistency of the migratory flows to selected centers in the United States. The annual count of aliens required by law includes all non-citizens regardless of the time of their arrival in the United States. Most of the immigrants, however, cannot acquire citizenship earlier than after 5 years of residence. The count includes, therefore, most of the recent arrivals in addition to the immigrants who, for various reasons, did not acquire citizenship. The count is further weakened by the fact that the penalty for non-registration is minimal. The annual variation of the numerical consistency reveals often puzzling changes in the totals of aliens which cannot be explained in any other way than by incomplete registration.

The total of 214,618 Italian aliens was registered in January 1965 (Table 1). The Northeast retained 72.6 percent of the total, while the lowest percentage was found in the South (4.4 percent). A comparison between the Italian-born counted in 1960 and the Italian aliens registered in 1965 would indicate the intensity of the recent migration where the ratio is high and a reduced recent migration where the ratio is low. The highest values are found in the New York area, and in Fairfield County, Connecticut. Lower values are encountered in Massachusetts and Rhode Island, in Ohio and California. The ratio therefore would indicate that the most recent intense flows are directed primarily toward the New York metropolitan area, and less to New England, to the interior, or to the Pacific coast.

While the Italians are the most numerous national group in the country, they rank fifth among the aliens, preceded by

---

[7] In 1965, during the discussion of the new immigration legislation, a detailed count (by counties) of registered aliens has been published in: The Immigration and Naturalization Service, Department of Justice. *Aliens in the United States* (*Number of Aliens in the United States, by States, Counties, and Nationalities, who reported under the Immigration and Nationality Act during January 1965*). Prepared for the subcommittee on Immigration and Naturalization of the Committee on the Judiciary, United States Senate. 89th Congress. Washington: Government Printing Office, 1965. 1014 pages. The information about the registered aliens is usually reported only on state by state basis.

immigrants from Mexico, Canada, the United Kingdom and Germany. This again would indicate that the postwar Italian migration was reduced as compared to the above groups. The counties with more than 1,000 Italian aliens include 13 of the 14 counties of the New York-New Jersey Consolidated Area; only Rockland has fewer than 500 Italian aliens. Nineteen other counties are found outside of the New York area and only nine outside the Megalopolis; each of them is a center of a larger metropolitan area: Rochester (Monroe County), Buffalo (Erie), Pittsburgh (Allegheny), Cleveland (Cuyahoga), Detroit (Wayne), Chicago (Cook), and San Jose (Santa Clara), Los Angeles, and San Francisco. These 32 counties, representing only one percent of all the counties of the country, contain almost three quarters of all the Italian aliens (74.1 percent), while the Italian stock in the same accounts for 62.3 percent. The difference can be interpreted by the preference of the new arrivals for the major metropolitan areas, while the second generation primarily is more dispersed reducing as a consequence the concentration intensity in the 32 principal counties. The most recent registrations for 1966-1968 substantiate the above reasoning. The number of registered Italian aliens has shown an increase in 1967 and 1968 over the 1966 figures due to the sizeable new immigration while the number of naturalized (and as a consequence removed from the obligation to register) remained virtually unchanged. The greatest absolute gain has been in the state of New York, 6,762 more in 1968 than in 1966, a gain of 8.4 percent, while the greatest relative gains occurred in Connecticut (17.1 percent) and Illinois (15.5 percent). In general, the gain is positively related to the size of the Italian group in the state.

The general conclusion derived from this examination indicates that the migratory movement of the Italians is being reduced to a few selected flows, with the minimum of dispersal to the rural areas, and with the distinct preference for the largest metropolitan areas, in spite of the fact that these might not offer the best economic opportunities to the new arrival. The existence of a strong Italian cluster is an incentive if not a prerequisite for any intense flow to materialize.

The basic geographic pattern of the Italian migrants in the United States was established at the turn of the century and was not greatly modified afterwards. With the slow vanishing of the migrants who arrived more than half a century ago, smaller centers are affected more than the larger

4

ones. The change in economic opportunities is already making its mark upon the reduced flows to the once prosperous mining areas of Pennsylvania, Illinois, Minnesota, Colorado and Montana, but is not affecting the Atlantic seaboard area, where new opportunities develop also for the new immigrants who frequently have to start at the bottom of the social and economic scale.

Selected Bibliography

The collection of immigration statistics has been subjected to different criteria in different countries and in the same country in different years. Even keeping this observation in mind, the trends and the volume of Italian immigration to the United States can be detected and computed with a fair amount of reliability from English and Italian language sources.

A panoramic view of the immigration movement is given in U. S. Department of Commerce, Bureau of the Census, *Historical Statistics of the United States*, Colonial Times to 1957 (Washington, D.C., 1960) and in the Continuation to 1962 and Revisions, (Washington, D.C., 1965). Also Robert Foerster's *The Italian Emigration of Our Times* (Cambridge, Mass. 1924) summarizes the entire emigratory flow in the first part of his book. Since 1892 the U. S. Commissioner-General of Immigration has published under various titles *Annual Reports* of yearly statistics on immigration and its effects. *Annual Reports* are now published by the U. S. Department of Justice, Immigration and Naturalization Service. The *Reports* present the volume of immigration as well as its distribution by State. An excellent analysis of census statistics relative to foreign born and native white of foreign or mixed parentage is the U. S. Department of Commerce, Bureau of the Census, *Immigrants and Their Children*, 1920, by Niles Carpenter, Census Monograph VI, (Washington, D.C., 1927). A recent bibliographical annotation of statistical studies on Italian immigration in Italy has been added to the essay by Giovanni Mazzocchi "Movimento migratorio con l'estero" in Istituto Centrale di Statistica, *Sviluppo della popolazione italiana dal 1861 al 1961*. Annali di Statistica, 94, VIII, Vol. 17 (Rome, 1965), pp. 769 and 787-88.

For the early period of immigration, see Commissariato Generale dell'Emigrazione, *Annuario Statistico dell'Emigrazione Italiana dal 1876 al 1925 con notizie sull'emigrazione negli anni 1869-1875* (Rome, 1926). Also, Leone Carpi, *Delle Colonie e dell'Emigrazione d'italiani all'estero sotto l'aspetto dell'industria, commercio, agricoltura, contrattazione di importanti questioni sociali* (Milano, 1874), Voll. 4; Leone Carpi, *Statistica illustrata dell'emigrazione all'estero del triennio 1874-1876 nei suoi rapporti coi problemi economico-sociali* (Rome, 1878).

Francesco Coletti, "Dell'emigrazione italiana", in *Cinquant'anni di Storia italiana*, MDCCCLX-MDCCCCX, Vol. III, pp. 1-284 (Milan, 1911).

For recent years, see: Istituto Centrale di Statistica, *Statistica delle migrazioni da e per l'estero*, reports from 1926 to 1937 continued from 1950 to date with the *Annuario Statistico dell'emigrazione*, 1950-1953 (Rome, 1955) and, the *Annuario di Statistiche del lavoro e dell'emigrazione* since then. Also, Anthony Trawick Bouscaren, *European Economic Community Migrations* (The Hague, 1969).

THE DISTRIBUTION OF ITALIANS IN THE UNITED STATES

Once the Italians arrived on our shores, they tended to become concentrated in ethnic communities or enclaves. Most of these communities were to be found in urban areas, especially within the northeastern states. Why did Italians congregate in the cities? How did they earn a living and prosper there? What kept them away from the agricultural occupations to which they had been accustomed in Italy? What factors affected the distribution of Italians in the United States? According to the first paper in this section, the *padrone* system was a significant factor in the dispersion of the immigrants. Together with the second paper, it explores the consequences of settlement patterns for both the Italians and the receiving or host population.

The Padrone and Immigrant Distribution

by Luciano J. Iorizzo *

At the beginning of this century virtually every state in the Union sought workers and, in particular, a large, floating, unskilled labor supply. Workers were needed to construct new railroads and extend the lines of old ones, to dig and enlarge canals and waterways, and to develop the water-supply systems in towns and cities. Hands were sought to assist in the cutting of timber. Harvesters were needed to bring in the ice from the frozen North and Northwest, as well as the fruits, vegetables, and grains from sunbaked fields throughout the nation. American natives and immigrants from Northern and Western Europe could not be depended upon to do the work described above. They were moving up the industrial scale, away from jobs which required little or no skill. By 1900 it was virtually impossible to find an English-speaking laborer doing common railroad work. The demand for such labor was met principally by the immigrants from Southern and Eastern Europe.[1] Despite unprecedented arrivals at Ellis Island, labor remained in short supply through World War I.

---

[1] U.S. Immigration Commission Reports (Dillingham Commission), *Immigrants in Industries*, Sen. Docs., 61 Cong., 2d Sess., No. 633, XVIII, Pt. 22, "The Floating Immigrant Labor Supply", 331 and 339 and F. J. Sheridan, "Italian Slavic and Hungarian Unskilled Laborers in the United States", *United States Bureau of Labor Bulletin*, No. 72, September, 1907, 380. The shortcomings of the summary reports of the Dillingham Commission have been incisively dealt with by Oscar Handlin, *Race and Nationality in American Life*, 1st ed. (New York, 1957), 93ff. In short, the conclusions reached were unwarranted by the facts. Beyond the summary volumes, however, the careful researcher will uncover extremely valuable descriptive and reportorial material nowhere else to be found.

---

* Luciano Iorizzo is Associate Professor of History at State University College, Oswego, N. Y.

The job situation in Syracuse, New York, was no exception. Influential Syracusans conducted a rigorous campaign to re-tain native and immigrant laborers, many of whom were desert-ing the city for greener pastures during World War I. They made melodramatic appeals to the Italian not to become a "floater" but to be true to his sense of loyalty to city, family, employer, and self by remaining in Syracuse and advised that the loyal laborer would be the one who would get consideration when peace came and jobs became scarce. (It seems ironic that in the face of these entreaties for immigrant labor, the United States would soon cut its flow to a trickle.) [2]

Attempts to provide an effective means of distributing im-migrants wherever needed throughout the United States came from all quarters. Those behind such efforts often had mo-tives other than the desire to supply industrialists with labor-ers or farmers with agricultural workers. Many thought the key to solving pressing social and political problems lay in halting the immigrant's tendency to congregate in large met-ropolitan areas. They believed that widespread immigrant distribution would help eliminate urban slums. It would alleviate the suffering brought about by exploitation and free the immigrants from the clutches of the padroni, who were numerous in large cities where the immigrants crowded into the ghettos. It also would remove a condition on which the politically corrupt could thrive and provide a setting more favorable for assimilation into American culture. [3]

The United States established the Federal Bureau of In-formation in 1907 "to promote a beneficial distribution of aliens . . . among the several States and Territories desiring

[2] La gazzetta di Syracuse, July 26, 1918, 4, and Constantino Ottolen-ghi, "La nuova fase dell'immigrazione del lavoro agli Stati Uniti d'Amer-ica," Giornale degli economisti, XVIII (Roma, 1899), 380.

[3] Letter dated April 19, 1894, Baron Fava to Walter Q. Gresham, Notes from the Italian Legation in the U. S. to the Department of State, 1861-1906, "National Archives," Microfilm 202; hereafter called "Notes from the Italian Legation." Letter dated July 11, 1905, Henry White to Elihu Root, Dispatches from U. S. Minister to Italian States and Italy, 1832-1906, "National Archives," Microfilm 90; hereafter called "Diplo-matic Dispatches." Report of the Commission of Immigration of the State of New York (Albany, 1909), 109-12 and 140ff. U. S. Commissioner General of Immigration, Annual Report, 1902-03, 121-22.

immigration." [4] The states were encouraged to maintain agents at the ports, but few did so. The responsibility for distributing immigrants then fell to the Division of Information (as the Federal Bureau of Information came to be called), which operated chiefly as an employment office, aiding both immigrants and natives to find employment, principally as unskilled laborers and farm hands. From 1908 to 1915 the Division placed about 5,000 men a year in such jobs. During the war it expanded into a nationwide system of employment offices and laid the foundation for the United States Employment Service, created in 1916. The Employment Service operated as a separate bureau in the Department of Labor and absorbed the Division of Information. At the end of the war, the Division of Information was nominally revived, only to be finally abolished in 1921. Over the years it placed thousands of workers, but Italians were never very numerous among them.[5]

In the 1890's the Italian government operated an Italian Bureau at Ellis Island. The main objectives of the Bureau were to help eradicate the padrone system and assist the Italian immigrant to find employment away from padroni-ridden New York City. Amid charges that the Bureau was seeking special privileges, that it was failing in its main objectives, and that it represented a foreign, and therefore intolerable, interference with the work of the Commissioner of Immigration, its operations were suspended in 1899.[6] Some even charged that the Italian Bureau was "a mere agency of the padroni." [7] The

---

[4] 34 Stat. 898; 8 U.S.C. cited in U. S. Department of Justice, Immigration and Naturalization Service, *Laws Applicable to Immigration and Nationality*, Washington, 1953), 300.

[5] Maurice R. Davie, *World Immigration* (New York, 1936), 462-66, and *Report of the Commission of Immigration of the State of New York*, 244-46.

[6] See Letters, November 16, 1895, June 20, 1899, October 31, 1899, November 4 and November 29, 1899, December 21 and December 26 (telegram), 1889, January 7 and January 8, 1900, "Notes from the Italian Legation."

[7] Letter dated June 20, 1899, Count Vinci to John Hay, "Notes from the Italian Legation." The Bureau was charged with instructing Italians on how to avoid obeying U. S. immigration laws. Moreover, the Industrial Commission claimed it had testimony of substantial witnesses that officers in Italy encouraged the *padrone* system, that they shared in its profits, and sent contract laborers to the United States. When the

truth of the matter is that the padrone system continued to exist despite the efforts of the Italian Bureau to do away with it.[8]

The Italian government worked in other ways to provide for the general welfare of its emigrants. On January 31, 1901, it created the Commissariat of Emigration and charged it with giving aid and protection to Italian emigrants throughout the world. The Commissariat did so by regulating the transportation of emigrants from Italy, providing information, and giving legal advice. It also supplemented the work of Italian embassies and consulates and private organizations which were also looking after the emigrants.[9] The Italian government could do little to directly influence the movement of its emigrants once they reached America. This was nowhere more evident than in its attempts to turn the tide of immigration from the large cities to rural areas especially. From the 1880's on, the Italian government became disturbed by attempts in the United States to restrict immigration. It felt such efforts were prompted by the crowding of immigrants in American cities and the evils that issued from such conditions. It also believed that such attempts were not aimed at the total exclusion of the "new" immigrants, but were designed to change the character of them. In other words, if these newcomers, Italians included, would give up the cities and go to the farms,

---

Italian Government protested and requested that these charges be proven true, the United States agreed to delete the unsupported objectional charges. See letters dated November 4, 11, 30, 1899, Fava to Hay, "Notes from the Italian Legation."

[8] For example, the Italian government requested the help of the U. S. government in putting an end to the operations of Gennaro Agnone, an Italian banker in New Haven, Connecticut, who sought to establish an international operation to promote clandestine emigration and defraud immigrants. To cite one such operation, bankers were to sell passports to Italian emigrants to the U.S. at a time when they were not required for leaving Italy or entering the U. S. See letter dated September 19, 1896, Fava to Richard Olney, "Notes from the Italian Legation." See also letter dated October 31, 1899, Fava to Hay, "Notes from the Italian Legation." Fava felt "so long as a large part of our Italian emigration comes from the southern provinces, represented mainly by the agricultural or rural classes, proverbial for their simplicity, there will always be those, both Italians and others, who are ready to take advantage of them. In other words, wherever there are lambs to be eaten, there are always wolves ready to eat them up."

[9] Elizabeth Cometti, "Trends in Italian Emigration," *Western Political Quarterly*, XI (December, 1958), 821-25.

they would continue to be welcome in the United States. To the Italian government, this change of character did not seem to be much of a change at all. Most of Italy's emigrants were trained farmers who could thrive and make themselves useful citizens, especially in the South and Southwest. Accordingly, the Italian government sent Ambassador Mayor des Planches to tour the area and report on the possibility of directing Italians there.[10]

Italians and the Southern States

The southern states had actively sought immigrant labor and gave des Planches a welcome befitting his stature. But serious difficulties barred the fulfillment of these international efforts to attain better agricultural distribution. The Southern States Immigration Commission, charged with bringing agricultural laborers to the South, was having little success. The Ambassador, reporting both the good and bad points of southern life from the immigrant viewpoint, advised that certain conditions be met prior to Italian migration to the South. Though sensible, these qualifications proved serious stumbling blocks. In short, des Planches wanted the Italians to have favorable working conditions, worked out in advance and guaranteed by contracts. In this way, the South could be made attractive to the Italians.[11]

The Italian attempt to effect better distribution through these means was frustrated. Such orderly distribution beyond metropolitan areas could come only if the Italians were certain, before leaving Italy, that they could obtain work and live near

[10] See letters dated July 11, 1905, August 31, 1905, January 3, 1906, January 25, 1906, White to Root, "Diplomatic Dispatches," (with enclosures).

[11] Mayor des Planches' activities in the South are related in his *Attraverso gli Stati Uniti* (Turin, 1913) which has been used extensively in Robert L. Brandfon, "The End of Immigration to the Cotton Fields," *Mississippi Valley Historical Review*, L (March, 1964), 591-611.

one another. The Foran Act (Anti-Contract Labor Act) prevented that. It made it

> ...unlawful for any person, company partnership, or corporation, in any manner whatsoever, to prepay the transportation, or in any way assist or encourage the importation or migration of any alien or aliens, any foreigner or foreigners...under contract or agreement, parol or special, express or implied, made previous to the importation or migration of such alien or aliens...to perform labor or services of any kind in the United States.[12]

Though the law was easily evaded,[13] it did present an effective impediment to the open operation of a contract system which would have had the sanction of both Italian and American governments and given a legal basis for protection of Italian immigrants. Italian efforts to get the United States to interpret the Foran Act so as to allow Italian emigrants to settle in rural areas on the basis of des Planches' recommendations proved futile. The South remained unattractive to the Italians.[14]

Italian immigrants were not the only ones who found the South unattractive. In fact, Italians, few as they were in the South, were among the leading immigrant groups in certain southern areas. In 1920, for example, Italians born in Birmingham, Alabama, were twice as numerous as the second foreign-born group, the English. The Italians numbered 1,653 and made up over 26 percent of the total foreign-born population. Moreover, the Italian population in the South was also highly significant percentage-wise. In 1920, Italians represented 11.6 percent of the foreign-born population in the United States. But in Lousiana the Italians accounted for 35 percent of the foreign-born population; in Mississippi, 22 percent; in Alabama, 15 percent; and in Tennessee, 13 percent.[15] One might well ask why more Italians did not go to the South. As

---

[12] 23 Stat. 322; 8 U.S.C. cited in *Immigration Laws*, 224-27.

[13] For a discussion of the evasion of the Foran Act and subsequent amendments to it see Charlotte Erickson, *American Industry and the European Immigrant, 1860-1885* (Cambridge, 1957), *passim* and Luciano J. Iorizzo, "Italian Immigration and the Impact of the Padrone System," unpublished Ph.D. dissertation, Syracuse University, 1966, 88ff.

[14] Letters dated August 31, 1905, January 3, 1906, White to Root, "Diplomatic Dispatches," with enclosures.

[15] U. S. Department of Commerce, Bureau of the Census, *Abstract of the Fourteenth Census, 1920*, (Washington, 1923), 50-51 and 310-17. For statistics on Italian distribution by states from 1850 to 1960 see Iorizzo, "Italian Immigration," 32-45.

elsewhere, the Italian going south need not have a penny in his pocket. The employer would, if necessary, advance the expenses of agency fees, subsistence, transportation costs, and so forth. Part or all of the transportation charge would sometimes be refunded depending on the length of the stay of the laborer. A stay of three, six or nine months usually meant a partial refund. A year's stay usually meant full refund of transportation costs. Though the Italian might object to high transportation costs to the South, this objection could be overcome by a long and profitable stay there. But conditions as to wages and treatment were found unsatisfactory once the Italian began work.[16] The prospects for a long and prosperous stay dimmed. The immigrant sought release from his job and complications immediately arose. Part of the trouble stemmed from the fact that Southerners, anxious to get Italian labor, misrepresented Italian immigrant life in the South. The Italian government warned its citizens of more than a few unscrupulous farmers and planters who took advantage of Italians in this manner and made contract-labor agreements with them in Italy. When the disillusioned Italians sought to depart from their southern jobs they were prevented from doing so by virtue of their debtor-employee relationship. State legislation gave the creditor-employer the right to have the debtor arrested or detained until the debt was worked off. The Italian had no choice but to pay off the money advanced to him for transportation, food, and lodging, or become a fugitive from justice. Under such conditions the Italian government asked its local authorities not to issue passports to immigrants going to the southern states.[17]

What particularly galled the Italian in the South was the personal treatment accorded him. If the Italian immigrant was a second class citizen in many parts of America, he must have been a third class citizen in the South. On the docks of New York an Italian might be called a "dago" or told that it takes two or three of him to make one "white man." In the South, people not only did this but often deprived the Italian of his civil liberties, as they did the Negro. The infamous lynching of eleven Italians in New Orleans on March 14, 1891, was only one of a number of such incidents. More than twenty-five lost

---

[16] Sheridan, "Italian Laborers" *Labor Bulletin*, No. 72, 422.
[17] Dillingham Commission, *Emigrant Conditions in Europe*, IV, 149-150. Passports were required from 1901 on.

their lives through mob violence in southern states: Arkansas, Louisiana, Mississippi, and North Carolina. Over ten were similarly killed in Colorado, Pennsylvania, and Illinois. (See Table I.)

TABLE 1
Mob Violence against Italian-Americans [a]

Date	Location	Number and Condition	Indemnity
12/17/1874	Buena Vista, Pa.	4 killed [b]	
3/28/1886	Vicksburg, Miss.	1 lynched [c]	
3/14/1891	New Orleans, La	11 lynched [d]	$ 25,000
7/ ? /1893	Denver, Col.	1 lynched [e]	
3/21/1894	Altoona, Pa.	200 driven from city [f]	
3/12/1895	Walsenburg, Col.	6 murdered by mob [g]	$ 10,000
8/11/1896	Hahnville, La.	3 lynched [h]	$ 6,000
7/20/1899	Tallulah, Miss.	5 lynched [i]	$ 4,000
7/11/1901	Erwin, Miss.	5 lynched, 1 wounded [j]	$ 5,000
11/18/1901	Marksville, La.	4 driven from city [k]	
5/14/1906	Marian, N.C.	2 killed, 5 wounded [l]	private settlement
9/20/1910	Tampa, Fla.	2 lynched [m]	$ 6,000
10/12/1914	Willisville, Ill.	1 shot and killed [n]	
6/12/1915	Johnson City, Ill.	1 lynched [n]	

[a] There were three major difficulties involved with aliens and mob violence: 1) denial of justice was likely in the failure of local or state authorities to afford adequate protection to aliens in custody; 2) failure to criminally punish the alleged violators of aliens; 3) denial of justice in not securing indemnity by state and local authorities. The U.S. government was able to remedy the third difficulty and did on a number of occasions. Originally it admitted of no liability for mob violence. But in 1891 the U.S. began paying indemnities "without respect to the question of liability." See Charles H. Watson, "Need of Federal Legislation in Respect to Mob Violence in Cases of Lynchings of Aliens," *Yale Law Journal*, XXV (May, 1916), 560-81.

[b] Letter dated December 17, 1874, Corti to Fish, "Notes from the Italian Legation." Armstrong Coal Works engaged 150 Italian laborers in New York. Former employees attacked the Italians and killed four as they were driven from the mine.

[c] Letter dated April 28, 1886, Fava to Bayard, "Notes from the Italian Legation," and letters dated May 6, 1886 and June 2, 1886, Bayard to Fava, "Notes to the Italian Legation." Federico Villarosa of Vicksburg was lynched on suspicion of having violated a 10-year-old girl.

[d] Correspondence on this affair is available from March 14, 1891, in "Notes from the Italian Legation," "Notes to the Italian Legation," and *Foreign Relations, 1891*, pp. 658-728. The infamous details are available in many printed accounts.

[e] Schiavo, *Four Centuries of Italian-American History*, p. 170.

[f] Letter dated March 21, 1894, Fava to Gresham, "Notes from the Italian Legation," and subsequent correspondence. Several hundred were driven from the city by an armed mob. Several were wounded and homes were burned. Circumstances causing action were not detailed.

g Letter dated March 13, 1895, Fava to Gresham, "Notes from the Italian Legation," and subsequent correspondence. Nine Italian-American miners were arrested on suspicion of murdering an American saloon keeper. One was found guilty at the inquest. Six lost their lives by violence after the inquest when settlers took the law into their own hands. See also *Foreign Relations, 1895*, II, 950.

h Telegram dated August 11, 1896, Fava to Olney, "Notes from the Italian Legation," and subsequent correspondence in that and in "Notes to the Italian Legation," Salvatore Arena, Giuseppe Venturella, and Lorenzo Saladino, jailed on suspicion of homicide, were taken out and lynched.

i Letter dated July 22, 1899, Vinci to Hay, "Notes from the Italian Legation," and subsequent correspondence. The five Italians lynched were Giovanni Cyrano, Francesco, Carlo, and Giuseppe Difatta, and Rosario Fiducia. A goat owned by the Difatta brothers (grocers in Tallulah), repeatedly climbed on the balcony of a house belonging to a local doctor. The doctor shot the goat; Carlo Difatta struck the doctor with his fist; the doctor then shot Carlo and in turn was wounded by Giuseppe who came to the aid of his brother. Carlo and Giuseppe hid, but were hunted out by a mob and lynched. The other three, who had taken no part in the fracas, were jailed. The mob then lynched them also. See also *Foreign Relations, 1900*, 715 ff.

j Letter dated July 15, 1901, Carignani to Hay, "Notes from the Italian Legation," and subsequent correspondence. Giovanni and Vincenzo Serio were killed by an armed mob, and Salvatore Liberto was wounded "under circumstances which constituted a lynching." A quarrel over a horse precipitated the incident. See also *Foreign Relations, 1901*, 282 ff.

k Letter dated November 18, 1901, Carignani to Hill, "Notes from the Italian Legation." Four Italians, doing well in the dry goods business, were warned to leave town. Accompanying the order to vacate were forty shots fired in their direction. They were given four days to wind up their affairs, then get out or be killed. Trade rivalry was the motive.

l Letter dated June 20, 1906, Montagna to Root, "Notes from the Italian Legation," and *Foreign Relations, 1906*, 919 ff. Sixty Italians tried to quit work for the Spruce Pine Carolina Co., a railroad construction company. They claimed the work was misrepresented, food was scarce, the dwellings were unheated, and they were forced to stay on the job by armed guards. When the Italians sought to set up a meeting time to discuss these conditions but got instead a reception from a company "posse," the outcome was two killed, five wounded, and nine jailed (all Italians) for "assault, battery, and conspiracy." Montagna was able to make settlement with the company out of court. In addition to a monetary indemnity to the heirs of the dead, the company agreed to dismiss its agents who were guilty of misdemeanors, ill-treatment and abuses of laborers, to adopt administrative reforms and take measures to remove the more serious complaints. It should be noted that this happened at a time when railroads, in general, began to take a more direct interest in hiring and supervising its laborers in answer to the pressures to rid the nation of padroni.

m *Foreign Relations, 1913*, 613-14. Two Italians, one Ficcarotta and Angelo Albano were taken from custody (in jail on suspicion of murder) and lynched.

n Watson, "Need of Federal Legislation," *Yale Law Journal*, XXV, 560-81. Albert Piazza, jailed on suspicion of murder, was shot and killed by an armed mob as he was being transferred to the county seat in Perry County in southern Illinois. Joe Speranza was lynched on suspicion of killing the father-in-law of a mine superintendent in the town of Johnson City, Illinois, not far from the murder scene of Piazza.

On other occasions Italians were just driven from town. In 1901 four Italians were fired upon and given a warning to leave Marksville, Louisiana, in four days or else lose their lives. It seems they were doing too well as merchants, making the competition too keen for the native businessmen.[18] A number of Italian shopkeepers were run out of town for similar reasons or because they were naive enough to want to allow Negroes and whites alike to frequent their stores.[19]

Other major deterrents to the Italian's settling in the South were the recurring outbreaks of yellow fever and the attempts by southerners to make the Italian an agricultural laborer, while the Italian had ambitions to become a land-owner.[20] The key to land-owning was to reap the rich rewards of industrial employment offered by the great cities of America, save money, then begin to accumulate land holdings.

One immigrant newspaper summed up the Italians' aversion to the South:

> If the governments of the southern states and other local-
> ities really wish to turn the current of immigration to their
> profit, they must show clearly that not only is there greater
> opportunity in their area than in others, but also that the
> workers enjoy there the same rights accorded the natives.[21]

Italian Immigrants in the North

National groups had their own private organizations which sought to facilitate the distribution of their own kind to prof-itable positions throughout the country. The Germans had an Immigrant Labor Bureau, the Irish had the Irish Immigrant

---

[18] Letter dated November 18, 1901, Francesco Carignani to D.J. Hill, "Notes from the Italian Legation."

[19] Letter dated January 15, 1900, Fava to Hay, "Notes from the Ital-ian Legation" with enclosures; and Gino Speranza, "A Mission of Peace," *Outlook*, LXXXVIII (September, 1904), 128-31. The Italians innocently threatened the social-economic structure of white supremacy in the South. Southerners saw in their behavior an important reason to echo the sentiments of northern restrictionists despite the need for immi-grant laborers in the South.

[20] Brandfon, "The End of Immigration," *Mississippi Valley Histor-ical Review*, L, *passim.*

[21] *Risveglio coloniale*, Syracuse, New York, May 15, 1909. The best states were listed as New York, Massachusetts, New Jersey, Pennsyl-vania and Ohio.

Society of the City of New York, and so on. Among the many
Italian societies, the Labor Information Office for Italians was
a non-political, non-sectarian organization which sought to
solve the problems of immigrant labor and eliminate the abuses
of the padrone system. It was incorporated in New York in
1906 and with a sizable subsidy from the Italian government
immediately began to place Italian emigrants in jobs. But
at no time did the numbers it placed become very significant.[22]

Religious societies, philantropic organizations, and state
labor agencies also sought to provide distribution of Italian
immigrants to needy areas. Once again, the efforts of these
groups were no more successful than any of the others mentioned. The major reason for the continued success of the
padroni was their ability to compete favorably against all
comers and successfully avoid prosecution under reform legislation.[23] Thus the padrone system flourished as the principal
distribution agency prior to World War I.[24]

The Dillingham Commission investigated construction
work in New York and New Jersey, railroad and other construction work in North Dakota, South Dakota, Minnesota,
Kansas, and Missouri, and construction work in West Virginia,
Tennessee, North Carolina. In each area — East, West and

---

[22] *Charities*, XVI (July, 1906), 402-03.

[23] Vineland, New Jersey, was founded as an Italian colony in 1878
by an Italian refugee, Signor Secchi di Casale. Thousands of Italians
came to Vineland, attracted by the profitable business of truck farming.
But there were too few such colonies to which Italians could go. See
U.S. Reports of the Industrial Commission, XV, (Washington, 1901),
499ff. Employers looked to padroni for a source of labor supply and
encouraged their activities. Agents and contractors split fees. And, of
course, the padroni provided personal services *par excellence.* Neither
the state agencies, nor the private ones could compete against all that.
Despite attempts by states, notably Illinois and New York, to curtail
labor abuses by padroni, the padroni usually managed to get around
these measures. For example, padroni claimed exemption from State
employment agency laws because they charged no fee and received no
compensation. Thus they did not even bother to take out licenses to
operate as labor agents though they continued to operate as such and
make a handsome profit by providing services for immigrants. See
Grace Abbott, "The Chicago Employment Agency and the Immigrant
Worker," *American Journal of Sociology*, XIV (November, 1908), 289ff.,
Report of the Commission of Immigration of the State of New York,
121-22, and Charles B. Phipard, "The Philanthropist Padrone," *Charities*,
XII (May, 1904), 470-72.

[24] Dillingham Commission, *Immigrants in Industries*, XVIII, Pt.
22, 425.

South respectively — Italian labor was provided by padroni. In the East the majority of labor was supplied by padroni. In the West and the South labor agencies supplied most of the immigrant laborers. But when Italian laborers were sought, the padrone system was used.[25]

The padrone would agree with a contractor or railroad representative to furnish the required labor. He then contacted his banker or labor agency associate in New York or Philadelphia. The latter would collect, assemble, and send the men to their destination. Sometimes the Italians came to him unsolicited; sometimes he would have to canvass an area of the city where immigrants were out of work and procure them himself. On other occasions he would have to call on his banking associates in Italy who kept in close touch with the sub-agents of steamship companies scattered throughout the Italian peninsula. Having once established himself with a contractor or railroad, the padrone would then usually remain with them, enlarge his business, and increase his profits on the commissary privilege granted him in the original contract. This was satisfactory to the employer who was insured of a labor supply, was relieved of the responsibility of hiring an interpreter, and obtained a hold, through the supervisory power of the padrone, on the men he would not otherwise have.[26]

That the padrone and the banker could be one and the same is seen in the case of two padroni who operated a bank and labor agency in Philadelphia and numerous commissaries

---

[25] *Immigrants in Industries*, XVIII, Pt. 22, *passim*. The most important means of immigrant distribution for all kinds of work was the mails. Armed with a letter from a friend or relative, the majority of Italian immigrants needed no direct contact to insure success in the U.S. He knew that "he need only go to the Italian quarter ... to get work." See Sheridan, "Italian Laborers," *Labor Bulletin*, No. 72, 439, and *Report of the Commission of Immigration of the State of New York*, 110. Under these conditions the padrone can indirectly be given much of the credit for distribution. For it should be remembered that the role played by the padrone in the Italian neighborhoods was a key one, especially in the writing and translation of letters.

[26] Dillingham Commission, *Immigrants in Industries*, XVIII, 393 and 426 and *Report of the Commission of Immigration of the State of New York*, 122ff. In cases where labor agencies furnished most of the labor they would have to use the services of the padroni to fill jobs when labor was scarce. It should also be noted that the control that a padrone exercised over an immigrant from the time he left Italy made for a very mobile labor force. The padrone could transfer his men from one job to another with ease to suit the requirements of the time.

in New Jersey. One remained at the work sites directing the commissaries, while the other gathered the men and shipped them where needed. As might be expected they also provided the usual immigrant bank services for their clients.[27] In another instance, prior to the prohibition of contract labor, a *Banco Italiano* official claimed to have imported 14,000 Italians from the Civil War to 1884. When necessary, travel expenses were advanced at 6 percent. How many immigrants were bound to bankers in this manner will probably never be known.[28]

The immigrant worker did not have to be afraid to travel in a foreign land or remain out of work for lack of money to go where there was activity. The padrone would make sure he was escorted to the work site and would maintain a close vigilance over him until the job was completed. For his troubles, he would get a fee, a rebate on the transportation costs (which he did not pass on to the immigrant), and most important, he would make a tidy profit on the commissary privilege. Moreover, he did not stand to lose anything if he had to advance transportation costs since contractors protected the padrone against loss by keeping the men on the job until they had worked out their transportation. Sometimes transportation was provided on a line upon which the immigrant was working. At other times transportation costs would be remitted, depending on the amount of time an immigrant would stay on, as an inducement to get a needed worker to remain on the job. The fact that the padrone did not charge the railroad or contractor for his services attests to the profitable nature of the commissary business.[29]

The padrone system was a widespread institution among the immigrants from southern and eastern Europe. What made the Italian padrone system unique was the commissary system. Other immigrants were willing to use the boarding trains of contractors and railroads. But the Italians demanded their own kitchen. They did so despite the exploitation that might result for two basic reasons. First, they preferred to cook and eat food to suit their own tastes. Second, and probably more important since the Italians were known to eat American food in their needy moments, they could eat cheaper this way. The

---

[27] Dillingham Commission, *Immigrants in Industries*, XVIII, 393.
[28] Erickson, *American Industry*, pp. 84ff.
[29] Dillingham Commission, *Immigrants in Industries*, XVIII, 419ff.

non-Italian laborer willingly paid $18 a month for room and board, which included three full meals a day. The menu included ham and eggs, roast beef, vegetables, fish, oatmeal, bread, butter, pie and coffee. The Italian bought his own food, cooked it, and ate it. At times he even baked his own bread. He could room and board for as little as $6.90. That represented a saving of $11.10 on the cost of absolutely essential items to non-Italians. But the savings were not due to low overhead alone. The Italian hardly ate one full meal a day. For example, the monthly menu of one laborer included twenty loaves of bread, various quantities of bologna, sausage, sardines, cheese, lard and coffee. Others might follow the typical menu prepared from items purchased from the padrone's commissary:

Breakfast: coffee and dry bread
Lunch: bread, bologna, sausage and onions
Supper: macaroni, rice with tomatoes, potatoes or beans.

Two days a week the menu might be supplemented with some boiled meat for supper. The Italian willingly "underfed" himself since, in many cases, he was still eating better than he had in the old country. He could spend as much as $3 a month on beer, cigars, and tobacco and still have enough surplus to send remittances to his family or bank in Italy.[30]

Immigrants paid $1 a month for housing. Railroads furnished ordinary box cars with windows about eighteen inches square cut for ventilation. The cars had a stove in the center around which from ten to fourteen bunk beds were placed to accommodate the workers. Though the box cars were furnished free, the padrone was allowed to charge his workers a monthly room rental, usually $1.[31]

The Italians in this country who elected to put themselves under the care of a padrone could start from New York City, for example, without any money. They could go virtually anywhere in the United States, even Alaska, provided their

---

[30] *Ibid.*, and Sheridan, "Italian Laborers," *Labor Bulletin*, No. 72, 462ff. The Italians might also use the boarding boss system whereby "the boarding boss buys all the food from the commissary and at the end of the month each man's proportion is deducted from his wages by the commissary clerk."

[31] Dillingham Commission, *Immigrants in Industries*, XVIII, 397-99 also contains descriptions of other types of housing like shanty towns.

labor was required. They could get food, clothing, lodging, and luxury items such as beer and cigarettes on credit. When pay-day came, be it weekly, bi-monthly, or as was usually the case, monthly, the padrone would present his bill to the contractor or railroad paymaster. The latter would deduct from the workers' wages what was due the padrone and give the balance to the workers. In some cases, the padrone drew the wages for his men and paid them after deducting what was due him. Deductions might be charged off to employment fees (which ran as high as $2.50 and were paid once per job), trans-portation costs, commissary items, and so forth. When all was done, the Italian saved more than any other immigrant group. From a monthly salary of $35, the Italian could save $25 or more. Other immigrant groups were reported as saving $20. The difference saved by the Italian was due generally to his utilization of the padrone's services.[32]

Though the Italian worked and settled mainly in the East, he did not ignore the advantages around the country. Padroni were active in the mid-West and West, particularly in Chicago as one study of the clearing house activities of that city's employment agencies demonstrated. Most of the agencies in-vestigated were located in steamship and immigrant bank of-fices or near saloons and cheap lodging houses, clearly indicat-ing the many functions of the Italian go-between: padrone-banker, steamship agent, saloon keeper, and so on. All in all, 70 percent of the agencies in Chicago which placed immigrant labor were connected to the padrone in one way or another. Chicago became a clearing house for the seasonal workers of America.[33] Furthermore, sometimes Westerners had a direct contact with a labor supplier in Italy. A labor syndicate in Denver, Colorado, had agents in Italy in order to obtain hands for railroad and public works projects.[34]

---

[32] *Ibid., passim. Report of the Commission of Immigration of the State of New York*, 123 and Memorandum of interview with Anthony Smith, Syracuse, New York, January 29, 1964. Smith is a descendant of a padrone.

[33] Grace Abbott, "The Chicago Employment Agency and the Im-migrant Worker," *American Journal of Sociology*, XIV (November, 1908), *passim*. Illinois law prohibited labor agencies to operate from a saloon. So 45 percent of them operated above, below or next door to saloons.

[34] *Laborer Enquirer*, Denver, January 1, 1884, and February 9, 1884, cited in Erickson, *American Industry*, p. 84. The immigrant would have to pay his own passage, a deposit fee of from $3 to $10, and contract to pay his importer 20 percent of his wages for three years.

At the end of the nineteenth century padroni controlled two-thirds of the Italian laborers in New York City. Each year they sent thousands of them to work areas as far west as Nebraska and as far south as Florida. As a rule only a small number of the workingmen went to the southern states of Florida, Virginia, North Carolina, South Carolina, Alabama, Tennessee, Georgia, Maryland, Mississippi, Kentucky, and Louisiana.[35]

Industrial Pursuits of Italian Immigrants

The labor force that was employed for the industrial expansion of the United States at the turn of the century was drawn in large part from southern and eastern Europe. Most of the wage earners engaged in manufacturing and mining at that time were foreign born. These immigrants worked in the iron and copper mines of the Mid-West, Southwest and South. They were found in the steel plants and glass factories of the Middle West and South. They worked in the mines, mills, and factories of the East, and traveled throughout the country providing the labor force for temporary and seasonal needs. The Italians were most conspicuous among that labor force. In the West and Mid-West they did construction work or harvest work from spring to fall. In winter they kept busy at logging camps or brought in ice off the Great Lakes. In the South most Italians worked on the railroads, carrying crossties, shifting tracks, and doing pick and shovel tasks. Others served as general laborers, cotton pickers and sugar cane cutters. About 10 per cent performed the skilled work of carpenters, stone masons, plasterers, marble carvers, and the like. In the East, Italians were to be found in every conceivable type of occupation.[36]

Throughout the United States in 1900 Italian-born males were more concentrated in domestic and personal service jobs than any other immigrant group. This was due to their concentration in the laborer category. Except for the Hungarians they were least massed in agriculture. In separate job cat-

---

[35] Nathan Glazer and Daniel Patrick Moynihan, *Beyond the Melting Pot* (Cambridge, 1963), pp. 190-94 and Sheridan, "Italian Laborers," *Labor Bulletin*, No. 72, 416ff.

[36] *Ibid.*, and Dillingham Commission, *Abstracts*, I, 493.

egories, Italians "were in highest proportion among hucksters and peddlers, followed by tailors, miners, and quarrymen,
laborers, masons, and steam-railroad employees." They also
herded sheep and homesteaded land. But, in these occupations, as in most of the others, they made up only a relatively
minor proportion of the labor force.[37]

The occupational distribution of Italian-born in the city
of Oswego, New York, about that time was probably typical
of what one would find in any city where Italians were beginning to settle. In 1905 there were 399 Italian-born in Oswego,
a city of 23,000. About 200 Italians were classified as day
laborers or railroad laborers. A few dozen or so Italians were
employed in the various factories and mills in the city. A
handful were shopkeepers, and a few could be found working
as blacksmiths, masons, carpenters, machinists, gardeners, and
music teachers. There were no Italian-born farmers — that
is, farm owners — either in the city or the county of Oswego.
However, many Italians did provide their services, in season,
to the native farmers in the area. And of course, there were
Italian bankers.[38]

The number of native born males of Italian origin in the
United Sates labor force was small. In many respects their

----

[37] E. P. Hurchinson, *Immigrants and Their Children* (New York,
1956), p. 178. Letters dated March 5, 1903, des Planches to Hay, "Notes
from the Italian Legation," and July 14, 1964, L. G. Giacomini to this
writer. Giacomini is a descendant of an Italian family which homesteaded in Padroni, Colorado, in the late 1890's. Not a few Italians served
in the military forces. They helped put down the Indians and also
served in the Spanish-American War. And, of course, they continued to
serve in the military bands. Our diplomatic correspondence with
Italy is rich with references to such activities, but see, in particular,
letters dated July 25, 1873, April 24, 1874, March 23, 1875, October 23,
1898, May 2, 1899, April 8, 1900, July 9, 1900, March 27, 1903, "Notes
from the Italian Legation."

[38] New York State Census, "Manuscript Books of the County and
City of Oswego," 1905. Memorandum of interview with Lydia Karpinski, September 10, 1964. Mrs. Karpinski is the widow of Henry Karpinski, farmer and dry cleaner. He employed seasonal Italian laborers on
his farm about 1905. She has a picture of about fifteen Italians working on the farm where they did everything from hoeing to harvesting.
Italians did not begin to work their own farms until a decade later in
the opinion of Dominic Santoro, muck farmer, Oswego, New York.
See Memorandum of interview, September 28, 1964. By 1915 there were
34 Italian-born farmers in the County of Oswego. See New York State
Census, "Manuscript Books of the County and City of Oswego," 1915.

jobs were different from those of their fathers. They were still most concentrated in domestic and personal service, though less than the foreign born, and had only moderate employment as laborers. They were also highly concentrated in trade and transportation and attained less than proportionate representation in the professions.[39]

Examination of the Twelfth Census, 1900, reveals more particularly where and what kind of work the descendants of Italian-born performed. The following table shows an occupational distribution of workers of Italian parentage in six states representing the various sections of the United States:

TABLE 2

Total Males of Italian Parentage 10 Years and Older in Gainful Occupations

	Ala.	Calif.	Colorado	N.Y.	La.	Nev.
Agriculture . . .	36	5,849	443	966	4,287	427
Professional service	6	233	49	1,664	64	3
Domestic and personal . . .	59	4,475	953	47,268	1,956	201
Trasportation and trade	159	2,839	490	17,849	2,368	282
Manufacturing and mining . .	310	4,020	2,615	28,237	1,122	181
Total	573	17,416	4,550	95,984	9,797	1,094 a

a Adapted from 12th Census, 1900, *Special Reports: Occupations*, 190 ff. The leading specific occupations with each category for workers of Italian-born are: Agriculture: laborers, Professional: musicians, Domestic and Personal: laborers, Transportation and Trade: retail merchants, Manufacturing and Mining: miners, quarrymen, and bootmakers.

[39] Hutchinson, *Immigrants and Their Children*, p. 178. The sons of Italians were chiefly messengers, hucksters and peddlers, saloon keepers, bartenders, printers, and tailors. Though they had almost attained full representation in the professions by 1900, the impression should not be left that they had their full share by mid-century. In 1950 those of Italian foreign stock were still under-represented in the professions when compared to the occupations of the total foreign stock in the U.S. This has been particularly upsetting to those Italian descendants who are in the professions and wish to believe otherwise. But see U.S. Department of Commerce and Labor, Bureau of the

The sons of Italians continued to stand out in the domestic and personal category in New York where as common laborers they constituted about half of the total Italian parentage work force. Less than 1 percent farmed or did agricultural labor. In Louisiana, Nevada, and California, on the contrary, descendants of Italian immigrants were most numerous as farmers or agricultural laborers and least numbered in professional service. In the other major categories, they were about equally divided. In Colorado and Alabama, they were most numerous in manufacturing and mining, where they served as miners, quarrymen, and iron and steel workers. Again they were least numerous in the professions and fairly well distributed in the other major categories. The Italian-born had provided the United States with a progeny that was to help fill the needs of expanding America. The jobs that those of Italian parentage took were in no small way determined by the needs of the communities in which they were raised.

Italian immigrant labor, padrone labor included, which was attracted to urban America did not close its eyes entirely to rural America. A good number of the men and women who picked rags, collected bottles, did railroad work, or worked in box factories or textiles in the wintertime, were ready by springtime to embark on the migrant trail. From May through October they would go berry picking as the crops matured: strawberries, blackberries, raspberries, and cranberries. In one particular operation, the padrone's role was described clearly by Mina C. Ginger of the Newark Bureau of Associated Charities. Farmers would converge on Philadelphia in early spring for the purpose of making contracts with padroni in order to insure themselves of enough harvesters. The padroni would then canvass the neighborhoods and induce immigrants to sign up with them by offering them free shelter, straw with which to fill their bed ticks, inexpensive fruits and vegetables, and probably most important, a net profit for the season of

---

Census, *Special Reports*: *Occupations at the Twelfth Census*, 190 ff. and Hutchinson, *Immigrants and Their Children, passim*. One group remains, however: those native-born Americans who have no direct link to Italian born and who are not born of foreign parentage. These people, whose grandparents were foreign born or of foreign parentage, are known in some circles as Italian-Americans also. The number of such persons engaged in the professions is virtually impossible to ascertain for the simple reason that they are classified as native Americans in the census reports.

from $150 to $400. The padroni would get a nominal salary of $1.50 to $3.00 a day from the farmer for whom their crews worked. But they obtained their major income by providing the usual commissary, transportation, and banking services to their workers. Their "earnings" were supplemented by whatever they could wring from their charges as "presents" — at the end of the season each family "willingly" gave one padrone $6. It was not unusual for a padrone to make over $3,000 a season.[40]

What made this possible, of course, was the willingness of the Italians to become migrant workers despite the "inconveniences" the padroni might cause them. The reason is not hard to find. As migrant workers, a family could triple its income by putting to work the children (if there were any) who were unable to work in the city. Mothers and fathers were known to be eager to have their children work in the fields (often against the wishes of the farmers who feared the youngsters would trample more than they would pick), so as to add to the family income. The following list shows the operation of one family:

	Age	Average pecks of berries picked per day
Father	39	20
Mother	38	17
Daughter	17	15
Son	15	13
Daughter	13	10
Daughter	11	5
Son	8	3
Daughter	7	4

This family (with only the father and three children working) made $24 a week in the city. On the farm tour they averaged $65 to $70 a week.[41]

Distribution of Italian Agricultural Pursuits

Though the Italians largely neglected agricultural pursuits in America, there were many Italian agricultural communities

---

[40] Mina C. Ginger, "In Berry Field and Bog," *Charities*, XV (November, 1905), 162-69; Alexander E. Cance, "Immigrant Rural Communities," *The Survey*, XXV (January, 1911), 587-89; Owen R. Lovejoy, "The Cost of Cranberry Sauce," *The Survey*, XXV (January, 1911), 605-10.

[41] Lovejoy, "The Cost of Cranberry Sauce," *The Survey*, XXV, 605-10. The author points out that vast stretches of marsh land in central

spread over every state in the Union. More Italian rural communities (about a dozen altogether) were found in Texas in 1908 than in any other state. New York and California ranked second, Louisiana, Mississippi, and Arkansas had sizable rural communities. The largest, and one of the most successful of all, was located at Vineland, New Jersey.[42]

How did Italian agricultural communities originate? In about half of the communities mentioned in Table 3 the Ital-

TABLE 3

*List of Italian Rural Communities in the United States
1900-1910* [a]

State	City or Town
Alabama [b]	Daphne
	Lambert
Arkansas [b]	Gracie
	Sunnyside
	Lambert
California [c]	Asti
	Madeira
	and scattered groups in the Sacramento and Visitation Valleys
Colorado [d]	Denver
	Pueblo
Connecticut [b]	South Glastonbury
Delaware [e]	Wilmington
Louisiana [b]	Independence
	Kenner
	Millikens Bend
	Shreveport
Maryland [e]	Baltimore

New Jersey, formerly useless and barren, were now overrun in season by padrone labor.

[42] Dillingham Commission, *Abstracts*, I, 560 and Ernest Peixotta, "Italy in California," Scribner's Magazine, XLVIII (July, 1910), 75-84. For the names of specific communities see Table 3. The Commission made a searching inquiry into Federal and State Census Reports, interviewed government officials, industrial agents and so forth. That these sources were not definitive on the subject was seen by the fact that the Commissioners still uncovered fluorishing little settlements of Italians about which there was no data available. For the subject of agriculture, with regard to the impact of the padrone, see U.S. Immigration Commission Reports, *Immigrants in Industries*, Sen. Docs., 61 Cong., 2d Sess., No. 633, XXI and XXII, Pt. 24, "Recent Immigrants in Agriculture."

TABLE 3 (continued)

Mississippi [b]	Delta Region
	Gulfport
	Long Beach
	Bay St. Louis
Missouri [b]	Knobview
	Marshfield
New York [b]	Canastota
	Lyons
	Clyde
	Albion
	Port Byron
	Geneva
	Oneida
New Jersey [b]	Hammonton and vicinity
	Vineland and vicinity
North Carolina [b]	St. Helena
	Valdese
Rhode Island [b]	Olneyville
Tennessee [b]	Memphis
	Paradise Ridge
Utah [d]	Salt Lake City
Texas [f]	Arcadia
	Alta Loma
	Beaumont
	Bryan
	Dickinsen
	Hitchcock
	Lamarque
	League City
	Little York
	Montague
	San Antonio
	Victoria
	Dallas
	Galveston
	Houston
Virginia [e]	Norfolk
Wisconsin [b]	Genoa
	Cumberland
Wyoming [d]	Cheyenne
Washington, D.C. [e]	

[a] The location of many Italian rural communities was never recorded but it should be noted that virtually no city with market garden possibilities did without truck products raised by Italians. See Eliot Lord, et. al., The Italian in America (New York, 1905), 123-24.

[b] These communities were investigated by the Dillingham Commission, 1909, Abstract, I, 560.

[c] Peixotto, "Italy in California," Scribner's, XLVIII, 75-84.

[d] Report of the Industrial Commission, XV, 500-505.

[e] Lord, Italian in America, pp. 121 ff.

[f] Ibid., 125, and Dillingham Commission, Abstract, I, 560.

ians came directly from Italy.[43] Both cotton and sugar plan-
tation owners sought to replace Negro labor with foreign white
labor and advanced passage money for the transportation of
Italian families. Though the Southerners met with no great
success, enough immigrants were attracted to form nuclei from
which other Italian agricultural communities developed. Several colonies were developed from the one at Sunnyside,
Arkansas, originally formed with the importation of 100 families from northern Italy. Other Italians, disembarking at New
Orleans, obtained immediate work on plantations and gained
the necessary money and skill to form the bases of other successful colonies in the future.[44] But how were the other southern Italian rural communities developed, and what of those in
the other states? The other Italian farm settlers were drawn
mostly from those who were engaged in some kind of day
labor. In addition, a few skilled hands moved from the trades
or industry on to farms. These Italians were persuaded to
join the farm ranks by philanthropists seeking to relieve the
congestion of the cities, by land companies, and by interested
Italian leaders.[45] Many from this group were originally padrone employees. Many Italians who worked for padroni,
either as industrial day laborers or migrant farm hands, eventually broke with them to enter agriculture on their own, either
full or part time.[46] For example, Italian railroad laborers,
after finishing a job for the Houston and Texas Railroad, set-

---

[43] Dillingham Commission, *Abstracts*, I 567.

[44] *Ibid.*, 568.

[45] For example, Austin Corbin, millionaire philanthropist, was associated with Sunnyside; when many Italians began to fail at Sunnyside,
the Reverend Father Bandini came to their aid and helped establish
a new Italian agricultural community at Tontitown, Arkansas; the
North Carolina Truck Garden Company sought to colonize an area
near Wilmington. These examples and others are documented in
virtually all of the sources used in this paper. In particular see: Alice
Bennett, "Italian-American Farmers," *The Survey*, XXII (May, 1909),
172-75; John L. Mathews, "Tontitown: A Story of Conservation of Men,"
Everybody's Magazine, XX (January, 1909), 3-13; Alfred H. Stone, "Italian
Cotton Growers in Arkansas," *Review of Reviews*, XXXV (February,
1907), 209-13.

[46] Brandfon, "The End of Immigration," *Mississippi Valley Historical
Review*, L, 594 suggests the same thing. "In the early 1880's padroni
had been active in bringing laborers from northern cities to work on
the Mississippi levees. Some of these laborers might have formed the
nucleus of the Delta's first Italian agricultural settlement at Friars
Point (Coahoma County) in 1885."

tled in Bryan, Texas, and established a cotton colony there in 1880. Many other Italian tenant and independent farmers in Texas were also originally railroad day laborers initially sent to Texas by padroni agents in New York, Chicago, and St. Louis.[47] In the settlement of strawberry growers in Tangipahoa Parish, Louisiana, were many former berry pickers who worked out of New Orleans, a city not free from the touch of the padroni.[48]

The Italian rural community of South Glastonbury, Connecticut, developed after the efforts at part-time farming by railroad day laborers proved successful. Two of the highly successful Italians were John Carini and Luigi Piro, both of whom went into farming in the 1890's. Carini saved enough as a railroad worker to buy his own farm and subsequently built it into a 1500 acre "estate" on which he raised peaches, apples, plums, pears, grapes, and some small fruits and vegetables. Piro went to work in 1896 for J. H. Hale, one of New England's largest fruit growers, and by 1908 became Hale's partner. These were only two of the many Italians who became farmers in the area and were considered sober, industrious, and productive members of the community.[49]

In 1908, Vineland and Hammonton, New Jersey, were rated among the most promising Italian settlements east of the Rockies. They were both settled by former Italian berry pickers, who, having become land owners, hired Italian itinerants at harvest time. Originally the colony was formed by northern Italians who purchased new, uncleared, unoccupied land, but by 1908 they were giving way to the Sicilians. Both groups

---

[47] Moroni, "Il Texas e l'emigrazione italiana," 30; C. Nicolini, "Texas," from "Gli italiani nel distretto consolare di Nuova Orleans," *Bollettino emigrazione*, 1, 1903, 17-20; *Report of the Industrial Commission*, XV, 500.

[48] Dillingham Commission, *Abstract*, I, 568.

[49] The citizens in South Glastonbury did not have a high regard for Italians at first. On the contrary many thought the Italians would prove to be the ruin of Hale since Italians were considered inferior, lazy and untrustworthy. In time, many came to assess these new immigrants as did Hale: "(Italians) are delightful people, and one of the best handlers of the soil for horticultural purposes, and are getting more out of it than any other class of foreigners that are coming to our shores .... In less than ten years 500 acres which had always been too difficult to cultivate on account of rocks and stumps will be worth $250 an acre." See Alice Bennet, "Italians as Farmers and Fruit Growers," *Outlook*, XC (September, 1908), 87-88.

who had the "magic of property" and "turned sand into gold," built an oasis in a waste of sand and lowland by raising grapes, peaches, and sweet potatoes. Some among them, of course, succeeded more than others. Many of their sons showed an interest in new machinery, subscribed to agricultural journals and joined farmer co-ops. They were indeed progressive "American farmers." [50]

By the beginning of the twentieth century hundreds of Italians left their mining and railroad laboring jobs and took to the soil in and around Denver and Pueblo in Colorado, Salt Lake City, Utah, and Cheyenne, Wyoming. As truck farmers, they soon monopolized the business of furnishing vegetables to the people of those metropolitan areas.[51] In Nebraska many padrone laborers eventually became truck farmers *par excellence.*[52]

In New York State, many Italians turned to the soil in Lyons, Clyde, Port Byron, Oneida, Canastota, Oswego and other sites located along the Barge Canal and railroad lines, the building and maintenance of which attracted large gangs of padrone labor. In many instances, American owners were unwilling to undertake the clearing and draining of the muck land, abundant in these areas, at a great expense of hard labor. They had no need to do so since they profited from the uplands. The Italians saw a great opportunity here. They purchased the unused and unproductive land rather cheaply, cleared it, drained it, and began raising crops, particularly onions. Soon they made productive land which native farmers had considered worthless. The success of these Italians is remarkable for they contributed to the economic well-being of the communities and displaced none of the orginal American agricultural population in the process.[53]

[50] Cance, "Immigrant Rural Communities," *The Survey,* XXV, 587-89.
[51] *Report of the Industrial Commission,* XV, 500-03.
[52] Alphonse T. Fiore, "History of Italian Immigration in Nebraska," Abstract of Ph.D. Dissertation, 1938, in University of Nebraska, Dissertation Abstracts, XII, (1942), *passim.*
[53] Cance, "Immigrant Rural Communities," *The Survey,* XXV, 487-95, and Dillingham Commission, *Abstract,* I, 563. Cance was in charge of the Dillingham Commission reports on "Recent Immigrants in Agriculture." Much of what is in his article is in the Commission reports.

Most of the above communities were within range of the well-known padrone in Syracuse, Thomas Marnell.[54] Some of the original farm settlers in Canastota were known to be padrone employees out of Syracuse, at a time when Marnell was extending his padrone operations.[55] In the Oswego area, hundreds of Italian railroad and day laborers preceded the emergence of the Italian muck farmer. They relied on a number of bankers, contractors, and steamship agents, among whom the best known were Luigi Tremiti, Ralph Campo, John Lapetino, Angelo Peluso, Rosario D'Angelo, and Guy D'Alia. The last three operated when Marnell was still alive and were connected with his operations in one way or another.[56]

Joseph Loschiavo, a modern day muck farmer, related to this writer how he (and many others) got into truck farming. He was born in Messina, Italy, on November 9, 1893, and came to this country in March, 1913, destination Oswego, New York. For four years he worked at manual labor for Italian contractors in Oswego and tried his hand at factory work in New Jersey and Delaware, to which some of his cousins called him. He soon returned to Oswego, settled on factory work, and married in 1919. His wife supplemented the family income by picking raspberries, beans, and cherries. By 1924 he was supplementing his factory income by sharecropping with lettuce and by 1925 had enough confidence in the future of the muck that he earned his living full-time through agriculture after

---

[54] Marnell was an Italian immigrant who rose from common laborer to kingpin of the Italian community in Syracuse in two short decades. By virtue of his ability to deliver the Italian vote, he was appointed to the Executive Committee of the State League of Republican Clubs in the important election year of 1904. For a brief glimpse at his life and influence, see Iorizzo, "Italian Immigration," 125-33.

[55] The padrone influence in the development of Canastota can be seen in Joseph T. D'Amico, "The Italian Farmers of Canastota," unpublished Masters' Thesis, Syracuse University, (1939), 31-38.

[56] When Italians in Oswego had to get something done it was to Marnell in Syracuse that they eventually had to turn. Alfred E. D'Amico tells of the husband who sought to prevent his wife from joining him in Oswego because he had picked up with another woman. Marnell was able to successfully thwart the departure from Italy of the wife through his international connections. Eventually, however, the wife learned what was preventing her departure and was able to reach America through "unreachable" officials. Interview with Alfred E. D'Amico, February 7, 1964, Oswego, New York. See also New York State Census Manuscripts, City of Oswego, 1892, 1905, 1915, and Oswego *City Directory*, variously titled, 1864-1926.

that. Though he had lean years, he profited sufficiently to set up his wife in a dry goods business and pay for a couple of trips to the old country. Significant in Loschiavo's story is the dependence on padrone-type (he didn't call them padroni) individuals that he acknowledged: contractors, grocery store operators, and so forth. Though he sometimes forwarded remittances back home through the United States Postal Service, he more frequently utilized services of the Italian contractor for whom he worked or the grocer with whom he dealt — even though it cost him a little more money. Whether he did so out of loyalty to those people who provided him with services or because it was expected of him if he wished to continue to find day labor employment was not made clear. The impression that this listener received was that as late as the 1920's many features of the padrone system were still highly operative in Oswego. Today Loschiavo makes a comfortable living off the muck on his twenty acres. He deals mostly in lettuce and employs up to half a dozen Puerto Rican migrants through the season. He is only one of the untold numbers who, initially depending upon padroni, eventually found their way into agriculture.[57]

Another revealing story is that of Dominic Santoro, one of the largest muck operators among the Italians in Oswego today. He got his start in agriculture by inheritance from his father, Onofrio Santoro. Onofrio came to the United States in 1903 and began working out of New York City, up the Hudson, and then across central New York. He worked on the canals, the railroads (which brought him to Oswego), and on the rebuilding of Fort Ontario in that city, a job which utilized much padrone labor. He saved enough money to open a grocery store and bakery and began part-time farming. By 1919 he was able to buy fifty acres of abandoned, run-down farm land and, with the help of his children, the above mentioned Dominic and another son Anthony, he cleared the land of rocks and shrubs. This was one of the earliest known Italian-owned farms to operate in Oswego. The Santoros raised strawberries, corn, beans, peas, celery, potatoes, and lettuce. They sold their produce to stores and peddled it from door to door. Today Dominic specializes in onions on his 150 acre plot. He ships his onions anywhere in the country, even over-

---

[57] Memorandum of interview with Joseph Loschiavo, August 31, 1966, Oswego New York.

seas. His business is worth somewhere around $300,000. From his own experience and from what his father told him, Dominic Santoro recalled that a majority of the Italians who went into agriculture worked first for the railroads as his father had.[58]

The Italians were not uniformly successful on the land. They achieved no marked success in general farming or in raising staple crops like wheat, corn, rice, sugar, and oats on large farms. But on small acreage farms, where the entire family could be productive and where they could concentrate on one or two crops like onions or lettuce, they did rather well. As farm hands the Italians were criticized by American employers because they showed too little initiative and required too much supervision. Yet their work proved

> ...very satisfactory on truck farms, nursey farms, and the farms of canning companies. Here where little machinery in used and most of the work is done by hand, they are worked in gangs. Many farmers prefer them to Americans because, it is stated, the Italians work more steadily and are more reliable and more easily handled than American farm hands.[59]

The Italian was able to cultivate carefully and economically. He had the willingness and ability to farm intensively and make kitchen gardens and small store accounts pay off. To a southern cotton "share hand" this could be valuable indeed, perhaps the difference between success and failure.[60] The Italian then would certainly have been an asset to agriculture in the United States, and especially in the South which was plagued with "more or less shiftless, thriftless . . . methods," or wherever his particular talent, for reclaiming land given up as useless, could be called on.[61] William Dean Howells spoke of mobilizing the potential genius of the army lying dormant in tenements for distribution

---

[58] Memorandum of interview with Dominic Santoro, September 28, 1966, Oswego, New York, and Oswego County, "Land Records: Deed Books," 1861-1925.

[59] Dillingham Commission, *Abstracts*, I, 575 and Cance, "Immigrant Rural Communities," *The Survey*, XXV, 594-95 claimed the Italian on the farm was not usually quarrelsome, suspicious, and mendacious as in labor gangs.

[60] Cance, "Immigrant Rural Communities," *The Survey*, XXV, 591-92.

[61] *Ibid.*

to country districts.[62] This might have been done had the Italians been given an opportunity to become not farm workers, but independent farmers and small land owners. But there was an "utter lack of facilities for the immigrant to acquire land and settle in the agricultural districts as a farmer."[63] That the governments of the United States and Italy could not agree on a plan for distributing Italian immigrants for the mutual benefit of all concerned was unfortunate.

Yet the solution to the problem of immigrant distribution would not have been that easy. The New York Commission on Immigration briefly summarized the aversion for agriculture exhibited by Italians. Citing reports which showed that laborers could clear $190 in eight months' work as opposed to farm employees who took a full year to clear only $155, the Commission concluded:

> From this and other statements presented to the Commission it appears that low wages, social isolation, and short seasons of the year largely explain the indisposition of aliens to meet the demand for farm labor. The present condition will probably continue until the inducements for farm labor compare more favorably with those of the factory and even of the contractor for common labor and until adequate protection is given to the laborer leaving the cities.[64]

By now one must wonder why the padroni's role in distributing permanent farm workers was not more significant. Without doubt, padroni had little interest in promoting such operations. If many Italians accepted jobs as year-round farm hands, they would have been provided with room and board

---

[62] Howells read a paper to the New York Society for Italian Immigrants parts of which Alice Bennet quoted in her "Italian-American Farmers," *The Survey*, XXII, 172.

[63] Gustavo Tosti, "The Agricultural Possibilities of Italian Immigration," *Charities*, XII (May, 1904), 472-76. Tosti was acting Consul-General of Italy in New York City. See also Dillingham Commission, *Abstracts*, I, 562-72. Most Italian immigrants came to this country to improve their economic lot. In many cases, they depended on the padrone-banker-steamship agent to provide them with jobs, money, provisions, and transportation inland if needed. Even if they burned with desire to turn to the plow, they had not the sufficient capital, or knowledge of the country to go immediately into agriculture for themselves. Clearly, the padrone provided "facilities" to serve industrial America. It was to industrial America that the Italians came mainly.

[64] *Report of the Commission of Immigration of the State of New York*, 138-39. It should be noted that $190 was a bare minimum. The immigrants often made much more than that. It was difficult for a worker to make more than $155 on a farm however.

by the farmers for whom they worked. The commissary privilege, one of the most profitable of padrone operations, would have been lost to the padroni. Moreover, the Italians would have been exposed to American ways and given the opportunity to become Americanized much more quickly than if they had remained under the tutelage of padroni. Other lucrative padrone operations would then have been jeopardized as the Italians turned to the use of American banks, travel agencies, and notaries public.

Certainly if anyone could have moved the Italians out of the tenements onto the farms it was the padroni. The padrone system could have been legalized and regulated to give the padroni the opportunity to become dignified, efficient, and honest labor agents. In this manner, the padroni could have made up in employment fees what they missed with the loss of commissary privileges and the like. Or, the padroni could have been put in charge of the proposed Italian agricultural communities which Italian government officials and many American social workers hoped would become a reality in America. Both of these possibilities would have involved changing the nature of the padroni. Most of the Italian officials and social workers were not out to change the hated padrone system. They wanted to destroy it.[65] That was one of the major reasons they desired to establish permanent agricultural communities for Italians in the first place. They were not about to sanction a system they were intent on eliminating.

There are serious doubts here that American agriculture could have competed successfully with industrial America for the services of the padroni and for Italian workmen, even if those concerned persuaded the padroni to attempt to lead their followers on to the farms of America. The disappointment is that they did not even try.

Conclusion

The impact of the padrone on agricultural America is virtually impossible to determine. He certainly played a key role in supplying America's farmers with temporary labor. We might call it migrant labor with a twist. His impact on permanent agriculture was less definite, but was more negative than

---

[65] For a proposal to make padroni bona fide labor agents see Speranza, "A Mission of Peace," *Outlook*, LXXVIII, 130-31.

positive. On the positive side, the padrone's influence was generally indirect. In distributing day laborers and seasonal workers he was often the first to place Italians in an area in which they later turned to farming. Thus many Italian padrone laborers worked in cities and eventually become part-time farmers, either as tenants or sharecroppers in the surrounding countryside. If successful on the land, they soon bought their own land and turned to farming full time. More often than not, they became truck farmers providing urbanites with fruits and produce.

On the negative side, the padrone was not interested in pointing out to the Italians the profitable possibilities of agriculture. He directed their attentions to industrial America. He made it possible for Italians to take advantage of the better economic and social advantages which urban America offered and enabled them to throw off the shackles of agricultural life which they came to consider as undesirable as a "cruel stepmother." [66] Paradoxically, the padrone, who was often one of the fiercest exploiters of his countrymen, offered the Italian an opportunity to escape agricultural life, which in Italy was synonomous with degradation, humiliation, and virtual starvation.

The impact of the padrone on industrial America was significant. Unquestionably, he was the primary distribution agent of temporary laborers (Italian) throughout the United States. In the main, these were the unskilled railroad and street workers who with their picks and shovels filled the gap in American labor that had to be filled if the United States was to industrialize as rapidly as it did. The padrone was less important in filling the needs of America's permanent labor supply. But here, as in agriculture, the padrone's indirect influence cannot be ignored. Just as many padrone workers turned to agriculture, so too many of them turned to white collar, blue collar, and professional work, in areas throughout the United States — areas they never would have been able to reach had it not been for the padrone. Early Italian settlers in many cities throughout the United States had been definitely traced to the padrone system: Lincoln and Omaha, Nebraska; Paterson and Newark, New Jersey; Cortland, Syracuse, and Oswego, New York; Boston and Lawrence, Massachusetts;

---

[66] See Baron Saverio Fava, "Le colonie agricole italiane," *Nuova Antologia*, CXCVII (October, 1904), 468.

Detroit, Michigan and many communities along the railroad lines in the Mississippi Valley.[67]

Overall the padrone played a vital role in stimulating and directing Italians to America. He was among the first to stir the masses and open their eyes to the tremendous opportunities awaiting them in the United States. He insured that once the Italians got here distribution throughout the United States would not be by chance. He directed Italians, particularly in the 1800's, to wherever a need arose for their labor, through an institutional mechanism which brought and kept Italians together all over America. Some padroni sought to exploit and enslave their countrymen. The vast majority provided the immigrants with work and services and represented security for them. As the years went on, Italians became more and more self-reliant, less and less disposed to depend on the padroni. But they continued to settle and expand in those areas originally opened up by the padrone laborers — the vanguard of

[67] See studies of Italian immigrants: Fiore: "History of Italian Immigration in Nebraska"; Carlo C. Altarelli, "History and Present Conditions of the Italian Colony of Paterson, New Jersey," Unpublished Master's Thesis (Colombia University 1911); Charles W. Churchill, "The Italians of Newark," unpublished Ph.D. dissertation (New York University, 1942); Giovanni Schiavo, *Four Centuries of Italian-American History* (New York, 1952), p. 162. Evadene B. Swanson, "Italians in Cortland, New York," *New York History*, XLIV (July, 1963), 266-68. Donald B. Cole, *Immigrant City, Lawrence, Massachusetts, 1845-1921* (Chapel Hill, 1963), p. 69. John C. Vismara, "The Coming of Italians to Detroit," *Michigan History Magazine*, XI (January, 1918), 118-19. Grace L. Pitts, "The Italians of Columbus — A Study in Population," *The Annals of the American Academy of Political and Social Science*, XIX (1902), 154-59 claimed that the Italians there did not work under a padrone system. Apparently she meant a highly formalized one for she spoke of many Italian saloons, railroad laborers, organ grinders, and many other elements connected with the padroni. Curiously enough Padroni, Colorado, was not founded by padroni. It was named after its founder, Thomas Padroni, who went to Logan County about 1895 and homesteaded a tract of land near the present site of the town. Apparently he made a success of his irrigated farm business. See letter from L.C. Giacomini, July 14, 1964, to this writer and *The Colorado Magazine*, XIX (July, 1942), 141.

Italian migration.[68] The wonder is not that the majority of Italians remained in the Northeast, but that so many moved on and made their homes in every sector of the country.

----

[68] John S. MacDonald and Beatrice D. MacDonald, "Urbanization, Ethnic Groups, and Social Segmentation," *Social Research*, XXIX (1962), 435 ff. say the padroni first brought Italians together, then chain migration took over as padroni declined, i.e., "the process by which prospective immigrants learned of opportunities, were provided with passage money, and had initial accommodation and employment arranged through previous immigrants." The decline of the padroni was hastened by the attempts to regulate emigrant distribution which was discussed at length in Iorizzo, "Italian Immigration," *passim.* These attempts were also measures designed to eliminate the padrone system. However, the constant pressures applied by the United States government, state and local governments, the Italian government, philanthropic, charitable, and social work societies, and the like, to rid America of padroni were not the only sources of dismay for the Italian go-betweens. Their decline was ensured by the Americanization of Italians, the increasing opportunities in factory work which deprived the padroni of the chance to serve or exploit his countrymen, the successful move to organize Italian labor, both skilled and unskilled, especially after the turn of the century, the development of chain migration practices, and very important, the curtailment of padrone operations by railroads which increasingly assumed from 1906 on direct responsibility for recruiting labor, paying wages, and regulating work camp conditions. See also Humbert S. Nelli, "The Italian Padrone System in the United States," *Labor History*, V (Spring, 1964), 164-67; Sheridan, "Italian Laborers," *Labor Bulletin*, No. 72, 451 ff.; Koren, "The Padrone System," *Labor Bulletin*, No. 9, 124 ff.; Rudolph J. Vecoli, "Contadini in Chicago: A Critique of the Uprooted," *The Journal of American History*, LI (December, 1964), 404-17.

Italians in Urban America

by Humbert S. Nelli *

Nearly four million Italians entered the United States between 1890 and 1921, when restrictive legislation enacted by the federal government ended the period of free and large-scale immigration to this country. Contemporaries expressed deep concern about the influx of this alien horde, composed, many claimed, of criminals, paupers, ignorant peasants and illegal contract laborers, all congregated in closely-packed colonies where they infected American life by perpetuating old world traits and compounding city problems. Few discerned that settlement in America's urban environment profoundly affected not only the receiving society, but newcomers as well.[1]

Life centered around the family in southern Italy and Sicily (and eastern Europe), where needs and problems were handled from the standpoint of the family group or its individual members. Political scientist Edward C. Banfield, in a recent study widely accepted by immigration scholars and students of Italian history, described a Sicilian-southern Italian society dominated by amoral familism. Banfield found peasants and gentry alike unwilling to act "for any end transcending the immediate, material interest of the nuclear family." If this study is accurate, one can reasonably conclude that community and ethnic consciousness found among Italians and Sicil-

---

[1] A sampling of available literature includes: Frank Julian Warne, *The Immigrant Invasion* (New York, 1913); M. Victor Safford, *Immigration* (Boston, 1912); Jacob A. Riis, *How the Other Half Lives* (New York, 1890); Samuel P. Orth, *Our Foreigners* (New Haven, Conn., 1920); Henry Cabot Lodge, "Efforts to Restrict Undesirable Immigration," *Century Magazine*, LXVII (January, 1904), 466-469; Frank E. Sargent, "The Need of Closer Inspection and Greater Restriction of Immigration," *Century Magazine* LXVII (January, 1904), 470-473.

---

* Humbert S. Nelli is Associate Professor of History at the University of Kentucky in Lexington.

ians in the United States was not an old world transplant, but a development of the new world.[2]

In the United States, one leader of a Sicilian-southern Italian community described his neighborhood in Chicago as possessing "unusual unity and strength." He believed that his colony had "to a very very great extent the same kind of warmth, friendliness and intimacy in our community life that was to be found in the small towns of Sicily from whence our parents came." It is ironic that this community feeling, which developed in response to the American environment, was assumed to be a carryover of old world habits.[3]

Because it served as a staging area where new arrivals remained until they absorbed new ideas and habits which made possible their adjustment to the alien environment, the community of the immigrant generation fulfilled a vitally important function both to its inhabitants and the receiving society. It bridged the gap between rural (old world) traditions and the new urban world; it acquainted a succession of immigrant groups with American ideas and values, although obviously not all members of any group reacted in the same way to the colony, its available institutions, or its urban surroundings.

Urban Patterns of Settlement

The pattern of Italian settlement in cities east of the Mississipi and north of the Ohio began with the founding of the immigrant community by northern Italians, who tended to predominate until the 1880's; after that time, southerners and Sicilians formed the bulk of the new arrivals. The original enclave started in or near the city's central portion — that is, the business area — and was characterized by the movement of economically successful newcomers out of the settlement

---

[2] William I. Thomas and Florian Znaniecki, The *Polish Peasant in Europe and America*, I (Chicago, 1918), 87-89; Edward C. Banfield, *The Moral Basis of a Backward Society* (Glencoe, Ill., 1958), p. 10. Among others who accept the Banfield position are Herbert J. Gans, *The Urban Villagers: Group and Class in the Life of Italian-Americans* (New York, 1962), p. 203 and Norman Kogan, *The Politics of Italian Foreign Policy* (New York, 1963), pp. 4-5.

[3] Statement by Dr. A.J. Lendino, quoted in William Foote White, "Social Organization in the Slums," *American Sociological Review*, VII (February, 1943), 36.

and into the American community. New arrivals from overseas swarmed into the colony, filling vacancies and creating or aggravating overcrowded, rapidly deteriorating neighborhoods.

In general, settlement in Chicago typified the Italian experience in urban America.[4] Northern Italians, most of them from Genoa and Tuscany, formed the early colony in the years after 1850. Whether from the north, in the first three decades of immigration, or from the south and Sicily after the 1880's, newcomers tended at first to settle along the same streets and in the same tenements. They lodged according to town or province of origin, doubtless seeking familiar faces, names and dialects. They lived together and — if possible — worked together.[5] This early concentration broke down as immigrants met and mingled with newcomers from other towns and provinces in the homeland and with non-Italians who lived and worked in close proximity. In the process, they began for the first time to think of themselves as Italians rather than as members of a particular family or emigrants from a particular locality. This new concept comprised a considerable expansion of provincial horizons, and was one of the first results of Chicago's impact upon them.

---

[4] U.S. Senate, *Reports of the Immigration Commission*, XXVI (1911); George La Piana, *The Italians in Milwaukee, Wisconsin* (Milwaukee, 1915); Frederick A. Bushee, "Italian Immigrants in Boston," *Arena*, XVII (April, 1897), 722-734; Walter I. Firey, *Land Use in Central Boston* (Cambridge, Mass., 1947), chap. v; Charles Loring Brace, *The Dangerous Classes of New York* (New York, 1872), chap. xvii; Charlotte Adams, "Italian Life in New York," *Harper's Magazine*, LXII (April, 1881), 676-684; Charles W. Coulter, *The Italians of Cleveland* (Cleveland, 1919).

[5] U.S. Commissioner of Labor, *Ninth Special Report. The Italians in Chicago, A Social and Economic Study* (1897); Frank O. Beck, "The Italian in Chicago," *Bulletin of the Department of Public Welfare of Chicago*, II, No. 3 (February, 1919), 2-12; Alessandro Mastro-Valerio (at times Mastrovalerio, Mastro Valerio, and Valerio), "Remarks upon the Italian Colony in Chicago," *Hull House Maps and Papers* (New York, 1895), pp. 131-139; Edith Abbott and Sophonisba P. Breckinridge "Chicago Housing Conditions, IV. The West Side Revisited," *American Journal of Sociology*, XVII (July, 1911), 1-34; Grace Norton, "Chicago Housing Conditions, VII: Two Italian Districts," *American Journal of Sociology*, XVIII (January, 1913), 509-542; Natalie Walker, "Chicago Housing Conditions, X. Greeks and Italians in the Neighborhood of Hull House," *American Journal of Sociology*, XXI (November, 1915), 285-316; Esther Quaintance, "Rents and Housing Conditions in the Italian District of the Lower North Side of Chicago," unpublished Master's thesis, University of Chicago, 1925.

Not only did they live and work with Italians from throughout the Kingdom as well as with Irishmen, Poles, Germans, Scandinavians and others; many went to church with these "foreigners" and their children attended the same schools. In contrast to the homeland tradition of seeking a spouse from the same place of birth, they began to intermarry with "outsiders" from elsewhere in Italy. Despite strong northern prejudices, by 1900 marriages had begun to take place between Tuscans (and other northerners) and Sicilians (and other southerners). On occasion newcomers even married non-Italians. Both choices represented a shifting away from old world attitudes, although of individually varying significance.[6]

Continuing the pattern set by their predecessors, southern Italians and Sicilians who obtained the financial means moved away from the colony. If migration from the ethnic settlement — a sign of economic mobility and an indication of desires for better housing and living conditions — did not take place in the first generation, it generally occurred in the second or third.[7] Nevertheless, the continued presence of numbers of Italians in neighborhoods led contemporaries to the erroneous conclusion that Italians, their children and their grandchildren after them, remained on the same streets and in the same tenements from the time they arrived in the city until they died. Americans also assumed that compact, unchanging settlements grouped according to place of immigrant origin. While this description fitted the initial phase of settlement, new relationships quickly formed, both with other Italians and with members of different nationality groups. A major cause of this constant regrouping and expanding of relationships was the fact that the composition of Italian colonies (like that of other ethnic groups) remained in constant flux, with at least half the community residents changing their place of dwelling each year.[8]

---

[6] Observations based on examination of marriage records of parishes in Italian communities.

[7] Edith Abbott, *The Tenements of Chicago, 1908-1935* (Chicago, 1936), p. 97, maintained that while the second generation was moving from immigrant colonies to communities such as Columbus Park and Oak Park, many members of immigrant generations refused to move away from "the Italian church and their circle of old village cronies."

[8] Jane Addams, *Newer Ideals of Peace* (New York, 1907), p. 67; Chicago Department of Public Welfare, *First Semi-Annual Report to the Mayor and Aldermen of the City of Chicago* (Chicago, 1915), p. 89.

Contrary to popular belief, Chicago, like other urban areas, contained few blocks inhabited exclusively by Italians, and even fewer solidly Italian neighborhoods.[9] Between 1890 and 1920, only limited sections of certain Chicago streets held a 50% or higher concentration of Italian immigrants and their children. The population density of Italians in the city's various Italian districts fell considerably below 50%.

Throughout the four decades following 1880, the Near West Side community in the vicinity of Hull House made up the largest and most heavily concentrated Italian group in the city. According to the City Homes Association *Report* of 1901, this " Italian district " extended from Polk to Twelfth Street and Halsted to Canal. Here, while first and second generation Italians constituted 50% to 70% of the population in portions the size of blocks or slightly more, they formed only one-third of the area's total population. This mixture of nationalities, of course, brought about innumerable contacts among members of different nationality groups. By 1920 the major Italian community had shifted to the west of Halsted, where similarly scattered concentrations could be found.[10]

Observers of immigrant life in Chicago and other cities ignored or did not recognize the gradual shift in location of Italian districts. Thus the area discussed in one study often differed from that in another, even though the colony in both instances might be labelled "The West Side" or "The North Side" community. In addition, the composition of Italian communities underwent rapid and continual change. Hence the miserable, poorly fed and ragged residents described in one survey probably were not the same individuals examined in subsequent studies of the same area.

Rural Ventures

Americans, concerned over slums and the effects which incoming European peasants might have in perpetuating miser-

---

[9] New York City was a possible exception, but there is every reason to believe that the remarks that follow in the text apply to that city as well. See, for example, Leo Grebler, *Housing Market Behavior in a Declining Area* (New York, 1952), pp. 135-137, 245-246, on Manhattan's lower east side Italian community during the period from 1910 to 1930.

[10] Robert Hunter, *Tenement Conditions in Chicago. Report of the City Homes Association* (Chicago, 1901), pp. 56, 188, 195-196; Ernest W. Burgess and Charles Newcomb (eds.), *Census Data of the City of Chicago, 1920* (Chicago, 1931).

able conditions and multiplying city problems, sincerely believed that urban difficulties could be alleviated or even solved
by encouraging immigrants to move into rural surroundings.
Shifting Italians into agriculture appeared to be "the natural
solution of the problem of Italian concentration in the slums,"
wrote I.W. Howerth in 1894. "Henceforth the tendency of
Italians to congregate in large cities will decrease." In order
to bring about this desired event, the Italian and American
governments, individual states and private agencies (such as
local Italian-American chambers of commerce) supported the
establishment of agricultural colonies for Italian immigrants
throughout the United States and especially in Texas, Arkansas, Mississippi, Louisiana and Alabama.[11]

Despite auspicious beginnings and official support, most
rural ventures came to nothing. For example, Alessandro
Mastro-Valerio (later editor of *La Tribuna Italiana Transatlantica* of Chicago, and head of the Italian Chamber of Commerce's
Agricultural Section) founded an Italian agricultural colony
at Daphne, Alabama, in 1892. This enterprise received counsel
and financial aid from Jane Addams and the residents of
Hull House. Italian inhabitants of Chicago, however, gave it
little support and soon it failed. Truck gardens in the vicinity
of large urban centers of the east and middle west, and in
California, achieved a greater measure of success than did
efforts to attract immigrants to rural colonies.[12]

---

[11] I. W. Howerth, "Are the Italians a Dangerous Class?" *Charities
Review*, IV (November, 1894), 40. The U. S. Bureau of Immigration
published *Agricultural Opportunities. Information Concerning Resources, Products and Physical Characteristics* (of various states) (Washington, 1912-1920). Under the direction of Allessandro Mastro-Valerio, the
Agricultural Section of the Italian Chamber of Commerce of Chicago
was very active in its efforts to settle Italians in rural colonies located
in the southern states. See also A.H. Stone, "Italian Cottongrowers in
Arkansas," *American Monthly Review of Reviews*, No. 35 (February,
1907), pp. 209-213; L. Mathews, "Tontitown," *Everybody's Magazine*, No.
20 (January, 1909), pp. 3-13; G. Rossati, "La colonizzazione negli Stati di
Mississippi, Louisiana ed Alabama," *Bollettino dell'Emigrazione* (hereafter *Boll. Emig.*), No. 14 (1904), pp. 3-30; G. Moroni, "Gli italiani in Tangipahoa," *Boll. Emig.*, No. 7 (1910), pp. 3-7; Luigi Villari, "Gli italiani nel
distretto consolare di New Orleans," *Boll. Emig.*, No. 20 (1907), pp. 3-47;
U.S. Congress, *Industrial Commission*, XV (1901), 405-507; U.S. Senate,
Immigration Commission, Vol. XXI.

[12] Adolfo Rossi, "Per la tutela degli italiani negli Stati Uniti," *Boll.
Emig.*, No. 16 (1904), pp. 74-80; *Hull House: A Social Settlement, An
Outline Sketch* (pamphlet dated February 1, 1894), p. 21; Florence Kelly,

Contemporaries wondered why more Italians did not move to farms. Some maintained that "new" immigrants, trapped in cities, lacked the strength, ability and knowledge required to take advantage of the marvelous agricultural opportunities offered in the United States. According to this thesis, "old" immigrant groups had seized these opportunities and thus had proven themselves to be superior to "new" arrivals. In this vein, labor economist and historian John R. Commons observed that " in the immigrant stage they [Italians] are helpless." In contrast, " immigrants from Northwestern Europe, the Germans and Scandinavians," had been from the start " the model farmers of America " because of their " thrift, self-reliance, and intensive farming." He added, " The least self-reliant or forehanded, like the . . . Italians, seek the cities in greater proportions than those sturdy races like the Scandinavians, English, Scotch and Germans." [13]

Commons believed that serious consequences would follow the massing of recent immigrants in American cities because cities did not create the spirit of independence and initiative achieved by farm workers. He not only distrusted new immigrant groups, but also feared the phenomenal growth of urban areas and the changes being wrought there by technology and increasing populations. "The dangerous effects of city life on immigrants and the children of immigrants cannot be too strongly emphasized," he wrote. Foreigners in urban centers "are themselves dragged down by the parasitic and dependent conditions which they [cities] fostered among the immigrant element." [14]

Others held similar views and expressed them in magazines, books and reports. "The illiterate races, such as the Hungarians, Galicians, and Italians, remain in the cities to lower the standards of the already crowded Atlantic territory," declared one. Said another, "The illiterate immigrants congregate chiefly in the slums of our great cities.[15]

"The Settlements: Their Lost Opportunity," *Charities and the Commons*, XVI, No. 1 (April 7, 1906), 80; Alberto Pecorini, "The Italian as an Agricultural Laborer," *Annals of the American Academy of Political and Social Science*, XXXIII (March, 1909), 383-384.

[13] John R. Commons, *Races and Immigrants in America* (New York, 1907), pp. 133, 166.

[14] *Ibid.*, pp. 167-168.

[15] U.S. Congress, Senate, *Report from the Committee on Immigration*, 54th Congress, 1st Session, 1896, Rept. 290, p. 9; Lodge, "Efforts to

Alessandro Mastro-Valerio reported to the United States Industrial Commission in 1901 that Italian immigrants wanted desperately to farm but did not know "how to get the land and the means to work it until it produces." Consequently, he said, they remained caged in cities. Because most of the immigrants had engaged in farm labor in Italy, it seemed logical that they should hope to settle on the land in America. As country people, "they should have been established in the country." Americans, he said, had a responsibility for moving immigrants out of urban areas and into agriculture.[16]

An Italian visitor to an early farming settlement in the American south indicated some reasons for the immigrant preference for crowded cities rather than rural "opportunities":

> The colony lives in poorly constructed houses, made of wood, without the most elementary precautions against the weather; frequently...the dwellings are really tents, where members of the colony sleep together without distinction as to age and sex.... Hygiene is unknown.... Our people are eternally deeply in debt...and the current agricultural contracts for sharecropping or renting are not to the advantage of the Italians.[17]

Overwhelming as these disadvantages appear, Robert Foerster has shown that factors such as ignorance of opportunity, unfamiliar climate, squalid living conditions and cost of land did not form the primary deterrents to successful farming colonies. In Argentina, for example, Italians overcame similar obstacles and farmed to great advantage, adapting without difficulty to new world crops, soils, markets and rural living conditions. Another and more important factor contributed

---

Restrict Undesirable Immigration," p. 468. See also Jeremiah W. Jenks and W. Jett Lauck, *The Immigration Problem* (New York, 1912). The authors argued on the basis of the findings of the U.S. Immigration Commission, of which both were members, that the "old" immigration naturally went into agriculture while the "new" immigrants remained in the cities (p. 26).

[16] U.S. Congress, *Industrial Commission*, XV, 497. Mastro-Valerio's argument was open to question, as he himself ought to have recognized, since both colonies that he founded in Alabama failed. For a view similar to Mastro-Valerio's see G.E. Di Palma Castiglione, "Italian Immigration into the United States, 1901-4," *American Journal of Sociology*, XI (September, 1905), 183-206.

[17] Giovanni Preziosi, *Gl'Italiani negli Stati Uniti del Nord* (Milan, 1909), p. 81.

to inmigrant distaste for settlement in the county: most Italians simply did not emigrate to North America with hopes or intentions of farming.[18]

Like the majority of immigrants, "old" as well as "new," Italians arrived seeking economic opportunities. In the last decades of the nineteenth century and the early ones of the twentieth, prospects of financial gain existed in commercial and industrial centers of the north and east and not in agriculture. This fact resulted in the failures of agricultural colonies, such as the one at New Palermo, Alabama, as reported in *L'Italia* of Chicago on May 21, 1904. The immigrants, reported the paper, who "went with the delusion of finding riches," instead "found nothing but misery." The United States Industrial Commission recognized the desire for economic betterment in its summary volume, published in 1902, where it examined the factors responsible for immigrant concentration in cities. The Commission noted first "the general movement of all modern industrial peoples toward urban life — a movement quite characteristic of the American people themselves." For the foreign-born, additional factors reinforced this trend: (1) the isolation of farm life in the United States, in contrast with more crowded conditions in rural areas of Europe; (2) immigrant memories of "hardship and oppressions of rural life from which they are struggling to escape"; (3) ready employment in cities directly upon arrival and for higher wages than those paid farm laborers.[19]

In the period after 1890, as English historian Frank Thistlethwaite has pointed out, the great migrations proceeded "from farm to factory, from village to city, whether this meant from Iowa to Chicago, Silesia to Pittsburgh or Piedmont to Buenos Aires." Writing in 1906, demographer Walter F. Willcox found no evidence that "immigrants tend disproportionately toward cities." He claimed that recent immigrants showed no stronger tendencies to crowd into cities than earlier groups. Nevertheless, during the years between 1890 and 1905, writers and speakers repeated the idea that immigrants — especially illiterate ones — clung to the slums of large cities. The American public in general accepted this view.[20]

---

[18] Robert F. Foerster, *The Italian Emigration of Our Times* (Cambridge, Mass., 1919), pp. 370-371.

[19] U.S. Congress, *Industrial Commission*, XIX (1902), 969-971.

[20] Frank Thistlethwaite, "Migration from Europe Overseas in the Nineteenth and Twentieth Centuries," *Population Movements in Modern*

The cultural problem of adjusting to new living patterns, the result of moving to an urban environment, constituted a key factor responsible for immigrant difficulties in urban America. Contemporaries failed to recognize that adjustment would have been necessary had the villagers migrated to a city in Italy or to some other European city rather than across the Atlantic. Americans of rural background who moved to urban areas faced many of the same problems encountered by Sicilians who journeyed to the new world, to Milan, or to other cities in the Italian peninsula and Europe.[21]

Significantly, Americans and Italians who encouraged agricultural colonies did so at least in part because of the conviction that foreigners would become Americanized more rapidly and completely in a rural setting than in a city. Commissioner-General of Immigration Frank Sargent maintained that "if, instead of crowding into our large cities," immigrants would go to rural areas, "there would be no need to fear for the future." [22] Probably the opposite was true. As the experience of German agricultural colonies in Pennsylvania and the Middle West made clear, assimilation slowed or halted in rural environments where there existed only limited contacts with outside agencies and individuals. In sparsely populated areas, an ethnic community is forced in upon itself, or can maintain a desired isolation. In cities, on the other hand, contacts of one type or another are (and were) virtually impossible to prevent.

University of Chicago sociologist Robert E. Park noted in 1921 that the rural experience "is naturally in the opposite direction" of the urban. Country life "emphasizes local differences, preserves the memories of the immigrants, and fosters a sentimental interest in the local home community." An

---

European History, ed. Herbert Moller (New York, 1964), reprinted from XIe Congrès International des Sciences Historiques, Stockholm, 1960, Rapports V: Histoire Contemporaire, p.91; Walter F. Willcox, Studies in American Demography (Ithaca, 1940), pp. 159, 169, 174. This is from chap. x, "The Foreign-Born," which is largely a reprint of an earlier article by Willcox, "The Distribution of Immigration in the United States," Quarterly Journal of Economics, XX (August, 1906), 523-546.

[21] Pauline Young, "Social Problems in the Education of the Immigrant Child," American Sociological Review, I, No. 3 (June, 1936), 419-429. P. 420 discusses urban adjustment problems of rural Americans.

[22] Sargent, "The Need of Closer Inspection and Greater Restriction of Immigration," p. 470.

expert on foreign-language newspapers, Park cited the example of the "German provincial press, which is printed in a dialect no longer recognizable by the European press, and which idealized German provincial life as it existed fifty years ago and still lives in the memories of the editors and readers of these papers." This comment paralleled an observation made several years previously by John Foster Carr, who noted that by 1906 "only two poor fragments remain of the numerous important German and Irish colonies" that had flourished in New York city in the 1870's and 1880's. In contrast, "the ancient settled Pennsylvania Dutch, thanks to their isolation, are not yet fully merged in the great citizen body." [23]

Clearly, new arrivals to the United States faced the basic problem not of escaping from a mythical urban "trap" or of finding agricultural jobs, but rather of settling into a new way of life, that of the city community.

Italo-American Institutions in Urban Areas

Italians who, in the Kingdom, never considered the possibility of cooperation or even of contact with co-nationals from other towns and provinces, found themselves forced to deal with urban difficulties in the United States as members of groups. In the process, newcomers modified familiar institutions (like the Church), organized some which had scarcely touched their lives in Italy (such as the press and mutual benefit societies), and established agencies which did not exist in the home country (notably the immigrant bank). Thus while some immigrant institutions had counterparts in the old world, southern Italians and Sicilians either came in contact with them for the first time in America or cast them in new molds.

Many Americans assumed that ethnic communities and their institutions reproduced homeland surroundings and encouraged "isolated group life"; hence through "churches and schools, and in social, fraternal, and national organizations," immigrants could maintain "the speech, the ideals, and to some extent the manner of life of the mother country." In reality,

---

[23] Robert E. Park, "Cultural Aspects of Immigration. Immigrant Heritages," *Proceedings of the National Conference of Social Work*, XLVIII (1921), 494; John Foster Carr, "The Coming of the Italian," *Outlook*, LXXXII (February 24, 1906), 429.

of course, the colony represented an important step away from old world patterns. Because the city prevented isolation, neither the community nor its institutions were fully Italian in character; nor were they American. They served an interim group, the immigrant generation with its old world traditions and new world surroundings.[24]

Community institutions of all new immigrant groups in the United States resembled each other and native American counterparts more closely than they did any homeland organizations. Mutual benefit and fraternal societies, for example, existed among Poles, Ukrainians, Lithuanians, Jews and others. Italian publishers used similar techniques and faced the same problems as those of other foreign-language press groups. Non-Italians also depended upon services provided by immigrant bankers and padroni. "In America," sociologist Robert E. Park noted, "the peasant discards his [old world] habits and acquires 'ideas.' In America, above all, the immigrant organizes. These organizations are the embodiment of his needs and his new ideas." [25]

Many newcomers sought to solve life's complexities by joining benefit groups. These were not "transplanted" insti-

---

[24] Edith Abbott and Sophonisba P. Breckinridge, *The Delinquent Child and the Home* (New York, 1912), p. 55. Constantine M. Panunzio, himself an immigrant, wrote of an Italian colony in which he had resided in Boston: "This was in no way a typical American community, neither did it resemble Italy." *The Soul of an Immigrant* (New York, 1922), p. 231.

[25] Grace Abbott, *The Problem of Immigration in Massachusetts. Report of the Commission on Immigration* (Boston, 1914), pp. 202-207, presented an examination of the various institutions mentioned here among Greeks, Italians, Jews, Lithuanians, Poles and Syrians in Massachusetts. Robert E. Park, "Foreign Language Press and Social Progress," *Proceedings of the National Conference of Social Work* (1920), XLVII, 494. On the foreign-language press among other immigrant groups see Thomas Capek, *The Czechs in America* (Boston, 1920), pp. 172-173 and Edmund G. Olszyk, *The Polish Press in America* (Milwaukee, 1940).

The padrone and the immigrant banker are examined in detail elsewhere and will not be discussed here. For an analysis of the activities and role in the community of the former see Humbert S. Nelli, "The Italian Padrone System in the United States," *Labor History*, V, No. 2 (Spring, 1964), 153-167, and the banker in Nelli, "Italians and Crime in Chicago: The Formative Years, 1890-1921," *American Journal of Sociology* LXXIV, No. 3 (January, 1969), 380-382.

tutions carried by southerners to the United States.[26]   In southern Italy and Sicily, where strong family ties ensured aid in times of need, group life featured recreational activities in a few social clubs (*circolo sociale*), most of which had small memberships and limited community importance.[27]

The mutual aid society (*società di mutuo soccorso*), although known in Italy, existed almost exclusively among middle classes, and especially among artisans, in urbanized areas of the northern and central parts of the Kingdom. By the 1890's, mutual aid groups had begun to appear in the Italian south and Sicily, as J. S. McDonald has pointed out, but not in those portions of the south from which emigration flowed. The development of mutual aid societies among Italians in the United States contrasted with that in the homeland, where benefit groups closely intertwined with the growth of labor unions; societies were, in the words of historian Daniel L. Horowitz, "the linear predecessors of the trade unions in Italy." Societies in the United States, on the other hand, concentrated on insurance and social functions, and helped newly arrived immigrants to deal with sickness, loneliness and death rather than labor organization.[28]

Benefit societies in the United States antedated the period of large-scale immigration from southern and eastern Europe. Assessment mutual aid methods found popularity with working class Americans, native as well as foreign-born, by the middle

---

[26] Rudolph J. Vecoli, "*Contadini* in Chicago: A Critique of *The Uprooted*," *Journal of American History*, LI, No. 3 (December, 1964), 412, cites as proof an article which appeared in one of Chicago's Italian-language newspapers, *L'Unione Italiana*, on March 18, 1868. This date was at least ten years before southern Italians became an important element in Chicago and other urban centers.

[27] William E. Davenport, "The Exodus of a Latin People," *Charities*, XII, No. 18 (May 7, 1904), 466, and Banfield, *The Moral Basis of a Backward Society*, pp. 16-17.

[28] J.S. McDonald, "Italy's Rural Social Structure and Emigration," *Occidente*, XII (September-October, 1956), 443-446; Daniel L. Horowitz, *The Italian Labor Movement* (Cambridge, Mass., 1963), p. 12. The Italian background of the mutual benefit society is discussed in Edwin Fenton's excellent "Immigrants and Unions, A case study: Italians and American Labor, 1870-1920," unpublished Ph.D. dissertation, Harvard University, 1957. See also two sources on which Fenton relied heavily: Rinaldo Rigola, *Storia del Movimento Operaio Italiano* (Milan, 1946), pp. 9-22, and Humbert L. Gualtieri, *The Labor Movement in Italy* (New York, 1946), p. 137.

of the nineteenth century. Groups like the Mechanics Mutual Aid Society, founded in 1846, provided strong competition for regular life insurance companies. Benefit societies in America apparently grew out of English friendly societies, which provided working class points of view as well as sickness, old age and funeral benefits, along with features from secret societies, ideas about organization and self-government, and an interest in social activities, ritual and symbolism. "The prototype societies," according to insurance historian J. Owen Stalson, "were active in England while we were still colonies." American groups, however, developed a stronger social and fraternal character than English friendly societies. In a highly mobile country like the United States, vast numbers of the native-born as well as immigrants from Europe found themselves uprooted from familiar surroundings, people and life patterns. For them the lodge filled a great social and psychological void. Furthermore, the practice of "passing the hat" for unfortunate group members guaranteed aid in the event of need at minimum expense for all concerned, at least during the early years of the society when members were young and vigorous, and death or illness appeared to be problems of the distant future.[29]

Immigrants (and native Americans) who joined mutual benefit organizations contributed small monthly sums, usually between 25¢ and 60¢, to guarantee that the group would look after them when they were sick and provide a decent burial when they died. In addition, societies required all members to attend funeral services or pay a fine as penalty for nonattendance. In this way the organization assured each member of a proper burial and a well-attended service, with the result that funerals tended to become social events. Over the years the burial service grew into an opportunity for old acqaintances to gather at irregular intervals and to reminisce about old days. Since young and vigorous members predominated at first, most deaths resulted from accidents or disease growing out of employment conditions. Societies also generally handled

---

[29] J. Owen Stalson, *Marketing Life Insurance: Its History in America* (Cambridge, Mass., 1942), pp. 446-449; Josef M. Baernreither, *English Associations of Working Men* (London, 1889), chap. i, "Origins and General Character of Friendly Societies."

other related activities, particularly the payment of sickness and accident expenses.[30]

In early years of settlement, societies formed typically on the basis of place of origin, either town or province of birth. This development in itself indicated a significant movement away from old world distrust of anyone outside the family circle. In the new urban environment, and in the absence of sufficient family members to provide the resources necessary to meet all emergencies, immigrants found it necessary to cooperate with "outsiders." Consequently natives of a particular town or province — men who would have regarded each other as strangers in Italy — found that in the United States they possessed in common enough traditions to warrant banding together.

It is difficult to determine both membership figures and the number of societies in existence,[31] because of the basis of group organization — in many cases, not merely town or province of birth, but neighborhood and even street or building of residence — and the fact that some societies formed with goals other than mutual aid or recreation. Some existed to satisfy political, religious or military functions. Through necessity, small units which had organized on a town or provincial basis consolidated into, or were absorbed by, larger organizations encompassing all Italians regardless of place of birth or residence. In all these respects the Italian experience with societies paralleled that of other nationalities. Thus the merging of small groups into the Sons of Italy had its counterpart in the establishment, for example, of the Polish National Alliance.

The function and value of the "colonial" press (as those in Italy and many in the immigrant community referred to Italian-language newspapers in the United States) were tem-

[30] Antonio Mangano, "The Associated Life of the Italians in New York City," Charities, XII, No. 18 (May 7, 1904), 479-480; G. Abbott, The Problem of Immigration in Massachusetts, pp. 202-206; Giovanni E. Schiavo, The Italians in Chicago: A Study in Americanization (Chicago, 1928), p. 59. On the vital importance of death benefits to immigrants, see Robert E. Park and Herbert A. Miller, Old World Traits Transplanted (New York, 1921), pp. 124-128.

[31] "Le Società italiane all'estero," Bollettino del Ministero degli Affari Esteri (April, 1898), p. 7; " le Società italiane all'estero nel 1908," Boll. Emig., No. 24 (1908), p. viii; " Le Società italiane negli Stati Uniti dell'America del Nord nel 1910," Boll. Emig., No. 4 (1912), p. 20.

porary, specialized in nature, and vital only so long as a sufficiently large group needed its services. The press saw itself in a nobler role. According to Italian-American journalist Luigi Carnovale, the best and truest friend available to the immigrant was his Italian-language journal. "In the colonial press, in short, the Italian immigrants have always found all that is indispensible — wise advice, moral and material assistance, true and ardent fraternal love — for their success and triumph in . . . America." [32] The major significance of colonial tabloids lay on a less grand, but undeniably important level, that of easing the first critical years of immigrant adjustment to America. Articles about events in Italy and in towns and provinces of origin, news of other immigrant communities, reports of societies and listings of collections for needy newcomers, all helped Italian-Americans to develop and nurture a sense of belonging within their new surroundings. Information about local and national American events, emphasis on the values of education and participation in politics, and advice regarding behavior and modes of expression acceptable to Americans were editorial attempts to lessen adjustment problems for readers. The press served as a crutch for immigrants having difficulties in adapting to their new surroundings, or those unable to break away from homeland traditions. To many of the second generation and a number of self-reliant newcomers, colonial journals offered little of interest or value; hence readership reached its height during the first two decades of the twentieth century, the time of arrival of great masses of immigrants desperately in need of services which foreign-language newspapers could provide.[33]

During this period also, Italian-language tabloids employed technological advances pioneered by American papers in order to attract attention and hold readers. Immigrant periodicals

[32] Luigi Carnovale, *Il Giornalismo degli emigrati italiani nel Nord America* (Chicago, 1909), p. 34; also pp. 33, 74, 77. Carnovale worked for *La Tribuna Italiana Transatlantica* in Chicago, *Il Pensiero* and *La Gazzetta Illustrata* (a magazine) in St. Louis.

[33] *The Bulletin* (later changed to *The Interpreter*), I, No. 9 (December, 1922), 10, noted that not only did American-born children of immigrants prefer to read American papers, but also that "the foreign-born . . . as soon as they have acquired sufficient English, turn to the American papers for American and general news, depending on the press of their language for little more than news of the home country."

in the United States bore a stronger resemblance to the popular American press than to homeland journals, and featured headlines, brief articles, special columns, simple language and profuse illustrations. Because of inadequate staffs, they also contained typographical errors, slang, plagiarisms and unverified news items. Editors who valued literary excellence over sensational news, pictures and frequent protestations of loyalty to Italy generally lasted but a short time.[34]

Unlike the other institutions, the Church existed for newcomers before they left Europe, and formed an integral part of their lives. Yet it had undergone changes in the new world. Italians found the Church in America to be a cold and puritanical institution, controlled and often operated, even in Italian neighborhoods, by the hated Irish. Devout Catholics and critics of religion alike resented Irish domination of the Church, demanded Italian priests and sought to control churches in their communities. Liberals and nationalists decried the Roman Church's opposition to Italian unification and its continued refusal to recognize the Kingdom.[35]

By 1900, Italians appeared to be so dissatisfied that many Catholics believed the situation posed a serious threat to the Church's future in the United States. Laurence Franklin wrote an article for *Catholic World,* appearing in April, 1900, which showed how Italian disillusionment developed. The study contrasted the religious turmoil among immigrants in the United States with conditions in Italy. "At home a chapel or church stood at their very door," Franklin pointed out. "Their parish priest was their personal friend, who had baptized them at their birth, taught them their catechism, and watched over them like a father or elder brother." In an Amer-

---

[34] Carnovale, *Il Giornalismo,* pp. 33-34, 74, 77; Giuseppe Prezzolini, *I trapiantati* (Milan, 1963), pp. 62-63. These remarks refer specifically, of course, to the bourgeois press. Anarchist, religious and socialist papers reached a very small and specialized audience.

[35] *La Tribuna Italiana Transatlantica,* Jan. 14, 1905; June 4 and 18, July 2, Aug. 13 and 20, 1904; Apr. 22, 1905; Oct. 27, 1906; Aug. 24, Nov. 9, 1907; Feb. 29, 1908; *L'Italia* (Chicago), Nov. 1. 1890. Italian resentment over Irish control of the Church in the United States was shared by other Catholic groups as well. On the "Americanist controversy" see Thomas T. McAvoy, C.S.C., *The Great Crisis in American Catholic History, 1895-1900* (Chicago, 1957); Robert D. Cross, *The Emergence of Liberal Catholicism in America* (Cambridge, Mass., 1958); Colman J. Barry, O.S.B., *The Catholic Church and German Americans* (Milwaukee, 1953).

ican city, on the other hand, "they are suddenly thrown back upon themselves, without either tradition or public opinion to foster their sense of moral and social responsibility.... No church is to be found in the long row of tenements which form their horizon line, and the priests whom they meet speak another tongue." As a result of these factors, "like sheep without a shepherd, they too often go astray, wandering into some other fold, through interest or ignorance." [36]

In following years the Italian immigrant "problem" remained a source of deep concern within the Church. By early 1914 the *Catholic Citizen* of Milwaukee concluded that the religious condition of Italian immigrants and their children in the United States was "our biggest Catholic question," a view widely held among American Catholics. Between the beginning of the century and 1921, various aspects of the "Italian Problem" received frequent examination in the Catholic press, including discussion of religion in the homeland, parochial education in America, the need for Italian-speaking priests, and analyses of proposed solutions to the "Problem." [37]

Protestants saw in Catholicism's difficulties an ideal foundation for proselytizing. They lost no opportunity to proclaim Protestant recognition and support of the Italian Kingdom, in contrast to the attitude of the Church. Protestant clergy condemned the papacy as a reactionary institution — "it could not be the papacy and be anything else" — and branded Catholicism as a " papal cult," " fetish materialism," " image worship and spiritualism," entirely opposed to the simple truths of the Protestant interpretation of the gospels. [38]

---

[36] Laurence Franklin, "The Italian in America: What he Has Been, What he Shall Be," *Catholic World*, LXXI (April, 1900), 72-73.

[37] D. Lynch, "The Religious Condition of Italians in New York," *America*, X, No. 24 (March 21, 1914), 558. At least 25 articles appeared in *America, American Ecclesiastical Review*, and *Catholic World*, the leading Catholic scholarly reviews, during the years between 1900 and 1921.

[38] *La Fiaccola* (New York), Sept. 10, 1914; Sept. 19, 1912. See "Vatican Notes," a regular weekly feature of the journal. "The Vatican and Italy," Oct. 3, 1912, described the struggle between the Italian state and the Church. "Italian Evangelical Chronicle" was a regular feature devoted to Protestant activities among Italian immigrants in various cities of the U.S. On the growth of Protestantism among Italians see "The Secret of our Success," Oct. 31, 1912, and "The Italian Mission," Oct. 24, 1912.

Some Protestant sects, especially Methodists, Baptists and Presbyterians, worked actively among Italian immigrants in urban America, supporting a total of 326 churches and missions with more than 200 pastors, printing several Italian-language newspapers and publishing a steady stream of books, articles, pamphlets and leaflets in English and Italian.[39]

Contacts with Protestant settlements, social workers, public school teachers, ministers and missions profoundly influenced some Italians, who turned to Protestantism because it seemed to be one road to Americanization. Protestants believed that conversion formed an integral and essential element of immigrant adjustment; as one minister proclaimed in 1906, "If the immigrant is evangelized, assimilation is easy and sure." Nevertheless, despite costly and prodigious efforts by non-Catholic churches and settlements, relatively few Italians converted; those who did quickly transferred to American congregations.[40]

The tendency of many newcomers simply to turn away from all religious activities created a greater menace to the Church than did Protestantism. Undoubtedly what Father Joseph Schuyler calls "the stress of disorganization," the impact of migration and the influence of the American environment, distracted many immigrants from traditional organizations like the Church.[41]

Appearances to the contrary, the bulk of the Italian immigrants remained nominally or actually loyal Catholics, but in a way differing from other Catholic groups (like Irish- or Polish-Americans). National consciousness, which developed among all three groups in the United States, strongly influenced ethnic attitudes toward religion. While for Irish and Polish

---

[39] Aurelio Palmieri, "Italian Protestantism in the United States," *Catholic World*, CVII (May, 1918), 177-189; Antonio Mangano, *Sons of Italy: A Social and Religious Study of the Italians in America* (New York, 1917); Enrico E. Sartorio, *Social and Religious Life of Italians in America* (Boston, 1918); William P. Shriver, *Immigrant Forces: Factors in the New Democracy* (New York, 1913); Mary Clark Barnes and Lemuel Call Barnes, *The New America: A Study in Immigration* (New York, 1913).

[40] Local Community Research Committee. *Chicago Communities*, III, "The Lower North Side," Document 27; Howard B. Grose, *Aliens or Americans?* (New York, 1906), p. 256; *Literary Digest*, No. 47 (October 11, 1913), p. 636.

[41] *La Fiaccola*, Aug. 26, 1920; Joseph Schuyler, S.J., *Northern Parish: A Sociological and Pastoral Study* (Chicago, 1960), p. 228.

Catholics religion made up a central part of national loyalty, for Italians Catholicism and nationalism exerted opposing forces.[42]

At the same time that they attacked abuses of the Church both in Italy and the United States, Italian-Americans rallied to support the "Italian Church" against Irish "usurpers" and Protestants. One Protestant clergyman who worked zealously to convert Italians complained that some who talked and acted like "rationalists, atheists, free-thinkers and the like," called themselves Catholics, strongly opposed Protestantism, and urged other Italians to "stand fast to the traditions of their fathers' religion." [43]

Critics who "saw" an irreligious attitude in immigrant superstition and idolatry [44] ignored the fact that image-worship, especially of the Virgin, and anthropomorphic views of nature and religion made Catholicism comprehensible to the unlettered mind. In the same way, critics considered Italians' addiction to festivals, processions and feasts as a perversion of religion, although to participants they formed an integral part of worship. Immigrants who celebrated these functions in America did so not only in an effort to re-establish those elements of religion which had strongly appealed to them in Italy, but also to counteract Irish influences in their new churches.[45] Thus what seemed to Americans to be a falling away from religion was at least in part an adaptation of old habits to new conditions. Prior to 1921, however, the Catholic Church did not occupy the position of prestige among Italian-Americans that it later assumed, particularly after 1945.[46]

---

[42] Thus bourgeois and proletarian papers alike condemned the pope's temporal claims in Italy, the former primarily out of loyalty to the Kingdom. Protestant as well as left wing journals fully upheld the Kingdom, in part to embarrass the Church and in part to further their own particular objectives.

[43] A. Di Domenica, "The Sons of Italy in America," *Missionary Review of the World*, XLI (March, 1918), 193.

[44] Vecoli, *"Contadini* in Chicago: A Critique of *The Uprooted,"* p. 415. On the situation in Italy see Joseph M. Sorrentino, S.J., "Religious Conditions in Italy," *America*, XII, No. 1 (October 17, 1914), 6-7.

[45] Robert A. Woods (ed.), *Americans in Process* (Boston, 1902), pp. 228-229. Such celebrations met strong opposition from liberals and socialists within the Italian community. *La Tribuna Italiana Transatlantica*, Aug. 5 and 12, 1905; *Il Proletario* (Philadelphia), Aug. 11, 1909; *La Parola dei Socialisti* (Chicago), Nov. 8, 1913.

[46] François Houtart, *Aspects Sociologiques du catholicisme américain* (Paris, 1957), pp. 204-206.

In order to gain and hold the support of immigrants and their children, the Church in the United States found it necessary to offer a variety of services which were partly or entirely non-theological in nature and which were unnecessary in the static, unchanging homeland village. Among these new facilities were missions, hospitals, lay societies and organizations, and Sunday Schools. These expanded functions formed part of a general movement in the American Catholic Church during the period between 1890 and World War I toward providing social services in order to meet the needs of Slavic as well as Italian immigrants.[47]

Institutions and Assimilation

Identification with the colony, and use of its facilities and institutions, signified not only a growth away from homeland outlooks but also, for many newcomers, a vital step in assimilation. It is important to note, however, that Italians exhibited a variety of responses to urban America. Some ignored all community institutions and never expanded their loyalties or interests from the district of origin; even the Italian Kingdom lay outside their comprehension.[48] Others made full use of some or all existing community institutions and enlarged their personal horizons to include Italy, a concept which did not exist for them before their emigration from it.[49] A third group preferred to make limited use of press, societies and churches as intermediaries through which to learn American customs and ideas. Often this group of first generation arrivals came as young adults or children and absorbed or consciously adopted American habits and speech in the out-

---

[47] Andrew Shipman, "Immigration," *Official Report of the Second American Catholic Missionary Congress,* 1913 (Chicago, 1914), pp. 154-171; Aaron I. Abell, *American Catholicism and Social Action: A Search for Social Justice* (New York, 1960), especially chap. v.

[48] Park, "Cultural Aspects of Immigration. Immigrant Heritages," p. 495; Park and Miller, *Old World Traits Transplanted,* pp. 147-151. This last is a discussion of a colony of Sicilians living much as they did in their home village of Cinisi, a situation of note in the United States because of its uniqueness.

[49] C.A. Price, "Immigration and Group Settlement," *The Cultural Integration of Immigrants* (ed. W.D. Borrie; Paris, 1959), pp. 267-268; Prezzolini, *I trapiantati,* p. 63; Caroline F. Ware, "Cultural Groups in the United States," *The Cultural Approach to History* (ed. C.F. Ware; New York, 1940), pp. 62-65.

side community, from politics as well as schools, settlement houses and streets.[50]

From politics Italians gained patronage jobs and neighborhood conveniences like bathhouses as well as a voice in city government. In the early years of settlement, this influence extended only to occasional machine support for Italian candidates for precinct or ward positions, in exchange for delivering the vote for Irish politicians (who generally controlled Italian and other "new" immigrant wards).[51] With the passage of time Italians won control of Italian wards; victories in city-wide elections occasionally occurred, but not with any regularity until the 1930's and 1940's.[52]

Social workers reached and influenced many through classes in English, courses in sewing, handicrafts and other activities for women, the support of Italian theater groups, summer camps for children, and sponsoring of political and social clubs for men. Along with public schools, social workers and settlement houses offered alternate channels of contact with the American community to those provided by American political bosses, Italian "prominenti," bankers and padroni. Some reformers sought to establish and support free employment agencies for immigrants and to destroy the padrone labor system, while others worked to procure the passage of child labor laws and strict observance of compulsory education legislation.[53]

Italian immigrants won notoriety (and the wrath of social workers) because they seldom permitted their children to obtain adequate schooling. While complaining that their own

---

[50] Foerster, *Italian Emigration of Our Times*, p. 395. This third group of immigrants, comprised of those who adjusted quietly and with a minimum of difficulty, did not attract the attention of Americans.

[51] John Palmer Gavit, *Americans by Choice* (New York, 1922), p. 372: J.T. Salter, *"Boss Rule"* (New York, 1935), pp. 75-86; Humbert S. Nelli, "John Powers and the Italians: Politics in a Chicago Ward, 1896-1921," *Journal of American History*, LVII, No. 1 (June, 1970), 67-84.

[52] See Arthur Mann, *La Guardia: A Fighter Against His Times: 1882-1933* (Philadelphia, 1959), pp. 109-116; Samuel Lubell, *The Future of American Politics* (3rd ed., rev.; New York, 1965), pp. 77-83.

[53] Federal Writers' Project, Works Progress Administration, *The Italians of New York* (New York, 1938), pp. 105-107; Coulter, *The Italians of Cleveland*, pp. 32-34; Edward Corsi, *In the Shadow of Liberty* (New York, 1935), pp. 25-28; Jane Addams, *Twenty Years at Hull House* (New York, 1910), chaps. x and xiii.

lack of education kept them from getting better jobs, parents sent their offspring out to work in order to supplement family incomes. Although in time most Italians complied with minimum requirements of compulsory education laws, they secured jobs for their children after school hours. When Italian children reached the legal withdrawal age of fourteen, they were "to an alarmingly high degree" withdrawn from school and put to work.[54]

Despite dire predictions that Italians, caught in a "cycle of poverty," would remain destitute and a burden to society, by 1900 they had begun progressing from unskilled labor into commercial, trade and professional classes, including printing, bricklaying, carpentering, import and export, banking, law and medicine.[55] Notwithstanding complaints of reformers and laments of immigrant workers about education, financial success at this time did not depend entirely on schooling; ambition, hard work and cunning could, and did, overcome illiteracy.[56] Crime, one means of economic advancement independent of education, social background and political connections, provided for all classes of Italians opportunities for quick and substantial monetary gain and sometimes for social and political gains as well. Within the colony bankers and padrone labor agents, blackhanders and other lawbreakers all realized small but important profits by swindling or terrorizing compatriots. The "syndicate," business operations reaping vast profits from the American community, offered almost limitless opportunities within the hierarchy. Thus for some, crime

[54] Alberto Pecorini, *Gli Americani nella vita moderna osservati da un italiano* (Milan, 1909), pp. 397-398; Sophia Moses Robison, *Can Delinquency Be Measured* (New York, 1936), pp. 143-144; Beck, "The Italian in Chicago," p. 9. On attitudes toward education in southern Italy see Leonard Covello, "The Social Background of the Italo-American School Child. A study of the Southern Italian Family Mores and their Effect on the School Situation in America," unpublished Ph.D. dissertation, New York University, 1944, p. 399.

[55] Carr, "The Coming of the Italian," p. 429; Alberto Pecorini, "The Italians in the United States," *Forum*, XLV (January, 1911), 21-24; U.S. Congress, *Industrial Commission*, XV, 435-436; U.S. Senate, *Immigration Commission*, XXVIII, 169-176; Edwin Fenton, "Italians in the Labor Movement," *Pennsylvania History*, XXVI, No. 2 (April, 1959), 113-148 and "Italian Workers in the Stoneworkers Union," *Labor History*, III, No. 2 (Spring, 1962), 188-207.

[56] Filippo Lussana, *Lettere di illetterati* (Bologna, 1913); Letter from Grace Abbott to Julia Lathrop, January 14, 1913, located in the Papers of Edith and Grace Abbott, University of Chicago, Box 57, Folder 7.

offered means of advancement inside the ethnic community and for others, opportunities outside it.[57]

By the same process that many Americans believed Italians to be naturally criminal, contemporaries assumed that certain nationalities were predisposed to a particular occupation because of inborn traits or old world influences. The Irish, for example, were "natural politicians," although comparison with Irish experiences in other parts of the world would have challenged this belief. Irish immigrants and their children did not achieve political successes in London, Liverpool or other urban centers in England and Scotland (to which Irish immigration was "more numerous though less celebrated" than to American cities) comparable to their achievements in New York, Chicago and other cities in the United States.[58] Opportunities for political success were simply not present for Irish immigrants in England and Scotland, and Irish pre-eminence in American political life, like the later prominence of Italians in crime and Jews in the clothing industry, was due primarily to availability of opportunity rather than to inborn characteristics or old world habits.[59]

Conclusion

Willingly or unwillingly, immigrants began the process of assimilation as soon as they arrived in the urban environment. The community and its institutions fulfilled the function not of prolonging old world traits and patterns, but of providing important first steps in introducing newcomers to American life, and they did so most effectively. Schools and settlement houses introduced many directly to middle class ideas and living patterns and thus served as an outside force influencing the second generation and some of the more independent newcomers. Economic achievement played a vital role in fur-

---

[57] Nelli, "Italians and Crime in Chicago: The Formative Years, 1890-1920," pp. 373-391.

[58] Cecil Woodham Smith, *The Great Hunger* (New York, 1962), p. 266. For the presentation of a widely held (although exaggerated) view that the Irish dominated American urban politics, see John Paul Bocock, "The Irish Conquest of Our Cities," *Forum*, XVII (April, 1894), 186-195.

[59] On the role of the American environment in Italian criminal activity see William S. Bennet, "Immigrants and Crime," *Annals of the American Academy of Political and Social Science*, XXXIV, No. 1 (July, 1909), 120-121, and Nelli, "Italians and Crime in Chicago: The Formative Years, 1890-1920," pp. 386-391.

thering adjustment as well as in spurring movement out of early ethnic districts. Over the passage of years newcomers and their children moved up the economic ladder, progressing from unskilled labor into commercial, trade and professional lines. Channels of progress also appeared within organized labor and politics, while criminal activities provided a lucrative means of financial advancement, both within the Italian colony and in the larger urban environment. Critics complained of the slow upward progress of the immigrants, and compared Italians (and other "new" groups) with their predecessors, ignoring the fact that the "old" elements arrived in Chicago and other northern cities considerably earlier than did the bulk of Italians, Russian Jews, Poles, Lithuanians and Greeks. Thus they had the opportunity, as sociologist Richard Ford has pointed out, of profiting economically and socially in cities that had not developed rigid political or financial patterns. "The process of acculturation," notes Ford, "has been going on considerably longer for the Swedish, German and Irish immigrants than for the Italians and Russians." [60]

Like most recent immigrants, Italians appeared to move outward from the urban core more slowly and reluctantly than had Irish, Germans and other older groups. Contemporaries did not see the extensive amount of residential mobility among Italians and other late arrivals. From the early years of residence, movement took place not only inside colonies and

---

[60] Richard C. Ford, "Population Succession in Chicago," *American Journal of Sociology*, LVI (September, 1950), 160. It is tempting to compare the Italian experience with that of the American Negro. For Italians, as well as for other European immigrant groups, settlement in core area ethnic colonies formed the vital first step in the assimilation process. The core community has also functioned effectively for Negroes from the American rural South, but the process has typically ended at that point. The basic reason for this difference between the immigrant and the Negro urban experience was described in 1931 by a federal committee investigation of Negro housing conditions. In the case of the immigrant who had learned American speech and habits within the core community, movement "to more desirable sections of the city" was possible. "In the case of Negroes, who remain a distinguishable group, the factor of race and certain definite racial attitudes favorable to segregation, interpose difficulties to... breaking physical restrictions in residence areas." The President's Conference on Home Building and Home Ownership, *Report of the Committee on Negro Housing* 1931), p. 5. As Historian Gilbert Osofsky observed in his recent study, *Harlem: The Making of a Ghetto. Negro New York, 1890-1930* (New York, 1966), p. 131, this situation has continued to exist.

from one community to another, but also from the early, centrally located districts toward outlying areas of the city and even into suburbs. By the 1920's the suburban trend was noticeable and significant. World War I and the immigration laws of 1921 and 1924 closed new sources of immigration, and Italian districts began perceptibly to decline. The cumulative effect, noted by sociologist Harvey W. Zorbaugh in the late 1920's, was that "few Italians are coming to America.... The community without any influx from the old country is fast becoming Americanized." Depression in the 1930's and housing shortages in the 1940's slowed the pace of this dispersion from the ethnic colony, but it has again accelerated since 1950.[61]

---

[61] Local Community Research Committee, *Chicago Communities*, III, "The Lower North Side," Document 30 (excerpts from the notes of Harvey W. Zorbaugh). A similar situation existed elsewhere in urban America. See Caroline F. Ware, *Greenwich Village, 1920-1930. A Comment on American Civilization in the Post-War Years* (Boston, 1935), pp. 156-157.

Selected Bibliography

by Humbert S. Nelli

The literature on Italian immigration into the American environment is vast, and a separate volume would be necessary were all pertinent publications to be listed. Therefore this note will mention only the more significant or useful books, articles and published reports printed in English. Although many of the studies listed below cover more than one topic they will be mentioned only once in order to keep the bibliography within manageable limits.

The Italian background and factors influencing emigration are examined in Edward C. Banfield, *The Moral Basis of a Backward Society* (Glencoe, Ill., 1958); J. S. McDonald, "Italy's Rural Social Structure and Emigration," *Occidente*, XII (September-October, 1956), 437-456; Phyllis H Williams, *South Italian Folkways in Europe and America* (New Haven, Conn., 1938); Luigi Villari, *Italian Life in Town and Country* (New York, 1903); Leonard Covello, "The Social Background of the Italo-American School Child, A Study of the Southern Italian Family Mores and Their Effect on the School Situation in Italy and America," unpublished Ph. D. dissertation, New York University, 1944, which has been revised by the author and published by E. J. Brill in 1967.

An essential point of departure in any study of Italian immigration is Robert F. Foerster, *The Italian Emigration of Our Times* (Cambridge, Mass., 1919), which devotes four chapters (of a total of twenty-four) specifically to the United States and five to the Italian background. Unfortunately for the student of urban and immigration history, the study is out-of-date both in source materials and conceptual framework. Foerster made no use of a variety of primary works which urban historians and immigration scholars have found to be valuable, such as foreign-language newspapers, fraternal organizations and Catholic parish records, and precinct voting records. Although the rural experience of Italians in America was of minor importance compared with the urban, Foerster wrote an entire chapter about the former and examined the latter incidentally in other chapters. The book tends to concentrate on economic considerations, while political, social and cultural influence are ignored or unrecognized.

Other general studies of Italian immigration in the United States include Eliot Lord, John J. D. Trenor, and Samuel J. Barrows, *The Italian in America* (New York, 1905); Philip M. Rose, *The Italians in America* (New York, 1922); Francis E. Clark, *Our Italian Fellow Citizens in Their Old Homes and Their New* (Boston, 1919); Michael A. Musmanno, *The Story of the Italians in America* (Garden City, N.Y., 1965); Antonio Stella, *Some Aspects of Italian Immigration to the United States* (New York, 1924); Lawrence F. Pisani, *The Italian in America* (New York,

103

1957); Giovanni E. Schiavo, *Four Centuries of Italian-American History* (New York, 1952); Alberto Pecorini, "The Italians in the United States," *Forum*, XLV (January, 1911), 15-29; Max Ascoli, "The Italian-Americans," *Group Relations and Group Antagonisms,* ed. R. M. MacIver (New York, 1944); G. E. Di Palma Castiglione, "Italian Immigration into the United States, 1901-4," *American Journal of Sociology*, XI (September, 1905), 183-206; Eugene Schuyler, "Italian Immigration into the United States," *Political Science Quarterly*, IV (September, 1889), 480-495; Herbert N. Casson, "The Italians in America," *Munsey's Magazine*, XXXVI (October, 1906), 122-126; Edward Alsworth Ross, "Italians in America," *Century Magazine*, LXXXVIII (July, 1914), 439-445; Joseph H. Senner, "Immigration from Italy," *North American Review*, CLXII (June, 1896), 649-657.

Municipal, state and federal government authorities in the United States devoted a great deal of attention to conditions in Italian colonies in America. Among the more useful reports are Frank O. Beck, "The Italian in Chicago," *Bulletin of the Department of Public Welfare of Chicago*, II, No. 3 (February, 1919), 2-12; Grace Abbott, *The Problem of Immigration in Massachusetts. Report of the Commission on Immigration* (Boston, 1914); State of New York, *Report of the Commission on Immigration* (Albany, 1909); U.S. Commissioner of Labor, *Seventh Special Report. The Slums of Baltimore, Chicago, New York and Philadelphia* (1894) and *Ninth Special Report. The Italian in Chicago, A Social and Economic Study* (1897); U.S. Congress, *Report on Importation of Contract Labor*, 2 Vols. (1889) and *Reports of the Industrial Commission*, XV (1901), 473-492; U.S. Senate, *Reports of the Immigration Commission*, 41 Vols. (1911), especially XXVI and XXVII, "Immigrants in Cities." In the years since its publication, the Immigration (or Dillingham) Commission *Reports* have received much criticism, most notably from Isaac A. Hourwich, *Immigration and Labor: The Economic Aspects of European Immigration to the United States* (New York, 1912), and Oscar Handlin, *Race and Nationality in American Life* (Boston, 1957), chap. v, "Old Immigrants and New." Criticism has centered on the restrictionist bias of the Commission and its interpretation of data, while the statistical materials presented in the *Reports* have generally been accepted as accurate. Comparison of Dillingham Commission statistics with unpublished primary materials in various cities shows the Commission's figures to be inaccurate in many cases regarding Italians, and often distorted because of limited sampling.

Large numbers of books and articles have been written about the experience of Italians in individual cities. Studies on New York include Federal Writers' Project, Works Progress Administration, *The Italians of New York: A Survey* (New York, 1938); Charles Loring Brace, *The Dangerous Classes of New York* (New York, 1872), chap. xvii; Caroline F. Ware, *Greenwich Village, 1920-1930. A Comment on American Civilization in the Post-War Years* (Boston, 1935), especially chap. vi; Nathan Glazer and Daniel Patrick Moynihan, *Beyond the Melting Pot: The Negroes, Puerto Ricans, Jews, Italians and Irish of New York City* (Cambridge, Mass., 1963); Louise C. Odencrantz, *Italian Women in Industry: A Study of Conditions in New York City* (New York, 1919); John H. Mariano, *The Second Generation of Italians in New York City* (Boston, 1921); John C. Gebhart, *The Growth and Development of Italian Children in New York City* (New York, 1924); William B. Shedd, "The

Italian Population in New York City," *Casa Italiana Educational Bulletin*, No. 7 (New York, 1936); John J. D'Alessandro, "Occupational Trends of Italians in New York City," *Casa Italiana Educational Bulletin*, No. 8 (New York, 1936); Charlotte Adams, "Italian Life in New York," *Harper's Magazine*, LXII (April, 1881), 676-684; George J. Manson, "The 'Foreign Element' in New York City. V. The Italians," *Harper's Weekly*, XXXIV (October 18, 1890), 817-820; Viola Roseboro, "The Italians of New York," *Cosmopolitan*, IV (January, 1888), 396-406; John Foster Carr, "The Coming of the Italian," *Outlook*, LXXXII (February 24, 1906), 419-431.

On Chicago, see: Giovanni E. Schiavo, *The Italians in Chicago*: *A Study in Americanization* (Chicago, 1928); Harvey W. Zorbaugh, *The Gold Coast and the Slum* (Chicago, 1929); Alessandro Mastro-Valerio, "Remarks Upon the Italian Colony in Chicago," *Hull House Maps and Papers* (New York, 1895), pp. 131-139; Grace P. Norton, "Chicago Housing Conditions, VII: Two Italian Districts," *American Journal of Sociology*, XVIII (January, 1913), 509-542; Natalie Walker, "Chicago Housing Conditions, X. Greeks and Italians in the Neighborhood of Hull House," *American Journal of Sociology*, XXI (November, 1915), 285-316; Rudolph J. Vecoli, "*Contadini* in Chicago: A critique of *The Uprooted*," *Journal of American History*, LI (December, 1964), 404-417; Humbert S. Nelli, *Italians in Chicago, 1880-1930*: *A Study in Ethnic Mobility* (New York, 1970).

On Boston: Walter I. Firey, *Land Use in Central Boston* (Cambridge, Mass., 1947), chap. v; William Foote Whyte, *Street Corner Society* (Chicago, 1943) and "Race Conflicts in the North End of Boston," *New England Quarterly*, XII (December, 1939), 623-642; Herbert J .Gans, *The Urban Villagers*: *Group and Class in the Life of Italian-Americans* (Glencoe, Ill., 1962); Robert A. Woods, ed., *The City Wilderness* (Boston, 1898) and *Americans in Process* (Boston, 1902); Frederick A. Bushee, "Italian Immigrants in Boston," *Arena*, XVII (April, 1897), 722-734 and *Ethnic Factors in the Population of Boston* (New York, 1903); Vida D. Scudder, "Experiments in Fellowship, Work with Italians in Boston," *Survey*, XXII (April 3, 1909), 47-51; Robert A. Woods, "Notes on the Italians in Boston," *Charities*, XII (May 7, 1904), 451-452.

Studies of Italians in other cities in the East and Middle West include: Anthony J. Tomanio and Lucille N. La Macchia, *The Italian-American Community in Bridgeport* (Bridgeport, Conn., 1953); Irvin L. Child, *Italian or American? The Second Generation in Conflict* (New Haven, Conn., 1943), which is based upon an examination of the Italian population in New Haven; Blake McKelvey, "The Italians of Rochester; An Historical Review," *Rochester History*, XXII (October, 1960), 1-24; Charles W. Churchill, *The Italians of Newark* (New York, 1946); Emily W. Dinwiddie, "Some Aspects of Italian Housing and Social Conditions in Philadelphia," *Charities*, XII (May 7, 1904), 490-493; Joan Younger Dickinson, "Aspects of Italian Immigration to Philadelphia," *Pennsylvania Magazine of History and Biography*, XC (October, 1966), 445-465; M. Howe, "From Italy to Pittsburgh. Where the Pennsylvania Italians Come From," *Lippincott's Magazine*, LXXIII (1904), 200-208; Charles W. Coulter, *The Italians of Cleveland* (Cleveland, 1919); Grace Leonore Pitts, "The Italians of Columbus — A Study in Population," *Annals of the American Academy of Political and Social Science*, XIX (January, 1902), 154-159; George LaPiana, *The Italians in Milwaukee, Wisconsin* (Milwaukee, 1915).

An extensive literature exists in a variety of specialized topics, including the padrone system, organized labor, crime, politics, religion, societies, health and education. The following paragraphs provide a sampling of available studies.

John Koren, "The Padrone System and Padrone Banks," *U. S. Bureau of Labor Bulletin No.* 9 (March, 1897), pp. 113-129; Frank J. Sheridan, "Italian, Slavic and Hungarian Unskilled Immigrant Laborers in the United States," *U. S. Bureau of Labor Bulletin No.* 72 (September, 1907), pp. 403-386; Gino C. Speranza, "The Italian Foreman as a Social Agent, *Charities*, XI (July 4, 1903), 26-28; William E. Phipard, "The Philanthropist-Padrone," *Charities*, XII (May 7, 1904), 470-472; Domenick Ciolli, " The Wop in the Track Gang, *Immigrants in America Review*, II (July, 1916), 61-64. The foregoing are contemporary accounts of the padrone labor system. A recent effort to evaluate the contributions of the labor agent to American business as well as to immigrant workers is Humbert S. Nelli, "The Italian Padrone System in the United States," *Labor History*, V (Spring, 1964), 153-167. Italians and labor have been examined in two excellent articles written by Edwin Fenton, "Italians in the Labor Movement," *Pennsylvania History*, XXVI (April, 1959), 113-148 and "Italian Workers in the Stonecutters Union," *Labor History*, III (Spring, 1962), 188-207.

There exist numerous studies of Italians and religion. The "Italian Problem" of the American Catholic Church has received considerable attention: Bernard J. Lynch, "The Italians in New York," *Catholic World*, XLVII (April, 1888), 67-73; Laurence Franklin, "The Italian in America: What he Has Been, What he Shall Be," *Catholic World*, LXXI (April, 1900), 67-80; Kate Prindeville, "Italy in Chicago," *Catholic World*, LXXVI (July, 1903), 452-461; Edmund M. Dunne, "Memoirs of 'Zi Pre'," *American Ecclesiastical Review*, XLIX (August, 1913), 192-203; Albert R. Bandini, "Concerning the Italian Problem," *American Ecclesiastical Review*, LXII (March, 1920), 278-285; Henry J. Browne, "The 'Italian Problem' in the Catholic Church of the United States, 1880-1900," *United States Catholic Historical Society*: *Historical Records and Studies*, XXXV (1946), 46-72. These are representative articles only. For descriptions of Protestant activities among the immigrants: Antonio Mangano, *Sons of Italy*: *A Social and Religious Study of Italians in America* (New York, 1917); John B. Bisceglia, *Italian Evangelical Pioneers* (Kansas City, Mo., 1948); F. Guglielmi, *Italian Methodist Mission in the Little Italy of Baltimore, Md.* (New Castle, Md., 1913); Aurelio Palmieri, "Italian Protestantism in the United States," *Catholic World*, CVII (May, 1918), 177-189. For additional titles see the Mangano book, which contains an extensive bibliography of books, articles, pamphlets and leaflets.

Among the many works concerning crime and Italian-Americans, see: John H. Mariano, *The Italian Immigrant and Our Courts* (Boston, 1925); Arthur Train, *Courts, Criminals and the Camorra* (New York, 1912); John Landesco, *Organized Crime in Chicago, Part III of the Illinois Crime Survey* (Chicago, 1929); Frederic Sondern, Jr., *Brotherhood of Evil*: *The Mafia* (New York, 1959); Giovanni E. Schiavo, *The Truth About the Mafia and Organized Crime in America* (New York, 1962); The Italian "White Hand" Society in Chicago, Illinois, *Studies, Action and Results* (Chicago, 1908); Gaetano D'Amato, "The 'Black Hand' Myth," *North American Review*, CLXXXII (April, 1908), 543-549; Tomasso Sassone, "Italy's Criminals in the United States," *Current History*, XV

(October, 1921), 23-31; Humbert S. Nelli, "Italians and Crime in Chicago: The Formative Years, 1890-1920," *American Journal of Sociology*, LXXIV (January, 1969), 373-391, which lists additional titles.

Political activities of immigrants and their children are described in the following: Fiorello H. LaGuardia, *The Making of an Insurgent: An Autobiography, 1882-1919* (Philadelphia, 1948); Arthur Mann, *La Guardia: A Fighter Against His Times: 1882-1933* (Philadelphia, 1959) and *LaGuardia Comes to Power: 1933* (Philadelphia, 1965); John Palmer Gavit, *Americans by Choice* (New York, 1922); Samuel Lubell, *The Future of American Politics* (3rd ed., rev.; New York, 1965), chap. iv; and Humbert S. Nelli, "John Powers and the Italians: Politics in a Chicago Ward, 1896-1921," *Journal of American History*, LVII (June, 1970), 67-84.

For analyses of health problems in the Italian colony: Rocco Brindisi, "The Italian and Public Health," *Charities*, XII (May 7, 1904), 483-486; Antonio Stella, "Tuberculosis and the Italians in the United States," *Charities*, XII (May 7, 1904), 486-489. Education among Italians is examined by Jane Addams, "Foreign-born Children in the Primary Grades; Italian Families in Chicago," *National Education Association. Journal of Proceedings and Addresses*, XXXVI (1897), 104-112; Grace Irwin, "Michelangelo in Newark," *Harper's Magazine*, CXLIII (September, 1921), 446-454; Ellen May, " Italian Education and Immigration," *Education*, No. 28 (March, 1908), pp. 450-453. Societies are discussed in Antonio Mangano, "The Associated Life of the Italians in New York City," *Charities*, XII (May 7, 1904), 476-482, and Ernest L. Biagi, *The Purple Aster: A History of the Order Sons of Italy in America* (N.P., 1961).

Additional titles on these and other topics are listed in bibliographies of the major works as well as bibliographical compilations. In particular, consult: Ina TenEyck Firkins, "Italians in the United States," *Bulletin of Bibliography*, ed. Frederick Winthrop Faxon, VIII (Boston, 1915), 129-132; Joseph Velikonja, *Italians in the United States*, Occasional Papers No. 1, Department of Geography, Southern Illinois University (Carbondale, 1963); John Foster Carr, *Immigrant and Library; Italian Helps, with Lists of Selected Books* (New York, 1914).

INSTITUTIONAL TIES
OF ITALO-AMERICANS:
SOME CASE ILLUSTRATIONS

American society seeks to assimilate the immigrants admitted to its political and geographic confines. In time, therefore, it influences their institutionalized ways of thinking, feeling and acting. Similarly, when an immigrant group is powerful, it can influence American institutions — the economy, the schools, the political arena and the religious sphere. In what ways did Italians adjust, modify or completely change their old ways? In what ways were Italians, by dint of their group consciousness and ability to organize, able to bring about change in the "American Way?" The following five papers examine the experience of Italians in the United States as they met the challenge of its way of life. Specifically, they deal with the economic, educational, political and religious assimilation of Italo-Americans.

Italians and Organized Labor in the United States and Argentina: 1880-1910*

by Samuel L. Baily **

The Italian immigration to the Western Hemisphere is an extremely rich field for those interested in comparative migration studies. According to figures in the *Bolletino dell'Emigrazione* in 1912, 80% of the 5.5 million Italians abroad were in the New World. Of that 80% roughly two fifths were in the United States and the remaining number were divided between Argentina and Brazil.[1] In each country the immigrants encountered a different social, economic and political environment. Thus, if historians wish to determine the influence of a wide variety of variables on Italian immigrant experience a comparative study of these three areas provides an excellent testing ground.

My own particular interest is the Italians and the Argentine labor movement. However, I will place my remarks about Argentina in a broader context. The questions to which I wish to address myself are: 1) what was the contribution of the Italians to the organization and development of the major labor unions and federations in the United States and in Argentina during the period of mass migration at the turn of the century:[2] 2) was there a significant difference between

---

[1] Italian Republic, Commissariato dell'Emigrazione, *Bollettino dell'Emigrazione* (1912), No. 1, pp. 8-9.

[2] It is important to keep in mind that I am comparing the major labor federations and unions in each country. If, for example, one were to compare only radical unions in the United States with the Argentine labor movement one would come up with different results. See Edwin Fenton, "Immigrants and Unions, A Case Study: Italians and American Labor, 1870-1920," (Ph.D. Thesis, Harvard University, 1957), pp. 135-196 and Rudolph J. Vecoli, *The People of New Jersey* (Princeton: Van Nostrand, 1965), pp. 179-242.

---

* Paper read before the American Historical Association in New York City, December 28, 1966.

** S. L. Baily is Associate Professor of History at Rutgers, the State University.

the contributions of the Italians in the two countries: and 3) if there was a difference, how can we account for it?

Organized Labor in the United States

In its 47 volume report of 1910, the United States Senate Immigration Commission discussed, among other things, the relationship between the immigrant and the labor movement. It based its findings on census data, especially collected statistical information, and on the testimony of leaders of interest groups such as that of Samuel Gompers, John Mitchell, and other leaders of the American Federation of Labor.

The Commission concluded that the Southern Europeans, including the Italians, were hindering rather than contributing to the progress of organized labor. It argued that because of their lack of industrial training, their low standard of living, their thrift, their need to find employment, their desire for immediate gains, and their tractability, the recent migrants had been willing to accept conditions as they found them and had not, for the most part, joined unions. In addition, the Commission pointed out, the influx of large numbers of Southern Europeans had been so rapid that the labor organizations, in existence prior to the arrival .of the new migrants, had been unable to absorb them.

To support this conclusion, the Commission set forth union affiliation and nationality statistics on male wage-earners twenty-one years of age or over. According to its survey of 24,594 workers, 14.2% of the natives were affiliated with unions, 13.4% of the foreign-born workers in general were union members, and 39.8% of the Northern Italians but only 10.6% of the Southern Italians were organized. Thus the Commission reported that the Southern Italians, who constituted the overwhelming majority of the Italians in the country, were 18% less organized than native workers and 13% less organized than the foreigners in general.[3]

Since 1910, historians have attacked some of the Commission's reasons for explaining why the Southern Italians did not organize — particularly the assumption that something

---

[3] United States Senate Documents, 61st Congress 3rd. Session, Vol. 7 *Immigration Commission Report*, pp. 417-419, 530-531.

in their character prevented such organization — but few have questioned the data on the actual number that were organized.[4] It seems reasonable, therefore, to accept the Immigration Commission's data and to conclude that in the United States in 1910, the Southern Italians were not participating in union activity to the same extent as were the native born or the foreigners in general.

Organized Labor in Argentina

In Argentina the men who ruled the country from 1853 until Word War I devoted themselves to its transformation from what they considered to be a backward, Hispanic-creole area into a modern, progressive, European one. They sought to bring about this transformation by education, immigration and economic development.

Their ideas on immigration were embodied in the often quoted phrase of one of their members, Juan Bautista Alberdi — to govern is to populate. More specifically, Alberdi meant to govern is to populate the vast interior of Argentina with European immigrants. The Constitution of 1853, which Alberdi and others wrote, reflected this interest in immigration. Article 20 of the document guaranteed aliens the same civil rights as Argentine citizens. Article 25 stated that: "The Federal Government shall promote and encourage European immigration. It shall have no power to restrict, to limit, or to burden with taxes or charges of any kind, the flow to the territory of the Republic of any foreigners coming to cultivate its soil, to improve its industries, or to introduce and teach the sciences and arts."

The governments of the 1860's and 1870's made various efforts to encourage immigration, but it was the rapid economic development of the 1880's and early 1900's more than government policy that stimulated the mass migration. Between 1880 and 1910 Argentina was able to transform the grasslands of the pampa into a productive agricultural area which provided the basis for the development of the entire economy. As one historian summed up: "This agricultural conquest (of

---

[4] For example see Fenton, *Op. cit.* and I. A. Hourwich, *Immigration and Labor* (New York, 1912).

the pampa) created prosperity for many, provided the basis for commercial, industrial, and urban growth, and built Argentina into a leading power of South America."[5]

Before 1880 relatively few immigrants came to Argentina, but during the next three decades three and a half million immigrants entered and two-thirds of them remained in the country. These figures may seem small to historians of United States immigration, but in the Argentine context they are impressive. In 1869 the country had a population of about two million, 12.1% of which was foreign born. By 1895 the population had grown to four million with 22.5% foreign born. In 1914 the population had reached seven million and 30.3% were foreigners.[6]

In addition, the immigrant population concentrated in a few eastern provinces of the country and increasingly in the cities. Over 90% of the foreigners who came to Argentina during this thirty years period settled in the provinces of Buenos Aires, Entre Rios, Santa Fe and Córdoba. Nearly two-thirds settled within the province and the city of Buenos Aires. As a result Buenos Aires grew from a town of 180,000 in 1869 to a city of a million and a half in 1914, and throughout these years about half its population was foreign born. Given the higher percentage of adult males in the foreign population, this meant that in the eastern provinces and in the cities 50% to 70% of the economically active population was foreign born.[7]

At first the majority of foreigners went to the rural areas of the eastern provinces and engaged in agricultural occupations. Between 1871 and 1890 nearly three-quarters of the immigrants found their way into such persuits. But between 1891 and 1910 only half of the immigrants were involved in agriculture and the census of 1914 reveals that of the 800,000 male immigrants who stated their occupations, over half were

[5] James R. Scobie, Argentina: A City and a Nation (New York: Oxford University Press, 1964), p. 123.

[6] Argentine Republic, Dirección de Immigración, Resumen estadística del movimiento migratorio en la República Argentina, 1857-1924 (Buenos Aires: Ministerio de Agricultura, 1925), pp. 4-5; Gino Germani, Política y sociedad en una época de transición (Buenos Aires: Editorial Paidos, 1962), p. 185.

[7] Germani, op. cit., pp. 187, 212; Argentine Republic, Resumen, pp. 24-25.

in small industry, manual arts and commerce, and only a quarter in agriculture and livestock occupations.[8]

The Italians and Spanish were by far the most numerous, constituting between 78% and 90% of the total number of immigrants from 1880 to 1910. The Italians, however, were numerically the more important as they made up about half of all those who settled in Argentina during the period.[9] Robert F. Foerster estimated that the Italians plus their children represented 28% of the entire Argentine population in 1910.[10]

The distribution pattern of the Italians corresponded closely to that of the immigrants in general — nearly 90% lived in the eastern provinces. Up to 1900 most of the Italians — mainly Northerners — went into the rural areas, but enough remained in the cities to help swell the urban population. After 1900 the Southern Italians predominated and they for the most part remained in the cities. Thus, between 1869 and 1914, the Italians made up about a quarter of the population of the city of Buenos Aires and in 1906 they represented 22% of the population of Rosario.[11]

About 65% of the Italians who entered Argentina during the 1857-1895 period and who stated their occupation were farmers. Maybe a quarter of them were "golondrinas" — seasonal laborers — who came during the Italian winter to work and harvest the crops during the Argentine summer. Ten percent were merchants or engaged in small industry. The remainder held various kinds of jobs or were unemployed women and children.[12]

Labor organization in Argentina was almost completely the product of the mass migration during the 1880 to 1910 period. Italian, Spanish, German and French immigrants provided the ideologies, the leadership, and the majority of

---

[8] Argentine Republic, *Tercer Censo Nacional* (Buenos Aires: 1917), IV, pp. 396-397.

[9] Germani, *op. cit.*, p. 184; Argentine Republic, *Resumen*, pp. 8, 34.

[10] Robert F. Foerster, "The Italian Factor in the Argentine Race Stock," *Quarterly Publications of the American Statistical Association*, XVI, No. 125 (June 1919), p. 349.

[11] Germani, *op. cit.*, p. 184; Robert D. Ochs, "A History of Argentine immigration, 1853-1924," (Ph.D. Thesis, University of Illinois, 1939), pp. 163-170; Associazione per lo sviluppo dell'industria nel Mezzogiorno, *Statistiche sul Mezzogiorno d'Italia*, 1861-1953 (Rome, 1954, pp. 117-118.

[12] Argentine Republic, *Segundo Censo Nacional* (Buenos Aires: 1897), I, p. 643.

members for the country's first labor unions. Most of the workers' organizations were socialist, anarchist, or syndicalist, and they were concentrated primarily in Buenos Aires and Rosario. Approximately three-quarters of the labor leaders and two-thirds of the union members were foreign born, and they were occupied in small industry, manual arts, and transportation.[13]

The first efforts of the immigrant workers to organize were the mutual aid societies. By 1900 the Italians had established 79, the Spanish 57, and the other nationality groups about 40 or 50. Some of these societies, such as the Unión Tipográfica, were organized around a particular trade and were the first to use the strike to defend their interest. In addition to the mutual aid societies, several of the immigrant groups organized affiliates of the First International. But before 1880 none of these organizations was particularly effective in defending the interests of the workers.

The economic expansion of the 1880's brought thousands of workers to the cities and they began to form new organizations. In 1882 immigrants from Bismarck's Germany established the Argentine Vorwärts "to realize the principles and goals of socialism in accordance with the program of the Social Democrats of Germany." Bakers, masons, railroad engineers and others organized anarchist and socialist groups to protect their interests.

Toward the end of the 1880's a series of strikes, most of them in response to the tightening inflationary "squeeze," provided the background for the activities that led to the establishment of a labor federation. Stimulated by this working class militancy and by the establishment of the Second International in July 1889, Joseph Winiger, the president of the Argentine Vorwärts, assembled the working class organizations of Buenos Aires to form the Comité Internacional Obrero.

---

[13] These are estimates based on figures in Ciudad de Buenos Aires, *Censo General de 1904* (Buenos Aires, 1906), pp. 212-235; Argentine Republic, Repartamento Nacional del Trabajo, *Boletín*, Nos. 4-12 (1908-1909); Sebastián Marotta, *Movimiento sindical argentino* (Buenos Aires: Ediciones Lacio, 1961); Diego Abad de Santillán, *La FORA* (Buenos Aires: Ediciones Nervie, 1933); Martín S. Casaretto, *Historia del movimiento obrero argentino* (Buenos Aires: Vescovo, 1946); and Jacinto Oddone, *Gremialismo proletario argentino* (Buenos Aires: La Vanguardia, 1949).

The Comité held a May 1, 1890 demonstration and in July established Argentina's first labor federation. The federation did not endure very long because the ideological conflict between anarchists and socialists weakened it and the economic recession of the late 1880's and early 1890's forced many leaders and members to return to Europe. Within the decade the immigrant workers established three additional labor federations, but all of them failed.

In 1901, the workers of Buenos Aires plus some from Rosario and a few other cities, formed the Federación Obrera Regional Argentina (FORA) which within a year became an anarchist organization.[14] In 1903 the socialist and syndicalist workers established a rival labor federation, the Unión General del Trabajo (UGT), but it soon came under the exclusive influence of the syndicalists. These two organizations (the FORA and the UGT) — which at the peak of their influence in 1906 represented perhaps 70% to 80% of the organized workers and maybe as much as 50% of the workers in small industry and manual arts — provided militant leadership for the labor movement during the first decade of the twentieth century.[15] Between 1902 and 1910 they led a number of general strikes, some of which involved as many as 200,000 workers, and their affiliates participated in hundreds of individual strikes. As a result of this action and the prosperity of the period it seems that the real wages of skilled and semi-skilled workers increased, their hours decreased, and rents in some working class districts of Buenos Aires were lowered.[16]

---

[14] In 1901 the organization was named the Federación Obrera Argentina, but in 1904 it was changed to the Federación Obrera Regional Argentina. To avoid confusion, I have used the latter name throughout.

[15] These are estimates based on figures in the works cited in note 13. About 25% of the workers in small industry and manual arts were organized, but an additional 25% — very likely unwilling to pay union dues and thus to be counted as members — nevertheless supported the FORA and the UGT during the important general strikes. After 1906 there was a decline in the membership of the FORA and the UGT and an increase in the number of autonomous unions.

[16] There is some question as to whether real wages actually increased during this period. The statistics of the National Department of Labor (probably the best available), which compare salaries and hours for 1904 and 1909, suggest that there was in fact an increase in real wages and a decrease in hours. See Argentine Republic, Departamento Nacional del Trabajo, *Boletín*, No. 8 (March 31, 1909), pp. 16-30.

The governments of the period, representing the landed oligarchy, were alarmed by the wave of strikes and by the fact that the foreign workers were not apparently becoming assimilated. As a result they took the first steps to limit immigration since the writing of the Constitution of 1853.

On November 23, 1902, shortly after the first general strike, the National Congress passed the Ley de Residencia which empowered the government to deport all foreigners who had been convicted of crimes by foreign courts or whose conduct threatened national security or disturbed the public order. In addition, the law prohibited the entry of foreigners guilty of criminal offenses. On June 28, 1910, after several months of militant labor demonstrations connected with the celebration of the Centennial of Argentine Independence, the National Congress passed a second law to restrict working class immigration and radical labor activity, the Ley de Defensa Social. This law prohibited anarchists from entering the country and forbade those in Argentina from meeting or propagandizing in any way.

As a consequence of these laws, hundreds of labor leaders and workers were arrested and deported, union publications were suspended, and union headquarters were closed down. Although there are no reliable statistics on the number deported or refused entrance under these laws, one generally reliable authority claims that 500 workers were deported in 1910 alone.[17] In any case labor organization was severely weakened and did not recover for several years.

From the beginning the Italians, both Northern and Southern, provided many leaders and members for individual unions and for numerous labor federations, but due to the paucity of statistical data it is difficult to document this with precision. The National Census of 1914 does not list labor organizations and the National Census of 1895 gives only incomplete information on working class organizations and nationality groups. The Municipal Censuses of Buenos Aires contain the best information, but even they are far from complete. Therefore, I have relied heavily on the names of leaders and delegates of labor organizations and on the names of

---

[17] Among those deported were the following important Italian labor leaders: A. Zamorano, A. Zamboni, G. Pugliese, and C. Piccinini. See Marotta, *op. cit.*, II, p. 85.

affiliate groups to labor federations all of which are readily available in a number of Argentine labor histories.[18]   There are weaknesses to this kind of approach, but in the absence of better documentation this at least provides valuable hints as to the actual situation, and permits us to make some statements concerning the influence of the Italians in the labor movement.[19]

Before 1880 the Italians established 20 mutual aid societies in Buenos Aires and a smaller number in the interior.[20]   In 1873 Italians created a section of the First International, and although the French and Germans were most numerous within the Unión Tipográfica, 3 of the 9 organizers of the country's first strike — the printers strike of 1878 — were Italians.

During the 1880's and 1890's the Italians organized and were active in many working class groups. The Italian anarchists Errico Malatesta and Hector Mattei arrived in Argentina in 1885. In 1887 they organized a bakers' union in Buenos Aires and the next year they joined with other Italian and with French anarchists and socialists to establish the Circulo Socialista. Malatesta returned to Europe shortly thereafter, but Mattei remained in Argentina, helped organize other unions, and participated in the establishment of the FORA in 1901.

Italians were particularly active among the masons and 4 of the 7 leaders of the 6000 striking masons in 1889 were Italians. Italians, mostly from Genoa, made up the majority of the membership of the maritime unions — the sailors, firemen, stevedores, shipbuilders, etc. In addition, Italians were leaders among the painters, plasterers, harness makers, blacksmiths, mechanics, and stone cutters.

The Comité Internacional Obrera, which sponsored the May 1, 1890 workers demonstration and established Argentina's first labor federation a few months later, was dominated by German socialists and included many French and Spanish

---

[18] *Ibid.*; Abad de Santillán, *op. cit.*; Casaretto, *op. cit.*; and Oddone, *op. cit.*

[19] The quantitative approach is designed to raise questions and to suggest hypotheses which can be tested with further research. It is not the author's intent to minimize the importance or necessity of other approaches to the same subject.

[20] An excellent unpublished study of the immigrant societies in Argentina is Elizabeth Jelin, "Las comunidades de los extranjeros en la Argentina y sus asociaciones," (Buenos Aires, 1963).

workers. Nevertheless, 7 of the 28 leaders and representatives of the organization were Italians. More indicative, 16 of the 27 groups that supported the Comité's May 1 demonstration were Italian, and of those 16 at least 4 — Sociedad Figli del Vesuvio, Circolo Republicana T. Campanella, Union Calabrese, and Circolo Mandolinista Italiana — represented workers from Southern Italy.[21]

In 1890 the Italians were not as significant as the Germans, nor perhaps as the French and Spanish, as leaders of the embryonic labor movement, but they contributed a substantial number of members to almost all working class organizations. During the 1890's they became increasingly important as leaders of the various unsuccessful labor federations and in the first decade of the twentieth century they appear to have replaced the other nationality groups as the most important single leadership element within the working class. Thus among the 47 delegates at the founding congress of the FORA in 1901, 24 or 52% were Italian and 7 more may have been Italians. Of the 12 members of the Administrative Committee of the Congress, 7 or 8 were Italians. Among the 24 Italian delegates was the anarchist poet-lawyer Pietro Gori. Gori, who was in Argentina from 1898 to 1902 and who represented the railroad workers of Rosario, was one of the most influential men at the Congress and had much to do with the fact that it did not divide into anarchist and socialist sections. Hector Mattei, who represented the bakers of La Plata, was another of the 24 Italians.[22]

During the first decade of the twentieth century Italians were equally strong within the leadership of both major labor federations. A little less than half of the members of the Executive Committees of the syndicalist UGT and the anarchist FORA were Italians. In addition, Italians probably accounted for about the same proportion of members. The Buenos Aires Municipal Census of 1904 lists about a dozen Italian labor organizations with a membership of 10,000.[23] Keeping in mind

---

[21] These calculations are based on names in Marotta, *op. cit.*, I, pp. 79-81.

[22] These calculations are based on names in Marotta, *op. cit.*, I, pp. 107-108; Oddone, *op. cit.*, pp. 84-85.

[23] Ciudad de Buenos Aires, Censo General de 1904 (Buenos Aires, 1906), pp. 212-235.

that Italians were among the members of many other labor organizations and that there were a number of Italian groups outside of Buenos Aires it seems reasonable to estimate that they constituted about 40% to 50% of the approximately 50,000 organized workers in the country.[24]

Southern as well as Northern Italians were leaders and members of Argentine labor unions. The Southern Italians controlled a number of organizations in 1890, and many of the leaders throughout the period had names that would identify them with the South. Also, more than half of the Italians who came to Argentina after 1900 were Southerners and for the most part they remained in the cities. It is probable that about half of the organized Italian workers were from the South although very likely less than half of the leaders were Southern Italians.

There can be little doubt as to the importance of the Italians in the Argentine working class movement from the establishment of the first federation in 1890 to the temporary decline of organized labor in 1910. Unfortunately there are no statistics to document precisely what percent of the Italian or Argentine male wage earners over 21 joined unions, or what percent of organized labor was Italian. On the basis of the available information I have suggested the following: 1) about 2 out of every 5 organized workers in Argentina during the first decade of the twentieth century were Italians; 2) the Italians were the most important single leadership element within the labor movement during the same period; 3) the Italians were more active in labor organizations and in strikes than were the native Argentines; and 4) Southern Italians were as numerous as the Northerners within the unions, but the Northerners were probably more numerous as labor leaders.

The United States and Argentina Compared

Quite obviously there was a significant difference in the contribution of the Italians to the organization of the labor movements in the United States and in Argentina. In the United States they were of limited importance whereas in Argentina they were of primary importance. In the United States they were accused of passively accepting the conditions they

---

[24] This is an estimate based on figures in the works cited in note 13.

found and of hindering the organization of labor. In Argentina many were deported because they were influential labor leaders and because they had attempted to change the situation they had encountered.

The important, and at the present time not completely answerable question is why was there this difference between the Italians in Argentina and in the United States? Let us return to the reasons set forth by the Immigration Commission to explain why the Southern Europeans allegedly hindered the progress of organized labor: the lack of industrial training; the low standard of living; the thrift; the need to find employment; the desire for immediate gain; and tractability. All of these reasons would apply almost equally to the Italians in both Argentina and the United States and therefore do not, in themselves, explain the different contributions of the Italians to the respective labor movements. The Commission also mentioned that the influx of Southern Europeans was so rapid that labor organizations, which had been in existence before the new migrants had arrived, were unable to absorb them. In Argentina there were no significant labor organizations in existence before the massive Italian migration and so this might offer some kind of an answer. At the same time, however, the percentage of immigrants and of Italians was many times that of the United States and therefore presumably would have provided a more difficult problem of assimilation.

This indicates that the reasons set forth by the Immigration Commission are not of primary importance in explaining the fact that the Italians made only a limited contribution to the United States labor movement and forces us to seek our explanations among other variables as well. I do not pretend to provide the answer to the question, but let me briefly set forth a number of other variables — each one a fruitful area for further research — which combined may have accounted for the greater success of the Italian immigrants in the Argentine labor movement.

First, the Italians were an influential part of organized labor in Argentina from the beginning where as in the United States they arrived *en masse* after labor had begun to organize and never exercised decisive influence within the movement. In Argentina, therefore, they did not have to fight an established labor movement controlled by different and often hostile ethnic groups as well as the employer.

Second, the percentage of immigrants in Argentina was

twice that in the United States, and the percentage of Italians in Argentina about five times that in the United States. The relative strength in numbers of the Italians in Argentina apparently minimized prejudice and exclusion and gave them the power base upon which to develop a strong leadership element.

Third, the Italians, like all immigrants in Argentina, probably had greater economic bargaining power than did those in the United States. The United States experienced a recession toward the end of the first decade of the twentieth century whereas Argentina was experiencing one of its greatest economic booms. With rapid economic expansion there was a scarcity of workers of many types and so the workers had considerable bargaining power.

Fourth, the North Italians, experienced with labor organization, most likely played a different role in Argentina than they did in the United States. Apparently the Northern Italians in the United States remained aloof from the Southerners. In Argentina, however, the Northerners and the Southerners worked together in the unions and it is possible that the Northerners provided a bridge between the Southerners and the unions which facilitated organization.

Fifth, the labor union served a different function in Argentina and the United States. In the United States the craft unions of the AF of L were exclusive and job oriented. In Argentina the affiliates of the FORA and the UGT were not exclusive and were politically oriented. For the Italian in Argentina they may have served the function that a political machine or other organizations served for the Italian in the United States. Therefore, in Argentina there was additional incentive to join unions.

Finally, the culture of Argentina was more nearly like that of the Italians than was the culture of the United States. In Argentina the Italians did not have a major language problem, they were not subjected to religious prejudice, and they could understand the values of the society in which they were working. All of these things probably made it easier for them to organize and demand a greater share of the benefits of that society. The Italian immigrant coming to the New World at the turn of the century could, under favorable conditions, organize and lead labor unions as well as any other group. Perhaps if the Immigration Commission had devoted 12 volumes instead of 12 pages to Argentina it would have reached the same conclusion.

The Role of the Public School in the Assimilation of the Italian Immigrant Child in New York City, 1900-1914*

by Sr. Mary Fabian Matthews, C.S. **

In recent years, the works of Eisenstadt[1] and Gordon[2] have firmly established the distinction between cultural and social assimilation. Moreover, they have demonstrated the speed with which cultural assimilation (acculturation) takes place relative to social assimilation (acceptance). Other theorists have noted the significance of the school in fostering this phase of the assimilation process. However, Gans,[3] in his study of third generation Italians in Boston has suggested that the peer group and family take precedence over the school in shaping the behavior and attitudes of the working class community. Granting the seeming viability of his argument regarding the modern Italian community, the question still remains as to the influence of the school on the first generation.

For purposes of delimitation to a manageable size and scope, our research focused exclusively on the role of the public school in the assimilation of the Italian immigrant child in New York City, during the years 1900-1914. Information re-

[1] S. N. Eisenstadt, *The Absorption of Immigrants*, (Glencoe, Ill.: Free Press, 1955).

[2] Milton M. Gordon, *Assimilation in American Life*, (New York: Oxford University Press, 1964).

[3] Herbert J. Gans, *The Urban Villagers*, (New York: Free Press of Glencoe, 1962).

* This is a summary of results found in an unpublished doctoral dissertation by the same name done in the Department of Sociology and Anthropology, Fordham University, New York, 1966. I would like to express my graditude to Dr. Madeline H. Engel, Associate Editor of the *Review* and an Instructor of Sociology at Lehman College of the City University of New York for her comments regarding the first draft of this article.

** The author is chairman of the Department of Sociology, Mt. St. Vincent College, Halifax, Nova Scotia, Canada.

garding the role was gleaned from sources published in English, unpublished Board of Education statistical reports, and first-hand interviews with selected teachers and students personally involved in the City's school system during the first two decades of this century. In our research, attention was primarily directed toward the role of the school in facilitating both cultural and social assimilation vis-a-vis the role played by the family and the peer group. We were especially interested in learning about both the positive and negative consequences of assimilation. Thus, for example, a major concern was with evidence supporting or contesting the argument that the school helped to assimilate children but thereby disrupted their families and alienated them from their less assimilated, old-world oriented parents.

The Background of the Immigrant Child

If the child's assimilation is to be understood, something must first be known about his cultural heritage.

At the turn of the century, Italy was a new nation. Unification had scarcely begun; the provinces of Italy were radically unlike in character, customs, dress, thought, and speech. A variety of regional differences existed and the numerous dialects were a major factor in maintaining local differences. About four-fifths of Italian immigrants came from South Italy because profound economic disorders and abject poverty existed in this area. Nature and man had concurred in depressing and restricting living and income. While the principal industry was agriculture, rainfall was slight and often lacking for long periods of time. Heat and dry winds aggravated the situation. Malaria, earthquakes and the results of deforestation and erosion were ever-present problems. Foerster maintains that the most serious consequences of these conditions were psychological since a mood of helplessness or apathy was created which militated against progress and aspiration for mobility.[4] A complicated system of land ownership, the burden of heavy taxation and the rapid growth of population were additional factors that have to be considered.

Despite the hardships brought about by the lack of worldly goods and the vicissitudes accompanying the attempt to earn

---

[4] Robert F. Foerster, *The Italian Emigration of our Times*, (Cambridge, Massachusetts: Harvard University Press, 1919), p. 63.

one's livelihood, life for the Italian peasant had its compensations. The village in which he lived was his universe; he identified himself with the communal group with which he had been familiar from earliest childhood. The family was the central institution of Italian culture and formed an inclusive social world embracing relatives up to the fourth degree. The family, not the individual, was the unit of society but family relationships provided status and security for the individual. Strong family solidarity was a fundamental principle; anyone outside the familial group was considered a stranger and treated with indifference if not hostility.[5]

The entire regionalism called campanilismo strengthened family ties; marrying outside the immediate community was taboo. The father was the head of the family, tradition giving him patriarchal authority. Male dominance was the rule. The mother ruled the home as the interpreter of her husband's wishes and inculcated love for him in his children.[6]

One of the greatest handicaps facing the South Italian immigrant was his illiteracy. The reports of the Commissioner General of Immigration testify to the fact that, during the period from 1899 to 1909 inclusive, 54.2% of the South Italian immigrants fourteen years of age or over could neither read nor write.[7] Considering the place of education in Italy, these statistics are understandable.

> For decades the control of the government and the schools was in the hands of politicians from the northern and central provinces. The lack of understanding of the South and its people, the latent hostility and even open antagonism of the North for the South, the natural desire to benefit their own province or commune meant that the South received scanty consideration. Unification had not been a blessing to the South; it had simply added to its already heavy burdens. The consequences of this neglect of education in the South, when appraised in 1867, were evident in the 88% illiteracy in Compania, 89% in Sicily, 95% in Apulia, 98% in Basilicata.[8]

---

[5] Paul J. Campisi, "Ethnic Family Patterns: The Italian Family in the United States," *American Journal of Sociology*, LIII (May, 1948) p. 446.

[6] Phyllis H. Williams, South Italian Folkways in Europe and America (New Haven: Yale University Press, 1938), p. 77.

[7] Jeremiah W. Jenks and W. Jeh Lauch, 4th ed. rev. (New York: Funk and Wagnall Co., 1917) p. 35.

[8] Leonard Covello, "The Social Background of the Italo-American School Child," (unpublished Ph.D. dissertation, New York University, 1944), pp. 386-87.

Until approximately 1910, the average annual expenditure per inhabitant on education in the South was under two lire.[9] In 1877, a law was enacted making school attendance compulsory for all children between the ages of six and nine; in 1904 it was extended to the twelfth year but the law was difficult to enforce. Every city and town was left to provide and control its own educational system; the cities succeeded fairly well but the towns because of poverty and isolation were incapable of undertaking worthwhile education measures. Moreover, education contributed little to the struggle for existence. Even if the law were obeyed and the child attended school for three or four years, he lived in an environment in which he heard only his native dialect, he seldom had an opportunity to read Italian and the education he received gave him little more than rudimentary knowledge of arithmetic and the ability to write his name.

> The peasants saw no advantage in learning to read and write when the only occupation open to them was working in the field in time-honored fashion; and further, the officials, tied to tradition, had no mind to cooperate in any movement which would raise the standard of life among the peasants.[10]

Had the peasant himself an appreciation of the value of literary ability, he might have forced the issue but with that passivity consequent on living in abject poverty for generations, the contadino felt that the only security obtainable was achieved by following the rules of life received from his forefathers. Tradition was the all-important element and, of this, the family was the custodian and communicator. Desire for security in his way of living made the Italian peasant hostile to education from outside forces.

> Education in the south of Italy was aimed at achieving early social competence, for the child was a member of a society which had for its basic early economic maturity, early social adulthood, and very early social conformity.[11]

Thus, education was not fostered by the government or in the culture. Emigrating to and settling in a country such as

---

[9] Foerster, *op. cit.*, p. 515.

[10] Antonio Mangano, *Sons of Italy*, (New York: Missionary Education Movements of the United States and Canada, 1917), p. 100.

[11] Covello, *op. cit.*, p. 432-33.

the United States in which education had been and continued to be one of the major cultural values meant that the Italian immigrant would have to make an adjustment of extraordinary proportions in that sphere alone. And what was the educational situation in New York City at the time when immigration was at its peak? In particular, what was the educational situation in the crowded tenement-lined area of "Little Italy"?

The New York City School System

In 1898, the consolidation of the boroughs had been effected. The educational policies of the several boroughs were diverse and some measure of unification had to be accomplished especially since students moved from borough to borough as the transit system developed. At the same time, the number of students eligible to attend school was increased almost overnight by change in the compulsory education law and also the large numbers of immigrants arriving in the city. These problems happened almost simultaneously so that it was practically impossible to find solutions to any one of them before others just as great had to be faced. Schools were only one area in the network of city difficulties. Probably no other city at that time had such enormous burdens. The Italian child was only a part of the educational situation which required attention and assistance.

It was no secret that there were grave deficiencies in school facilities and these had existed for some time. In 1890, it had been estimated that the deficiency in school accommodations was about 10,000 sittings[12] and this was prior to both the changes in legislation regarding compulsory education (1895 and 1903) and also the greatest influx of immigrants. The lower part of the city showed a rapid abnormal increase in school population because of the tendency of the "new" immigrants to "colonize" in certain parts of the city. In 1905, over half the population of Greater New York, 53.76% resided within four miles of City Hall.[13] The largest number of Italians

---

[12] Letter of President of Board of Education to His Honor the Mayor Relative to Public School Accommodations, (New York: Office of the Board of Education 1890), p. 6.

[13] Thomas Adams, *Population Land Values and Governments*, Vol. II (New York: Regional Plan of New York and Its Environs, 1929) p. 17.

settled below 14th Street and hence it is the area chosen for our study.

One of the chief defects of the school system seemed to be that nowhere was there an exact record of how many children should be in school and were not. In 1895, by order of the Legislature, the first school census was taken and the law required that subsequently a school census be taken every two years. It was alleged that the law was forgotten as soon as it was made as the census was taken in 1895 and 1897 and not again until 1906. Discrepancies were so great in the figures of the 1906 census that the results were almost useless. Yet some classification and enumeration of the school population was essential.[14]

Italian Children in New York City School

In 1908, the United States Immigration Commission undertook a comprehensive survey of the immigrant in the United States and one of the fields was education. New York was one of the major cities chosen for the survey and the school population was studied. (See Table I)

TABLE 1
Population of Italian Birth or Italian Parentage in New York City - 1910

| | Total | | Foreign-Born | |
	Number	Percent	Number	Percent
New York City	544,449	14.5	340,765	17.7
Manhattan	307,795	16.0	199,757	18.1
Bronx	40,849	12.2	25,170	16.9

| | Native-Born | | Foreign-Born |
	Both Parents Born in Italy	One Patent Born in Italy	Italian Population-1900
New York City	191,545	12,139	145,429
Manhattan	102,687	5,351	95,930
Bronx	14,666	1,013	7,862 *

* U.S. Census Bureau, *Thirteenth Census*, 1910. *Supplement for New York*, pp. 598-99.

---

[14] John D. Haney, *Registration of City School Children* (New York City: Teachers College, Columbia University, 1910), pp. 105-106.

The principal object of the research was to determine any differences which might exist with respect to the school attendance and the school advancement of children of different nationalities. The Commission's report indicated that Italian children were present in all grades but most heavily concentrated in grades 1 to 4 as Table 2 indicates. Because there was no attempt to ascertain exactly how many Italian children lived in New York, there is no way of comparing the total in school with the total number of Italian children. But the Commission gave a more revealing picture of the school situation of the Italian children by listing the number of pupils in each grade according to age. Beginning with age six and the first grade the results of the study are shown in Table 3. The grand totals include a few students under six and over sixteen years of age.

The pattern for the ten percent of the population consisting of Italian children follows to a certain extent the pattern for the general school population. For both, the diminution is more rapid after the fifth grade and the eighth grade is less than one half as large as the sixth grade. But whereas for the general school population, the eighth grade is little more than a third as large as the first grade, for the Italian children the eighth grade is only about one tenth as large as the first grade.

TABLE 2
*Italian Children in Elementary School
In New York City, 1908*

Kindergarten	3,451	Grade 4	8,004
Grade 1	12,661	Grade 5	6,210
Grade 2	10,423	Grade 6	3,573
Grade 3	9,281	Grade 7	1,973
		Grade 8	1,191

High School

1st year	301
2nd year	123
3rd year	71
4th year	42
	537
Normal School	14
Special and Upgraded Schools	2,327
Grand Total	59,645 *

* U.S. Immigration Commission, *The Children of Immigrants in Schools*, XXXII (Washington Government Printing Office, 1911) p. 626.

TABLE 3

Number of Italian Pupils of Each Age in Each Grade in New York City, 1908

Age	Grade							
	1	2	3	4	5	6	7	8
6 years . .	5,230	68	1		10			
7	4,277	2,054	71	1	27			
8	2,053	3,642	1,312	93	11			
9	613	2,396	2,527	907	86	4		
10	245	1,308	2,418	1,850	689	64	1	1
11	113	522	1,481	2,055	1,441	440	44	2
12	39	282	872	1,700	1,744	1,069	365	428
13	23	104	402	952	1,399	1,173	732 *	303
14	14	34	150	361	666	664	595	121
15	5	13	42	77	123	137	199	14
16	—	—	4	8	14	16	33	3
Total . . .	12,661	10,423	9,281	8,004	6,210	3,573	1,973	1,191*

* *Ibid.*, pp. 631-35.

Considering the high school population, the following were the results:

TABLE 4

Italian Pupils in High School in New York City, 1908

Age	Grade			
	1st Year	2nd Year	3rd Year	4th Year
11 years	1			
12	2			
13	18	2		
14	78	17	2	
15	96	26	8	1
16	70	44	17	7
17	25	19	19	11
18	7	11	15	12
19	3	4	6	3
20	1	—	4	8
Total	301	123	71	42 *

* *Ibid.*, p. 656.

The remainder of the Italian children in New York City were distributed as follows:

	Total
Special Schools	162
Special Classes "C"	695
Special Classes "D"	333
Special Classes "E"	883
Ungraded Classes	254
Parochial School	8,301*

* *Ibid.*, pp. 670-83.

A conspicuous proportion of the children of Italian nationality were in the kindergarten. There was an unusually high proportion of Italians in the primary grades due to the recency of their immigration and the preponderance of children of early ages as well as those of the older children who had to learn the language. The Italians had less then two percent of the children in high school. The Commission warned that no inference should be made from the proportion of different ethnic groups in different grades because of the varying periods of residence in the United States of the families of the students. It was to be expected that the nationalities of the more recent immigration would show the largest proportion of their children in the elementary and intermediate grades, while a larger proportion of the children of the earlier immigrants would be in the higher grades.

Moreover, it was the practice at the time to place a child who could not speak English in the primary grades until he acquired some familiarity with the language. The supposition was that in the lower grades more time was spent on reading and the language arts and thus the foreign child would learn English more quickly. That the child might already have had some education in his native country or that he was far beyond the average age for placement in the lower grades did not seem to be taken into consideration. Such a practice was deleterious both to the American child and to the immigrant child. It is impossible to ascertain the number of foreign children so placed.

The problem of the overage pupil, or retardation, was first brought to official notice in 1904 when the first age-grade statistics were published for New York City Schools by Superintendent Maxwell, the first set of such statistics published in the United States for any school system. Maxwell found that from a total of 491,674 pupils in the regular grades, 192,143 or 39.1 percent were overage.[15] As Table 5 shows, the number of overage pupils increased through the grades from the first to the fifth years, then decreased to the eighth year. From age ten on, a considerable drop in the number of pupils is evident. Pupils in large numbers completed their schooling, whether overage or not, at thirteen or fourteen. The 8B group was about thirty percent of the size of 1A; only one in four entered high school; less than two percent of the 1A entrants graduated from high school. According to at least one writer several reasons accounted for this:

> While in large part such pupil elimination was due to economic reasons, to current popular opinion or tradition as to the length of the period of schooling, it also took care of the maladjusted pupils — the socalled misfits. It was an era of adjustment by elimination. Those who remained fitted in with the scheme of things. Those who didn't fit, got out.[16]

Pupils who were fourteen and had completed grade 5A or its equivalent could apply for employment certificates; at the age of sixteen they could leave school regardless of the grade reached. The consequence of retardation was that many pupils left with very limited schooling, having completed only grade four and a part of grade five.

In an effort to determine the causes of retardation, Dr. Leonard P. Ayres conducted a detailed study of the school records of 20,000 children in fifteen Manhattan schools. The results of the study were published in the book, *Laggards in Our Schools*. Slow progress was found to be the greatest factor and Ayres alleged that the course of study was geared to the unduly bright child, not to the average or to the slow child.[17] Ayres found Italians to be the most retarded of the nationality groups.

---

[15] Eugene A. Nifenecker, *A Review of Departmental Experience in Dealing with the Problem of School Maladjustment*, 1900-1934. Publication Numbers 27 and 28, (New York: Bureau of Reference and Research, 1936), pp. 11-13.

[16] *Ibid.*, p. 23.

[17] Leonard P. Ayres, *Laggards in Our Schools*, (New York: Russel Sage Foundation, 1909), p. 5.

TABLE 5
Age-Grade Distribution, Elementary Grades, 1904

Age	Kdg.	Gr. 1	Gr. 2	Gr. 3	Gr. 4	Gr. 5	Gr. 6	Gr. 7	Gr. 8	Total
4-5	1740									1740
5-6	9539	361								9900
6-7	3283	31352	1608	111						36354
7-8	79	35571	21126	3410	161					60347
8-9		13425	29379	17839	3246	248	5			64142
9-10		4117	17298	24185	13691	3187	304			62782
10-11		1636	8131	18321	20244	11799	3062	303	12	63508
11-12		647	3594	9929	16130	16206	9387	2591	269	58753
12-13		340	1896	5539	10788	14734	13514	7739	2402	56952
13-14		227	923	2629	6291	10215	11793	10815	7312	50205
14-15			299	839	2526	4382	5715	7488	8092	29341
15-16				157	494	802	1351	2500	4579	9883
16-17					46	77	189	467	1325	2104
17-18						16	21	37	203	277
18-19								1	23	24
19-20									3	3

Total	14641	87676	84254	82959	73617	61666	45341	31941	24220	506315
No. Overage	20392	32141	37414	36275	30226	19069	10493	6133		192143
% Overage	23.2	38.1	45.0	49.2	49.0	42.0	32.8	25.3		39.0*

Age-Grade Standards Used

Age	Grade	Age	Grade
6-8	1	10-12	5
7-9	2	11-13	6
8-10	3	12-14	7
9-11	4	13-15	8

Normal Age - Enclosed in horizontal pattern

Under Age - Above horizontal pattern

Over Age - Below horizontal pattern

* Nifenecker, *op. cit.*, p. 14.

TABLE 6
*Percentage of Retardation among Nationality Groups
in New York City, 1908-1909*

Nationality	Percent
German	16.6
American	19.6
Russian	22.9
Irish	29.5
Italian	35.5
Entire group	22.9 *

* *Ibid.*, p. 107.

In 1909-10, the Superintendent of Schools in New York City appointed a number of committees to study the question of overage in order to determine the probable causes. The findings of the Committees were published in the Twelfth Annual Report. Twelve causes were listed, among them irregular attendance, part-time classes, inefficient teaching, physical defects, excessive size of classes, late entrance and improper method of promotion. The culture of the immigrants or their peculiar problems were not mentioned.

A similar study made by the U.S. Immigration Commission published in 1911 concluded that the use of a foreign language in the home was an important factor in retardation. It also stated that "races" arriving later in the United States showed almost invariably a higher percentage of retardation than others. It warned that this was not an indication of less mental ability, but rather of some external circumstances that in another generation would disappear.[18]

In the area below Fourteenth Street, School Districts 1 and 9 contained large numbers of Italian children, adjacent districts in the same area contained large numbers of Jewish children as well as small numbers of other nationalities. Here the Associate Superintendent and principals with understanding and foresight, sought to initiate programs to assist the immigrant children in the districts. Such programs as English for foreign children, special classes, a more flexible curriculum were experimented upon before being introduced into schools

---

[18] U.S. Immigration Commission, *The Children of Immigrants in Schools*, 1911, p. 609.

in other parts of the city. However, investigations made indicated that the greatest criticism was directed toward the Board of Education because of failure to draw up a more flexible and practical course of study and also lack of attention to the need for industrial education. A uniform course of study is based on the assumption that the school population is homogeneous yet the metropolis had become more or less an aggregation of foreign colonies, and children who seldom heard English spoken at home went through the same routine as the child of native-born parents.[19] The inheritance of the Italian child was life in the open air and activity of body; upon entering school he was expected to sit still for long periods of time and listen to a perplexing foreign tongue.

In such manual training as the schools offered, in drawing and whatever required dexterity of fingers, the Italian children were leaders; they also had a finely developed artistic sense and were lovers of music. But the qualities in which these children could have excelled were wasted as they were not ones which the schools developed except in rare instances.[20] Scheduled duties occupied the time of the teachers and individual differences in the personality or group differences in the culture of the children were disregarded.

> Consequently, such extreme types as the Jews and Italians were educated in an almost identical manner. The nervous, flitting, uncertain little Italian received the same treatment as the steady, persevering, plodding little Jew.[21]

Despite their poor performance in school, evidence suggests that the ambition which would have been kept dormant in Italy by social tradition was aroused in the Italian children in America by the idea of "getting ahead" and this was revealed in their economic aspirations. At a large Italian school in Mulberry Bend, a social worker questioned the children as to what they would like to do for a living. The children questioned numbered one hundred forty-three, were among the poorest of Italian children and were the ones who had the

---

[19] William E. Grady, "Curriculum Making," *Psychological Clinic*, VII (May, 1913), p. 67.
[20] Lilian Brandt, "A Transplanted Birthright," *The Survey*, XII (May, 1904), p. 498.
[21] Thomas J. Jones, *The Sociology of a New York City Block*, (New York: Columbia University Press, 1904), pp. 127-28.

least opportunity.[22] Over three-fourths of the children possessed aspirations to earn a living in a higher level than that of
their parents and a number chose the professions. No follow-
up was indicated to determine how many were mobile and realized their ambitions but the expression of such aspirations
by so great a majority indicates that the children were respond-
ing, at least verbally to the cultural ideals.

Relative to economic and occupational aspiration, it should
be noted that one characteristic peculiar to the Italian population in New York City was the extent to which children were
employed before they left school. This was a natural consequence of the fact that so many of the Italian mothers did
piece work at home. The children assisted in such tasks as
pasting flowers, finishing coats, picking nuts, pulling bastings
or willowing feathers. It appears that instead of being kept
out of school to do the work, the child was kept at such tasks
before and after school hours; it was his duty to contribute to
the economic welfare of the family; the family was always of
primary concern. Working at home in this way had a marked
effect on progress in school — or lack of it.

Italian Immigrant Parents and the Schools

In a report on the visiting teacher which covered the years
1912-1915, an explanation of the Italian situation was given
which threw some light on the contradictory observations regarding the role of education and work in the eyes of Italian
immigrant children.[23] In the districts where the Italians lived,
three very distinct economic strata were represented. In the
first and lowest, the men were largely laborers, often unemployed and the women worked in garment factories under
Jewish employers. The standard of living was low, there was
much overcrowding and the full, nourishing Italian diet had
been reduced so that the children had stunted bodies and lag-
gard minds. Little ambition was evinced for education and
school was avoided as an evil whenever possible. In the second
stratum, while there was exploitation of children in tenement
manufactures, there were more men in skilled trades and fewer

---

[22] Brandt, op. cit., pp. 496-98.
[23] Harriet M. Johnson, The Visiting Teacher in New York City,
(New York: Public Education Association, 1916), p. 5.

women in factories. Dramatic clubs and art classes in the settlement houses showed groups of ambitious young boys and girls and graduating classes in the schools had a fair percentage of the children going to high school. These parents had a different attitude toward education. On the highest level were found men in skilled and unionized trades or city employees. There were no tenement industries and women in their homes did housework only. The parents were most ambitious for their children and most eager to cooperate with the school. This presents a somewhat different picture of the Italian immigrant than is found in much of the existing literature and one which would possibly fit any other nationality living under the same conditions. The most deprived are, as a rule, the least ambitious but this is due more to the relentless struggle for existence than any innate hereditary characteristic of nationality. Once the Italian parent understood the American way and had become acculturated to a degree, he lost the distrust of things American and was eager to cooperate that his children might profit by opportunity.

The general attitude prevalent at the time and which permeated the schools as well was that the immigrant was a one-generation difficulty; if the children got a good education, there need be no anxiety about the future. Assimilation was an educational process and the parents would be assimilated through their children. Ultimately this is true, in part at least, but what was not grasped was that the formal education of the child would not prove successful if his parents were neglected. Essentially assimilation is a spiritual, emotional, psychological and social transmutation and not only or not even primarily an intellectual one. To prevent family disruption the adults as well as the children had to be adjusted to the new environment; that the school did serve as the main channel through which the child was culturally assimilated, there can be little doubt. Evidence likewise would appear to substantiate the position that, except indirectly and through the children, the educational process did not ameliorate the plight of the immigrant parent who remained very much in ignorance of what the school was trying to do and who had little opportunity or incentive to obtain information about the purpose and aims of the type of instruction the children were receiving.

Italian parents were left untouched and outside the life of the school. Parents learned about America from their children but their contacts with the school were almost none. Not being able to speak English well if at all, ignorant of the mechanisms of the system, possessing little understanding of what transpired within the walls of the school, the parents stayed away. The school seemed to accept this state of affairs and so it prevailed. Few visits were paid by teachers to the home except in case of illness or death in the family.

Cut off in such a way from the school life of their children, not having an appreciation of education because of lack of opportunity and peasant background in Italy, imbued with the tradition that the family was the transmitter of knowledge and that a person succeeded by hard work, the Italian parent saw no additional value in advanced schooling. High schools had not been established in New York City until 1897; during the period under study, they were few in number and were considered as college preparatory courses; attendance at high school was rare for all children in the city. When seen against this background, the failure to prolong schooling cannot be interpreted as is the current phenomenon of dropping out.

One of the more serious charges against the school was that the school alienated the child from the parent. The consensus of our interviewees was that the problem was not as serious as some literature would imply. Furthermore, the vast majority of children of Italian extraction were in the grammar grades and hence would not have this type of problem which appears to occur later in the teens. The implications of Gans' research seem to be strengthened by the present study. The rift in parent-child relationships which was erroneously attributed to the influence of the school is in fact a consequence of an adult-centered society and the function of the peer group. The segregation of adults and children make the child's peer group more influential in decision making than are the parents. This accounts, at least in part, for the apparent indifference of the Italian parent toward school and for the parents' lack of pressure on the child to continue schooling. It also explains statements made by some of our interviewees that it was the example or urging of friends which was instrumental in their continuing or resuming their education. Gans maintains that in the case of an acculturating ethnic group, the segregation of children and adults lessens the conflict resulting from culture clashes between parents and children while, at the same time, the children are able to bring home some major dominant American culture patterns and are thus instrumental as an acculturating influence on parents. Information supplied by our interviewees seems to confirm this.

Conclusions

The school implicitly sought to assimilate the children, by the nature of the curriculum and the fact that the teachers were American, but had no *specific* programs aimed at resocializing the children. Upon the dominant cultural pattern of the first generation family, the school appears to have had little effect. In matters such as language, dress, habits of hygiene and such customs the school exerted an influence. Indirectly, as by the education of girls, for instance, the future would be affected but this would have resulted from contact with others in the economic sphere as well so that it is difficult to set the boundary between school and outside influences.

That the schools had little contact with the parents and that nothing was done to bring the parents into the educational process in so far as their children were concerned are now clearly recognized as defects of the system. In effect, the schools left the parents untouched except in those indirect ways by which the children brought home what they had learned of the new culture. Moreover, outside of the hours spent in the classroom, the children were minimally affected by the schools. Thus while the school acted as an effective agent of cultural transmission, its penetration into the area of social assimilation was negligible. Therefore, schools did not significantly increase the generational gap, nor did they severely disrupt family relations. Finally, if our data are representative and correct, the immigrant community played a far more important role in shaping assimilation and family life than any caretaking institution of the outside society including the school. This suggests previous studies may well have overemphasized the roll of formal education in the assimilation of first generation immigrants.

as an acculturating influence on its other... Information supplied by one informant seems to contradict...

Conclusions

The school implicitly sought to assimilate the child to the norms of life on the reserve, and the fact that the teachers were always there but do sustained programs aimed toward enabling the children... Upon reexamination cultural materials in the first generation until the school appears to have played little part in matters such as language, dress, habits of hygiene and such customs as are associated mostly or influenced chiefly the education of children to concentrate. Thus we can be reminded that the world is how much of front contact with others in these communities... so that it is difficult to set the boundary between school and outside influences.

That the school child would rather with the parents had the training was due to... for the parents too, the educational process is so far as they often felt they were culturally relinquished as individuals... the system... the absence of hierarchical or outward force in the culture gave by which the children brought home what they had extracted... the new culture. Moreover, outside of the hours spent in the classroom the children were not materially affected by the school. Thus, while the school acted as an effective agent of cultural transmission, it penetrated only into the area of social usability not into neighboring... therefore schools did not in reality increase the generational gap, nor did they severely disrupt family relations. Finally it is our data that we appreciate and accept the immigrant community played a far more important role in assimilation and family life than apparently in the function of the available society including the school. This suggests that the students were well into everything else... but not of formal education in the assimilation of first generation immigrants.

Case Studies of Ethnicity and Italo-American Politicians

by Salvatore J. LaGumina *

Politics affects our lives intimately, and precisely because of that fact, it behooves us to study the ethnic components of the body politic. Even if there is truth in the conclusion drawn by Nathan Glazer and Daniel P. Moynihan, that Italo-Americans have been slow and late in gaining important places in the consideration of party leaders, these authors readily acknowledge the tremendous importance ethnics play in the politics of New York City.[1] Ethnic identity is a basic element in all political equations.

Specifically, our attention is drawn to the political experience of the Italo-Americans in the belief that knowledge of this history can serve not only to enlighten us as to the dynamics of the process, but even further, to expand our understanding of such controversial movements as, for example, "Black Power." It is not inconceivable that the experiences of Italo-American politicians can be studied as models by other minority groups. Recently, Andrew Greeley, Director of the National Opinion Research Center at the University of Chicago, suggested that the study of ethnic backgrounds and differences may be the solution to the United States' racial problems. A recognition that ethnic differences are important led Greeley to say: "This may, in the final analysis, be the ultimate contribution that our multiple melting pot is able to make to the rest of the world."[2]

---

[1] Nathan Glazer and Daniel P. Moynihan, *Beyond the Melting Pot*, (Cambridge, Mass.: MIT and Harvard University Press, 1964).

[2] Long Island *Catholic*, June 27, 1968.

---

* Salvatore J. LaGumina is Professor of History, Nassau Community College, Garden City, New York.

Indeed, this phenomemon of Italian immigrants exploiting their ethnicity as the basis for political power has been recognized of late. For example, in 1958, *El Imparcial* "advised" Puerto Rican politicians in New York City to emulate the politics of Vito Marcantonio, as he represented his largely Italian constituency, if they wished to make a significant impact on politics.[3] Advocates of "Black Power" continuously refer to the necessity for Negroes to acquire the kind of power ethnic groups have attained, if they are ever to be recognized as equal partners in American life.[4] Only this continuing scholarly research further attests to the strength of ethnicity in politics. Michael Parenti, in a recent article entitled: "Ethnic Politics and the Persistence of Ethnic Identification," cautions against the temptation to relegate ethnicity to the historical past. His study suggests that ethnics continue to vote as ethnics, despite apparently increasing assimilation.[5]

In the case of Italo-Americans, ethnicity appears to remain very much alive today. Even when they decry it, foremost historians acknowledge its continuing influence in American culture. Recently, the renowned American historian, Thomas A. Bailey, had occasion to refer to ethnicity as a contributing factor in the perpetuation of myths in American history. He recognized that the hyphenates remain vocal "especially the Italian-Americans, who insist on having Columbus, rather than the Norsemen, discover America. The Italians are generally successful," wrote Bailey, "except in Minnesota, where the Scandinavians, clinging to their questionable Kensington stone, have more votes."[6]

One has only to reflect on some of the political events during 1968 to appreciate the continuing role of ethnicity. In February, 1968, Italo-American Democratic Representative John H. Dent of Pennsylvania, challenged incumbent Senator Joseph S. Clark, hoping, among other things, to capitalize on his na-

---

[3] *El Imparcial*, July 28, 1968.

[4] Nathan Wright, Jr., *Black Power and Urban Unrest* (New York, 1967), p. 9.

[5] Michael Parenti, "Ethnic Politics and the Persistence of Ethnic Identifications," *American Political Science Review* (September, 1957), 717-726.

[6] Thomas A. Bailey, "The Myth Makers of American History," *The Journal of American History* (June, 1968), Vol. XV, No. 1, p. 7.

tionality, especially since Clark was said to have alienated Italian voters four years ago with intemperate remarks about the ethnicity of Justice Musmanno.[6a] Within the last few months, the appointment of a successor to the seat held by the late Senator Robert F. Kennedy has been the occasion for a kind of campaign to convince Governor Nelson Rockefeller of the need to name an Italo-American. The fact that both of these attempts took place at all may be as important as the fact of their failure.

Even more recently, we have observed another demonstration of the tenacity of ethnics in political life when it came to the selection of a Republican Vice-Presidential candidate. Until the announcement that Governor Spiro Agnew of Maryland was designated by Richard Nixon as his running mate, speculation centered on Governor John Volpe of Massachusetts, as one of the favorites for the position. Highly placed Nixon intimates had admitted that Volpe was virtually assured a place on the ticket; they too were surprised by the designation of Agnew. In any event, this was the most serious effort in American history to nominate an Italo-American for the second highest elective office in the nation. Moreover, the strength of Volpe's candidacy was based on the relevant proposition that pertinent religious and ethnic factors indicated the wisdom of choosing an Italian-American Catholic for the vice-presidency. The thesis was based on a study which purported that analysis of recent presidential elections revealed that a combination of religious and ethnic factors were instrumental in the results of the 1960 presidential election, particularly in the populous northeastern industrial states.[7] Furthermore, the Democrats were also aware of the strength rendered their ticket by the inclusion of an ethnic (minority) representative. Although a Polish-American was eventually picked as the Democratic Vice-Presidential candidate, the Italo-American, Mayor Joseph Alioto of San Francisco, received serious consideration.[8]

[6a] *The New York Times*, February 25, 1968.

[7] Boston *Globe*, August 4, 1968, and Boston *Herald Traveler*, August 4, 1968. The study referred to is James F. and Constance S. Collins, *Comments on the Republican Vice-Presidential Nomination 1968*, n.d.; n.p.

[8] The New York *Times*, August 29, 1968.

Six Case Histories

In the present discussion, the case studies of Italian-American politicians, will be limited to those individuals who represented New York in the Congress of the United States until 1950. Special attention will be paid to Vito Marcantonio, because a substantial portion of my research has focused on his career. In addition, he was the most radical of Italo-American politicians, thus offering an extreme example by which the thesis of ethnic viability in politics can be tested. If it cannot be seen in the extremes it is difficult to see it in the average.

New York had sent only six Italo-Americans to Congress until 1950, and never more than two simultaneously. The paucity of the number of Italo-American representatives becomes even more glaring, when analyzed against the significant fact that by 1950 Italians constituted the largest nationality in the city, and probably in the state.

Francis B. Spinola, a Democrat, was the first Italo-American Congressman from New York, and the first in American history. Although the son of Italian immigrants, and despite his unabashed pride in his Italian ancestry, Spinola could hardly be considered a representative of the Italo-American community. Born in Stony Brook, Long Island, in 1821, he gained fame as a brigadier-general during the Civil War. Subsequently, he held a string of public offices, including alderman and supervisor of New York City, New York State Assemblyman, State Senator, and United States Congressman from 1887 to 1891.[9] Thus, his public career existed largely before the great tide of Italian immigration to this country. He could not, therefore, properly be called an Italo-American politician in the sense of reflecting the aspirations of a distinct immigrant minority striving to obtain a position of importance and prestige, and even a power base. During his Congressional tenure, Spinola displayed a warm disposition toward immigrants, taking to the floor of Congress to endorse the influx of honest and industrious immigrants, at a time when nativists were campaigning for their exclusion. Coming as it did at the

---

[9] *Biographical Directory of the American Congress*, 1794-1949 (Washington, 1950), p. 1849. See also a short biographical account in *Il Progresso Italo-Americano*, June 30, 1940.

threshold of massive Italian migration, it could be supposed that he was expressing genuine sympathy with the descendants of his forbears. Offsetting this impression, however, was his simultaneous failure to attribute priority to alleviating the problems of Italian immigrants. For example, although he was a member of a Special House Committee on Immigration, then conducting investigations regarding immigration problems in New York City (and this meant mostly Italian problems), he declined to attend the sessions. His explanation was that he had even more urgent duties to attend to in Washington — an unthinkable confession for one who placed the welfare of Italian Immigrants in the forefront.[10]

Fiorello H. LaGuardia was the second Italo-American Congressman from New York, and the third in American history. Only Spinola and Anthony J. Caminetti of California (1891-1895), preceded him. If Spinola did not qualify as an authentic representative of the Italo-American community, Caminetti was even less deserving of it. He emerged neither as a champion of Italo-Americans, nor as a sympathetic friend of immigrants in general. Thus, in many ways, LaGuardia merited the title of the first truly Italo-American representative. As Arthur Mann wrote in his lively and penetrating biography of LaGuardia, the "Little Flower," despite his bourgeoise background, empathized with the Italian peasant masses who migrated to the United States. Early in his life, he came to identify himself as an American proud of his Italian descent. He spoke Italian, ate Italian food, and played Italian music. There could be little question as to his acceptance by the city's Italo-American population.[11]

During his Congressional career, LaGuardia represented two New York City districts: the 14th on the Lower East Side and the 20th in East Harlem. In all his congressional campaigns, he appealed to the "foreign vote" which was predominantly Italian in his districts. Thus, while campaigning in 1916, he promised Italo-Americans that Italy would regain

---

[10] *Congressional Record*, 50th Cong., 2nd sess., Vol. 20, 999-1,000. For accounts of the Special House Committee investigation and the role of Italians, see The New York *Times*, July 28, 1888. There is no intention of criticizing Spinola of insensitivity, but to show rather that his primary concerns were in the realms of national defense and military affairs.

[11] Arthur Mann, *LaGuardia, A Fighter Against His Times, 1882-1947* (New York, 1950), pp. 25, 26 and 28.

Trieste. Reaction in Italo-American circles was vigorous. In 1921, the Italian newspaper, *La Domenica Illustrata*,[12] declared: "How proud our Italian brothers should be to have the privilege of voting for such a man." In LaGuardia, Italian immigrants possessed an undisputed Congressional champion of their cause. He forcefully condemned the quota system as bigoted, narrow-minded legislation. Energetically, he rebuked colleagues for displaying an Anglo-Saxon fixation, reminding them of the accomplishments of such Italians as Columbus. In a sardonic manner he utilized every opportunity to assail proponents of the National Origins Quota Act.[13] LaGuardia emerged as the first Italo-American politician to successfully challenge the political reign of the Irish-Americans, and properly stands at the forefront of the process through which Americans of Italian descent have come of political age.

The third Italo-American Congressman from New York was James Lanzetta, who served two terms 1933-1934 and 1937-1938. Lanzetta also had the distinction of defeating LaGuardia in 1933. Subsequently, he lost the congressional seat in 1934 to Marcantonio, won it against Marcantonio in 1936, and lost to Marcantonio again in 1938 and 1940.[14] Thus, he was one of a trio of Italo-Americans who represented East Harlem between 1921 and 1950. His two terms in Congress were undistinguished and unmemorable, especially when compared with the likes of the dynamic La Guardia and the fiery Marcantonio. Nevertheless, he paid homage to his ethnicity. His victory over LaGuardia was partially based on ethnicity. The Democrats deliberately selected him in an attempt to split the Italian vote. Since both he and LaGuardia were of Italian descent, neither had a monopoly on ethnic support. He had several assets which he brought to bear in the campaign against LaGuardia. He was born and raised in East Harlem, educated as an engineer and a lawyer, a practicing Catholic, and the recipient of support from Tammany Hall. Prior to his election to Congress, he held the elective position of Alderman. Although his record was inferior to that of LaGuardia, Lanzetta

---

[12] *La Domenica Illustrata*, July 30, 1921, found in Mann, *LaGuardia*, 134. Mann, p. 143, also refers to the pride expressed by the Italian paper *Il Vaglio*, as another example of the support rendered by Italian followers.

[13] Mann, *LaGuardia*, 188-190.

[14] *Biographical Directory*, p. 1437.

wisely expended efforts at making friends in East Harlem while LaGuardia remained busy in Washington. Important too were the inroads he made among younger Italo-Americans and the Puerto Ricans. In addition, the campaign was marked by violence, intimidation and fraud, unusual even for the tough East Harlem area. Even respected Democrat Judge Salvatore Cotillo acknowledged as much.[15]

Although leaving little lasting political impact, Lanzetta nevertheless spoke in behalf of immigrants during his congressional tenure. He proposed to extend beyond the statutory limitation of seven years, the validity of intention applications filed by immigrants while complying with naturalization procedures. He also called for the automatic admission to citizenship of aliens who had resided in the United States for many years, but had been unable to meet education requirements for naturalization. These issues were of high importance to his Italian constituency.[16]

The fourth Italo-American Congressman from York was Vito Marcantonio, whose career will be discussed later in the article. Louis Capozzoli was the fifth New Yorker of Italian descent to serve in Congress (1940-1944). In many ways he qualified as a typical Italo-American politician. Born in Cosenza, Italy, he emigrated to this country at the age of five. Although he came from humble, hard-working folk, he managed to study law and entered politics as a young man.[17] Ethnicity heavily impregnated his political career. As a resident of the 13th Congressional District in the Lower East Side of New York City, he joined the Democratic Party when Tammany Hall enjoyed unquestioned influence. Indeed, Christopher Sullivan, Tammany leader, held the congressional seat of the district for three decades before his voluntary retirement in 1940. In giving up his congressional seat, Sullivan

---

[15] For an astute explanation of why LaGuardia lost the election, see Mann, *LaGuardia*, 318. The campaign violence is treated in Lowell M. Limpus and Burr W. Leyson, *This Man LaGuardia* (New York, 1938), 351. Cotillo's observation is found in The New York *Times*, November 20, 1932.

[16] The New York *Times*, April 4, 1934 and April 7, 1937; *Congressional Record*, 73rd Cong., 2nd sess., Vol. 78, p. 3367; 75th Cong., 1st sess., Vol. 81, pp. 1179 and 4075.

[17] *Biographical Directory*, p. 947. *Il Progresso Italo-Americano*, October 23, 1940.

designated Capozzoli as the district's nominee for Congress, a selection which was tantamount to election because of the area's Democratic majority.[18]

Evidence that ethnic considerations were the overriding factors in Capozzoli's nomination is plentiful. Clearly, the Italians of the 13th Congressional District were successful in challenging the Irish for political control. It was nothing less than a political revolution for the leader of the illustrious Sullivan clan, a legendary power in the city, to surrender his congressional seat to the descendants of the Italian peninsula. Nor was the Italian community unaware of the significance of the action. *Il Progresso Italo-Americano* proudly acknowledged the nomination as a milestone in the political history of the Lower East Side: "When he was appointed the Democratic Congressional candidate of the 13th District a deep honor was bestowed not only upon himself, but upon the Americans of Italian extraction whom he represents." [19]

These developments constituted a recognition by Lower East Side political leaders, that the large Italo-American population in their midst could no longer be denied its share of political power. It is interesting to note that Capozzoli's nomination was engineered by James DiSalvio, Democratic district leader. DiSalvio's career itself is a classic example of the revolution then taking place. Earlier in his career, when he engaged in professional boxing, he was compelled to adopt the name of "Jimmy Kelly." As one political veteran explained it: "In those days it had been advisable for boxers of Italian or Jewish extraction to transform themselves into descendants of the Emerald Isle." [20]

Equally important in the nomination of Capozzoli was the concern felt by the national Democratic party leaders over the possibility of mass defection of Italo-Americans from Democratic ranks. This development had its roots in Franklin Delano Roosevelt's criticism of Mussolini for joining in the invasion

---

[18] The New York *Times,* July 2, 1940, and *Il Progresso Italo-Americano*, July 1, 1940.

[19] *Il Progresso Italo-Americano*, November 17, 1940.

[20] For information on DiSalvio, see Louis Eisenstein and Elliot Rosenberg, *A Stripe of Tammany's Tiger* (New York, 1966), p. 129. It is also interesting to note that the only potential challenge to Capozzoli among Democratic circles came from another Italo-American. See The New York *Times,* July 2, 1940.

of France in 1940. His remarks were interpreted as crude aspersions against the Italian character, with the result that Italo-Americans became probably the most anti-Roosevelt of all low-income groups. Against this backround, any move to assuage Italian feelings was welcome. The nomination of Capozzoli seemed to answer many problems for Democrats in the Lower East Side. Thus, it was with a great deal of relief that Sullivan read the election results, showing the party doing well in the Italian districts.[21]

Capozzoli made a few speeches in Congress, but when he did, he did not fail to pay his obligations to his ethnic compatriots. Accordingly, he condemned discrimination perpetrated against Italo-Americans in the employment picture of 1941. In 1942 he offered a bill to remove the "enemy" designation attached to Italian aliens. In 1943 he broadcast messages to the Italian people, advising them to resist compliance with Hitler. And in 1944 he urged United Nations aid for Italy.[22]

The sixth Italo-American Congressman from New York was Anthony Tauriello of Buffalo, the first of his nationality to represent that area of New York in 1949-1952. Here, too, ethnicity played an important role. Tauriello came from one of the most respected Italian families of the state's second largest city. He had exercised political influence among the city's Italo-Americans for many years. By 1948, Buffalo's political leaders were also compelled to grant the large Italian population a greater share in political power. Tauriello's election was highly praised by the Italian-American press. *Il Progresso Italo-Americano* exclaimed "Osanna" that the Italian community of Buffalo now had its own representative in Washington, and observed that his election presaged the steady growth to new political heights for that city's Italians.[23]

Tauriello responded by rendering service to his ethnic followers during his one term in Congress. He spoke forcefully

---

[21] Glazer and Moynihan, *Beyond the Melting Pot*, p. 214, discuss the Italo-American attitude in the 1940 election. For Sullivan's reaction to the election results, see The New York *Times*, November 6, 1940.

[22] *Congressional Record*, 77th Cong., 1st sess., Vol. 87, pp. 7523-7524; 77th Cong., 2nd sess., Vol. 88, A3311; 78th Cong., 1st sess., Vol. 89, A160. See also the New York *Times*, September 20, 1944.

[23] *Il Progresso Italo-Americano*, November 6, 1948. The Italian paper boasted of having given Tauriello extended coverage throughout the campaign. It also took note of the numerous important official positions of Buffalo's Italians.

against critics of the Italian character, and was a strong supporter of a bill to repatriate American citizens of Italian origin who, while visiting Italy, had voted in the crucial Italian elections of 1948.[24]

The Special Case of Vito Marcantonio

We now come to the fascinating career of Vito Marcantonio. An inveterate radical, an accomplished iconoclast, and a fiery exponent of socialist philosophy, Marcantonio might, on the one hand, appear to have been least influenced by purely ethnic considerations. Indeed, one's instinctive reaction would be to associate him with the Puerto Ricans as the group upon which his political power depended.[25] Those familiar with Negro politics in New York City would have difficulty in finding a more unyielding defender of Negro rights. Suffice it to note that W. E. B. DuBois, a foremost Negro scholar, gave eloquent testimony of Marcantonio's uniqueness among men.[26] There are instances also of Marcantonio's criticism of some ethnic traits of Italians.[27] Moreover, the Italian community itself could not be said to have been completely enamoured of him. Thus, he was severely criticized by City Council President Vincent Impellitteri for opposing the 1948 Italo-American drive, which urged Italians to vote against Communist candidates in Italy.[28] These incidents notwithstanding, the overwhelming evidence is that Marcantonio was a genuine champion of Italo-American rights and ringing proof of ethnic influence in American political life.

Ethnic influences constituted a major part of Marcantonio's youth. His mother and grandfather were immigrants, his friends were Italian, his heroes were Italian, and his home was in the most Italian neighborhood in the United States. Like LaGuardia, he spoke Italian, ate Italian food, and regaled in Italian customs. As a young high school student, he showed

---

[24] *Congressional Record*, 81st Cong., 2nd sess., Vol. 96, pp. 6319 and 1392.

[25] See, for example, Clarence Woodbury, "Our Worst Slums," *American Mercury* (September, 1949), 301.

[26] William E. B. Dubois, *In Battle for Peace* (New York, 1952), p. 44.

[27] See Antonio Arturo Micocci, "Vito Marcantonio," *Romanica*, Vol. 1, No. 4 (March, 1936), 8.

[28] *Il Progresso Italo-Americano*, November 3, 1949.

deep concern for promoting Italian-American causes. Thus, he joined with other Italo-Americans in high school, and became the founder and leader of Circolo Italiano, an organization designed to stimulate interest in Italian culture, while simultaneously working for Italian assimilation in the American social fabric. He continued his interest in Italian clubs in college, becoming president of Circolo Mazzini at New York University, and continuing as an enthusiast for the formation of an interscholastic organization of Italian clubs. So thorough was his ethnic identification, that he often performed in Italian plays while in school. As part of his extra-curricular activity, he became a citizenship education teacher in a project aimed at preparing Italian immigrants for active and responsible citizenship.[29] When, on one occasion LaGuardia visited his high school in his capacity as President of the Board of Aldermen, Marcantonio was selected as the student speaker of the day because of his ethnic background.[30]

As a LaGuardia protege, Marcantonio managed the Fiorello H. LaGuardia Political Association, which brought together a cross-section of Italians interested in promoting the political aspirations of their ethnic brothers. He was entrusted with the task of serving as LaGuardia's "eyes and ears" in East Harlem, a job which included a great amount of work in dealing with Italian constituents. Displaying uncommon zeal as LaGuardia's campaign manager, he mobilized Italo-Americans in support of LaGuardia's candidacy, making the LaGuardia Association the most effective political machine in the city. When LaGuardia ran for mayor in 1933, Marcantonio, although no longer his campaign manager, played a significant role by energetically and effectively circulating nominating petitions in Italo-American neighborhoods throughout the city. It was the virtually unanimous support of this ethnic group, cutting across party lines, which was largely responsi-

---

[29] Information regarding the East Harlem of Marcantonio's youth can be gleaned from Edward Corsi, "My Neighborhoods," *Outlook*, No. 141 (September 16, 1925), 90-91, and Leonard Covello, *The Heart is the Teacher* (New York, 1958), p. 180. For Biographical material on Marcantonio, see *Vito Marcantonio Papers* (hereafter referred to as *M.P.*), Box 19, Folder: Biographical Material. Accounts of his high school activities have come from interviews with his former school friends, Salvatore Cimilluca and Alfred Marra, both active in Circolo Italiano.

[30] Covello, *The Heart is the Teacher*, p. 153.

ble for electing New York's first Italo-American mayor.[31] To Marcantonio, LaGuardia's election was a necessary step to achieve political justice for the Italians of East Harlem. Moreover, it would demonstrate conclusively that Italians had passed the stage of factionalism, the result of a provincial attachment to regionalism, which had prevented unification earlier.[32]

When Marcantonio ran for Congress, he exploited his ethnicity to the fullest. Although his opponent was also an Italo-American, Marcantonio boasted of the endorsement from dozens of local Italian organizations and individuals, especially that of LaGuardia.[33] With the possible exception of LaGuardia, no other Italo-American worked as indefatigably in the halls of Congress, with a substantial amount of his efforts directed toward the advancement of Italo-American interests. During his first term, he emerged as the foremost Congressional defender of aliens and immigrants against the backdrop of a huge anti-alien drive then under way. Intense interest in immigration restriction had become intertwined with pressing economic questions by the middle of the 1930's. Indeed, that decade spawned some of the nation's severest restriction bills, some of which gained approval, while others failed in large part because of the strenuous opposition led by men like Marcantonio.

Desperately seeking a scapegoat to account for the Great Depression, many Americans found it easy to place the responsibility on immigrants. The views of Congressman Martin Dies of Texas expressed the attitude of dozens of other Congressmen and millions of Americans, when he said: "If we had refused admission to the sixteen and one-half million foreign born living in this country today, we would have no

[31] Mann, *LaGuardia*, p. 241; Mann, *LaGuardia Comes to Power, 1933* (Philadelphia, 1965), pp. 78, 86, 138, and 185. See also Howard Zinn, *LaGuardia in Congress* (Binghamton, 1959), 84, 156, and 248.

[32] See Antonio Arturo Micocci, "Vito Marcantonio," *Romanica*, Vol. 1, No. 4 (March, 1936), 8. Marcantonio also delighted in the ability of Italians in East Harlem to cooperate in ousting the Irish-dominated Tammany politicians from power as exemplified in the primaries of 1933.

[33] See, for example, *Il Progresso Italo-Americano*, October 26 and 31, and November 2, 1934.

unemployment problem to distress and harass us." [34] Against this kind of mentality, Marcantonio raised the strongest voice. Fully aware of his heritage as a representative of the second largest immigrant group, he understood that the Italo-Americans would be the foremost targets of discrimination, a problem intensified by their comparative aversion to naturalization. As a politician, he was also fully aware of the political significance in taking up the cudgels of immigrants. At the time he was the recepient of extensive communications from anxious Italo-Americans from East Harlem and throughout the city, imploring his assistance regarding clarification of naturalization statutes, applications for citizenship, aid in preventing deportation and other favors. [35]

On every issue regarding the welfare of immigrants, Marcantonio was on the liberal side. In 1935 he assailed a bill, authorizing the deportation of aliens, as a "vicious bill which presaged an avalanche of punitive alien and sedition bills aimed at further persecution of immigrants." He fought vigorously, and successfully, against another bill, designed to deport aliens who had entered the country illegally, but were otherwise of good character. He reminded his colleagues of the hardships such deportations would cause to native-born citizens, who were dependents of these individuals. Marcantonio succeeded in ending the official policy of making invidious distinctions between Northern and Southern Italians. He was instrumental in facilitating procedures for immigrants in numerous matters of technical detail. He fought doggedly against attempts to limit WPA benefits to citizens and legal aliens, again pointing out the injustice which would befall the innocent American dependents involved. "Starve the father and you starve his American children," he warned. Unfortunately, he was unable to stem the reactionary tide in this instance. [36]

---

[34] *Congressional Record*, 74th Cong., 1st sess., Vol. 79, pp. 10 and 229. See Lucille B. Milner and David Dempsey, "The Alien Myth," *Harper's Magazine* (September, 1940), Vol. 181, pp. 374-379, for an excellent journalistic appraisal of the anti-alien sentiment.

[35] Often those seeking help promised unstinting efforts in behalf of Marcantonio's candidacy at election time. See *M.P.*, Box 1, Folder: Immigration.

[36] *Congressional Record*, 74th Cong., 1st sess., Vol. 79, pp. 7708 and 14376; 2nd sess., Vol. 80, p. 6975, give examples of Marcantonio's involvement in immigration legislation. For information regarding the change

Marcantonio's concern for the welfare of Italo-Americans was never more manifest than during the years of World War II, when they became the objects of deep suspicion by so many Americans. For the non-citizen Italians, the situation was even worse, since they were officially classified as "enemy aliens." More than any other congressman, Marcantonio fought in their behalf, both inside and outside the halls of Congress. To be sure, there were three other Italo-Americans serving in Congress during that period, and two of them (D'Alessandro and Capozzoli) spoke out forcefully in favor of their ethnic constituents, but none had the national following, the influence, or the ability Marcantonio possessed. He, therefore, emerged as the national legislature's most consistent and conspicuous Italo-American spokesman. Eschewing the defensive, he objected to the denigration of Italo-American patriotism. Through diligent research, he sought out instances of acts of heroism by Italo-American servicemen, and brought these positive accomplishments to the attention of his colleagues. He cited the heartening response of Italians to war bond drives, and recounted episodes of wholehearted Italo-American participation in defense and war plans.[37]

Unstintingly, he fought for the right of Italo-Americans to employment in defense plants, castigating discrimination against them as a practice akin to "playing Hitler's game." Facing the issue head on, he exposed maligners and detractors of Italo-American patriotism for fostering discrimination which prevented the full mobilization of American power. Nor did he stop with speeches in Congress. He utilized the public media to instruct the public of Italy's enduring role in the history of democracy. Finally, he protested to Roosevelt himself repeatedly, until a degree of justice was rendered.[38]

Marcantonio's strong identification with Italo-Americans found him championing the cause of the land of their fathers.

in classification of Northern and Southern Italians, see *M.P.*, Box 19, Folder: Research Immigration, Letter from Marcantonio to Edward Corsi, January 4, 1936.

[37] *M.P.*, Box 14 Folder: International Relations, Italy General. Letter from Marcantonio to General J. A. Ulio, April 25, 1942; Letter from Alan Cranston to Marcantonio, April 27, 1942.

[38] *M.P.*, *Ibid.*, Letter from Navy Department to Marcantonio, May 18, 1942; Marcantonio speech entitled "The Role of the Italo-Americans in this War," July 17, 1942; Box 22, Folder: Italo-Americans in this War, Speech, August 6, 1943.

As Italy's defeat appeared imminent in 1943, he organized a group of Italo-Americans, which exhorted Italians to complete the overthrow of the fascist yoke. Anticipating criticism and jokes at the expense of Italians, because of their poor battle-field performance against the Allies, he retorted that Italians would fight bravely for freedom, but not for tyranny. Once Italy surrendered, he worked vigorously for a quick peace treaty and the acceptance of Italy as an ally, and the extension of generous aid to that country.

The revelation that Italy was compelled to accept rigid terms of unconditional surrender in September of 1943, found him joining with many Italo-Americans in condemning the pact. Simultaneously, he urged that Italian fighters be accept-ed as free men, rather than prisoners of war. His deep concern for the welfare of Italy was reflected in a radio message in which he demonstrated that Italian contributions comprised a glorious chapter in American history, from the discovery of Columbus to the 500,000 World War II service men and women of Italian descent.[39] As he summed it up: "They drill, hammer, forge, operate machinery, help turn out the ships, the planes, the tanks, and the ammunitions to win the war."

In 1944, he denounced the occupation conditions which Italy was forced to accept. He then introduced a resolution, asking for a resumption of diplomatic relations with Italy, as well as recognition of that country as a genuine ally, thus making her eligible for substantial aid. He rejected the "co-belligerency" status then prevailing, as a vague device which effectively prevented Italy from receiving much-needed lend-lease aid, and which was directly responsible for starvation, black marketeering, and military occupation.[40]

Realizing that action on his resolution would not come soon, Marcantonio found other ways of bringing succor to the Italian people. He joined with other prominent Italo-Amer-icans in asking President Roosevelt's personal intervention in facilitating the exchange of mail between Americans of Italian extraction and their relatives in Sicily and occupied Italy. Practically all Italo-Americans had needy friends or relatives in Italy, and were, therefore, most anxious to send packages of clothing and other useful items. Since his congressional dis-

---

[39] The New York *Times*, July 26, 1943; M.P., Box 22, Folder: Italo-Americans in this War, Speech, Aug. 6, 1943.
[40] *Congressional Record*, 78th Cong., 2nd sess., Vol. 90, pp. 8134-8136.

trict housed more Italo-Americans than any other district, Marcantonio labored incessantly for the resumption of mail. He pleaded passionately before Congress and, together with other Italo-Americans, forwarded appeals to the President, which soon bore fruit with the resumption of mail early in 1944.[41]

Marcantonio did not allow his resolution to remain pigeon-holed. His persistent efforts led to hearings on his resolution before the House Committee on Foreign Affairs in April, 1945. Moreover, Italo-American circles were unanimous in supporting his resolution. Obtaining Italo-American endorsement was no small accomplishment, when one considers the diversity, if not the antagonism, between Italo-American groups and the highly individualistic Italian mentality which normally militated against such united action. Thus, the hearings were a succession of witnesses from the Order of the Sons of Italy to prominent Italo-American leaders, traditionally critical of Marcantonio, calling for approval of his resolution. Marcantonio's own testimony correlated congressional approval of the resolution with the welfare of the United Nations' coalition, which had successfully waged the war. Continued cooperation between the Allies was indispensable in the pursuit of a postwar peace. He also voiced vigorous opposition to Secretary of State Byrnes' proposal to grant the city of Trieste to Yugoslavia, as an action which would be in violation of ethnic, economic and geographic considerations. The upshot of the hearings was that the House Committee of Foreign Affairs unanimously reported favorably on Marcantonio's resolution.[42]

A study of Marcantonio's activities in behalf of Italy and Italo-Americans during the war years is quite revealing. Often the subject of controversy because of his left-wing politics, and duly criticized for the same by many respected Italo-Amer-

---

[41] *M.P.*, Box 14, Folder: International Relations, Italy Communism After the War. Letter from Marcantonio to Franklin D. Roosevelt, February 12, 1944; *Congressional Record*, 78th Cong., 2nd sess., Vol. 90, p. 1563. Marcantonio was not the only one urging an amelioration of conditions for Italy. See for example, *Il Progresso Italo-Americano*, February 2 through 16, 1944, for evidence of how this issue galvanized the Italian-American community.

[42] United States Congress, House Committee on Foreign Affairs, *Hearings* on H.J. Res. 99, To Recognize Italy as an Ally and to Extend Lend Lease, passim.

ican leaders, nevertheless, when it came to the defense of the Italians, Marcantonio was second to none. On Capitol Hill, where policies affecting them were determined, he emerged as their leading champion. He was the first to call for a recognition of Italy, for its inclusion in the United Nations. He argued against imposing reparations on Italy, and prodded Administration officials to increase daily rations in the occupied country.

A committed left-winger, Marcantonio was not above urging political preference on the basis of ethnic identity. In 1943, for example, as leader of the left wing of the American Labor Party, then reigning as New York State's powerful third party, he obtained ALP support for Democrat Judge Thomas Aurelio for a Supreme Court judgeship, largely because of his insistence that the post go to an Italo-American. He maintained his support of Aurelio, despite revelations of the judge's connections with underworld boss Frank Costello.[43]

Sometimes his ethnic sensibilities found Marcantonio advocating policies inimical to the basic tenets of liberalism. While running for mayor of New York City in 1949, for example, he protested to the Roxy Theater against the showing of the film, *The House of Strangers*, as discrediting the good name of Italo-Americans.[44]

It is interesting to note that in the 1940's, Marcantonio continued to win elections in the face of an increasingly persistent and notoriously bad press. Virtually all the major New York dailies and the *Il Progresso Italo-Americano* opposed him. His ability to win repeatedly was due to his unstinting service to his constituents, for the most part, Italo-Americans. This support began to diminish in the late 1940's as a result of extremely poor publicity and the strident anti-Communist atmosphere. During the latter part of that decade, Puerto Ricans were entering the district in staggering numbers, and while he maintained unusually close relations with them, his strength at the polls was ebbing significantly. There was strong evidence that he was losing important support among East Harlem's Italian population. In 1948 he received approxi-

---

[43] The New York *Times*, July 24, August 29 and 31, 1943; Warren Moscow, *Politics in the Empire State* (New York, 1948), p. 163.

[44] *M.P.*, Box 14, International Relations, Italy Communism After the War, Communication of July 1, 1949.

mately 37 per cent of the total vote. It must be remembered that 1948 was a crucial year for Italy and Italo-Americans.[45]

The November congressional elections came only a few months after a tremendous letter-writing campaign by Italo-Americans, urging their friends and relatives in Italy to vote against Communist candidates. The large Italo-American population in East Harlem was deeply and emotionally involved in this campaign, and it was natural for them to follow this advice back home. Italo-American defection from Marcantonio's ranks was confirmed by a survey of the district undertaken by his own canvassers. They reported numerous instances of voter resistance to Marcantonio, based solely on the Communist issue.[46]

Even with these unfavorable circumstances, Marcantonio still remained a formidable power. Thus, when he ran for mayor in 1949 as the ALP nominee, both Democrats and Republicans expected him to attract a sizable vote. Marcantonio again tried to exploit his ethnicity. When the Brooklyn *Eagle* reacted to his complaint about a newspaper blackout on his campaign, saying: "It couldn't happen to a nicer fish peddler," Marcantonio immediately seized the comment as a base aspersion against all Italo-Americans. Democrats, in particular, expressed real concern over what appeared to be a "favorite son" candidate among the large New York Italo-American community. In fact, William O'Dwyer was forced to change his campaign strategy in the final weeks, resorting to a concerted effort to marshal Italian voters into the Democratic ranks.[47] However, New York politics once again proved the viability of the democratic process, as O'Dwyer won with a commanding lead over his Republican opponent, while Marcantonio was a distant third, with 356,000 votes, still bearing

---

[45] Marcantonio received 36,000 votes to 31,500 for Elis and 31,200 for Morrissey. For an account of the role of the Italian elections in the Marcantonio election, see Jonathan Bingham, *The Congressional Elections of Vito Marcantonio*, p. 112 (unpublished thesis at Harvard University). To realize how much of an impact the Italian election had on New York's Italo-Americans, see *The Catholic News*, July 2, 1949.

[46] *M.P.*, Box 49, Folder: Campaigns, the 1948 Campaign.

[47] Brooklyn *Eagle*, October 7, 1949. Examples of reactions to the campaign are to be found in the New York *Times*, October 29, 1949, and *New York Elections of 1949, Reminiscences*, George Combs section, (Oral History Office, Columbia University).

witness to the ALP's drawing power. Nevertheless, the inexorable law of politics dictated that the days of that left-wing party were numbered. So, too, were Marcantonio's.

Conclusions regarding Ethnicity and Politics

The careers of five of the six politicians examined demonstrated the results of the impact of ethnicity in politics. In these case studies, it became clear that the politicians exploited their ethnicity. But it was a two-way street. The Italian-Americans were conscious of the exploitation; however, they also realized that their influence in American society could increase to the extent that they wielded political power. While there were not a few non-Italian congressmen who were responsive to the needs of the large Italian minorities in their districts, it was natural for Americans of Italian extraction to believe that their cause would best be served by political leaders of their own kind.

The rise of political leaders to important national positions could alone instill a healthy pride in their ethnicity and a firm conviction in their ability to make meaningful contributions to their country. As one student of Italo-American life has observed, the ethnic basis of Italian-American participation in politics contained opposing potentialities. On the one hand, it could make for the conservation of Italian traits by allowing people to feel that they are being represented by fellow Italians and do not have to adjust individually to American political life. On the other hand, it could have important consequences in the direction of Americanization because of the ethnic group's participation in American political life.[48] Both consequences, in fact, do follow; however, the margin appears to be in the direction of Americanization.

---

[48] Irvin L. Child, *Italian or American, The Second Generation in Conflict* (New Haven, 1943), p. 40. See also Oscar Handlin, *The Newcomers*, (Cambridge, 1962), p. 38, for an observation concerning ethnic consciousness in New York City politics.

The Ethnic Church and the Integration of Italian Immigrants in the United States*

by Silvano M. Tomasi, C.S. **

The German sociologist Max Weber, who visited Chicago in 1904, noted its lawlessness and violence, the sharp contrasts between gold coast and slums, the steam, dirt, blood, and hides of the stockyards, and above all the "maddening" mixture of people: "The Greek shining the Yankee's shoes for five cents, the German acting as his waiter, the Irishman managing his politics, and the Italian digging his dirty ditches." [1] Scaled along a continuum of high and low acceptability in terms of race, class and religion, the immigrant groups that had come to the United States from the various regions of Europe were fiercely competing to reach the sources of wealth and power in their new country. The feverish desire to cross the ocean in order to escape social conditions incapable of fulfilling the new aspirations of peasants and artisans, had penetrated the poverty stricken villages of Southern Italy and pushed the migrants out of the Old Country.

In addition, the unification of Italy had brought about a serious economic and social upheaval. The artificial equilibrium of the economies of the old States of the Italian peninsula rested on the lack of external competition and the absence of mobility of capital and manpower. The sudden disappearance of frontiers and customs created a disastrous situa-

---

[1] Marianne Weber, *Max Weber: ein Lebensbuld* (Tubingen, 1926), pp. 296-300. Also H. H. Gerth and C. Wright Mills, eds., *From Max Weber: Essays in Sociology* (New York, 1958).

---

* This article is based on a paper read at the Symposium on Italian Emigration to North America, May 27-29, 1969, University of Florence.
** Silvano M. Tomasi, C.S., Division of Social Sciences, Richmond College of the City University of New York.

163

tion for industry and agriculture in Southern Italy. The economic revolution demanded a process of readjustment for which the leadership of Southern Italy had neither the capital nor the initiative. The peasants, on the other hand, — victims of *la miseria*, malnutrition, malaria and illiteracy, — were left with only the capacity to work and a tradition of servitude. Faina concludes the governmental inquiry into the condition of Southern peasants thus: "In the general restlessness of all classes to achieve economic advancement, the southern peasant was left with only three alternatives: he could either resign himself to his *miseria*, or he could rebel, or, he could migrate."[2] The attempt to rebel had failed. Ascetic resignation to a fate of acceptance, suffering and poverty had ended as well. A Sicilian *giornaliero* (day-laborer) reflected the soul of the people forced out of the island they loved: "For the inhuman way the *signori* treat us, they should all be set in front of a cannon, with the exception of the Church (not the priests) and the Saints. We are subjected to them like slaves." [3]

The Risorgimento broke the centuries old impasse of bitter fatalism and slowly awakened "the awareness of one's own right." [4] Emigration became linked to "a secret and instinctive upsurge of the lower strata of the population toward greater well-being, forcefully stimulated by political turmoil and bandit warfare." [5]   It became the only feasible choice for the southern peasants. The escape from oppression and poverty remained the haunting dream of the immigrants, a preoccupation blocking other initiatives, as Catholic, Protestant and Socialist organizers repeatedly complained. *Il Proletario* editorialized this feeling in 1905.

> Italians come to America with the sole intention of accumulating money. They live like sheep....Their dream, their only care is the bundle of money they are painfully increasing, which will give them, after 20 years of deprivation, the possibility of having a mediocre standard of living in their native country.[6]

[2] Francesco Coletti, "Dell'emigrazione italiana," R. Accademia dei Lincei, *Cinquanta anni di storia italiana* (Milano, 1911), vol. III, p. 121.

[3] *Ibid.*, p. 146.

[4] *Ibid.*, p. 157. S. Jacini, Relazione per le Calabrie e la Basilicata, vol. IX, fasc. 1, pp. XV-XVI.

[5] *Ibid.*, p. 157; S. Jacini, *op. cit.*, p. 66.

[6] Ilion, "Americani e Americanizzazione," *Il Proletario*, Anno IX, n. 23 (4 Giugno 1905), p. 1.

Thus, mostly for economic reasons, about four million Italians entered the United States between 1880 and 1924, crisscrossing the Atlantic and the United States with only the avowed purpose of making money, returning to their villages, and buying some land.

The expectations, however, were soon reshaped in the slums of the big cities of North America. There Italian immigrants found themselves bewildered and lost in an evironment whose language they did not understand, whose bureaucratic machinery frightened them and whose social and religious attitudes clashed directly with those of their traditional world. Dreams of instant fortune turned into nightmares of everyday survival. The painful experience of social rejection taught the newcomers to transcend their family clannishness and to join with other families from the same province in the home country, who shared the same dialect and patron saints, in order to find personal security in the strength of the group. The immigrants, in the total absence of opportunity for social participation, were forced to recall the only form of social experience they had known in their villages, the institutional type of the parish. With no knowledge of political maneuvering, unfamiliar with the methods and customs of big commercial enterprises and with the added burden of illiteracy, Italians in the States were, initially, ill-equipped to challenge the future with new institutions. Instead they had to fall back on and repeat the past. There could be no more striking contrast than that between the Puritan village and the urban villages of transplanted Italians. Sumner Chilton Powell writing on the formation of a New England town remarked:

> To emigrate from accustomed social institutions and relationships to a set of unfamiliar communities in the way in which Noyes and Ruddock shifted from England to Sudbury, and the latter from Sudbury to Marlborough, meant a startling transformation. The townsmen had to change or abandon almost every formal institution which they had taken for granted.[7]

The Puritan immigrants had a sophisticated theology to defend, an experience of debate and persecution and involvement in

---

[7]Sumner Chilton Powell, *Puritan Village: The Formation of a New England Town* (Middletown, 1963), p. 142.

courts, legal practices, and elective offices — a rich background out of which a new society could be structured. Little Italy, on the other hand, was born as a tentative and temporary substitute for the old world community. It had the familiar superstitions, smells, expressions, and, above all, institutional structures that made the world understandable again. The necessity, however, that had stimulated the creativity of the Puritans, gave a new twist to the reconstructed world of the peasants.

Interpretation of Italian Immigration

Analysis of the Italian experience had been approached from several angles: to demonstrate the American dream of democracy and success, to prove the benefits of capitalism, to express ethnocentric and filiopietistic devotion.

Bishop Dunne sums up the thinking of Gibbons, Ireland and their followers in the American Catholic hierarchy at the time of Italian mass immigration. "One thing certain, the Catholic Church ... is best qualified to weld into one democratic brotherhood, one great American citizenship, the children of various climes, temperaments and conditions." [8] This view is reflected in the writings of most historians, who, like Commager, interpret the Catholic Church as "one of the most effective of all agencies for democracy and Americanization." [9] On the issue of Americanization Latin immigrants encountered a united front, a clear line of demarcation between the "in" and the "out" groups, between morally "good" and morally "bad" people. In the eyes of the Southern Italian peasant the excitement over the Cahensley question and the flag-waving attitude of Irish pastors and bishops were not very different from the Protestant judgments which placed them outside the category of the "Elect." Father Peter Bandini, writing on the founding of the New York's St. Raphael Society in 1893, gives

---

[8] Edmund M. Dunne, "The Church and the Immigrant," in C. E. McGuire, ed., *Catholic Builders of the Nation* (Boston, 1923), vol. II, p. 15.

[9] Henry S. Commager, *The American Mind* (New Haven, 1950), pp. 193-194. Vincent P. De Santis, "The American Historian Looks at the Catholic Immigrant," in Thomas McAvoy, C.S.C., ed., *Roman Catholicism and the American Way of Life* (Notre Dame, 1960), pp. 225-234.

us his conclusion after years of dealing with American civic and ecclesiastical officials:

> What is interesting is that people in Italy seem to think the St. Raphael Society is greatly helped financially by Americans. These persons cannot realize that this project, because of its stated purpose, prompts Americans to think it must be helped instead by those who send us. This project, which facilitates the arrival on American soil of an element that, far from being desired, is one it would be more desirable to expel, represents an activity that must be as welcome to Americans as smoke is to the eyes.[10]

As late as 1917 the Archbishop of New York was advised by the Irish pastor of Nativity Church that

> The Italians are not a sensitive people like our own. When they are told that they are about the worst Catholics that ever came to this country they don't resent it or deny it. If they were a little more sensitive to such remarks they would improve faster. The Italians are callous as regards religion.[11]

From *The Catholic World* we learn that the Italians, at least in 1888, lacked some traits of the American character, "especially," says Bernard Lynch, "what we call *spirit....* They for the most part seem totally devoid of what may be termed the sense of respectability.... The shame of being thought a pauper is almost unknown among the Italian people of this quarter (Mott and Park Streets, New York City.)"[12] Italian clergy and immigrants alike were looked upon with suspicion and hostility. As an Irish pastor remarked: "Italian priests here must be servants."[13]

But the Anglo-Saxon evaluation of the Italians was far more radical and destructive than that of the Irish. Southern European immigrants, the necessary unskilled labor needed in the expanding industrialization of the nation, were feared as a threat to America's free institutions. This fear was tempered by the conviction that the alien population could be evangelized

---

[10] Letter dated February 10, 1893, Fr. Pietro Bandini to Fr. Francesco Zaboglio, General Archives of the Congregation of St. Charles, Rome (ACSC).

[11] Letter dated March 4, 1917, Rev. B. J. Reilly to Cardinal Farley, Archives of the Roman Catholic Archdiocese of New York (AANY).

[12] Bernard J. Lynch, "The Italians in New York," *The Catholic World*, XLVII, (April, 1888), p. 68.

[13] Letter dated May 24, 1888, Fr. Marcellino Moroni to Archbishop Micheal A. Corrigan, AANY.

and properly Americanized.[14] It was a duty demanded by the
Church and the Republic "to bring the Gospel in its purity to
these masses from Southern Europe, who are, to a large extent,
both ignorant and superstitious." [15] If "Christianized," the
Italians would qualify for entrance into American society, and
this, in turn, would help America carry out her messianic
task.   Once the immigrants were evangelized,

> this nation, together with the rest of the Anglo-Saxon race,
> fully brought under the power of the Gospel and in the spirit
> of a true consecration going forth to conquer the world for
> Christ, with God's presence and blessing would prove ir-
> resistible.[16]

The eagerness to Christianize the immigrants had also a
less idealistic motive:

> Public schools, mission schools and churches will do the
> work to evangelize the immigrants.
> And it must be done. Business pleads for it, patriotism
> demands it, social considerations require it.[17]

Since bad men cannot be good patriots and since love for
and devotion to the country requires intelligence, sympathy and
character, observes John Dixon, the problem arises: Whence
will these newly made Americans get these qualities?   The
answer is clear: surely not by retaining their language and by
being crowded into the manufacturing and mining centers,
but by being properly evangelized.[18]   The behavior of social
workers reflected the ideological convictions of the first decade of the century.   The gap between the foreign colonies and
the dominant group in the large cities was wide and deep.   It
derived from the poverty (akin to immorality in the Calvinist
tradition) and the unfamiliar cultural and religious manifesta-
tions of the immigrants.

---

[14] John Willis Baer, "The Peaceful Invasion of America: Some Facts;
Some Figures; Some Fears," *The Assembly Herald*, X, n. 5 (May, 1904),
p. 233.

[15] ———, "Who are Coming? — To What?"; "Character of Immigration," *The Assembly Herald*, IX, n. 2 (August, 1903), pp. 381-384.

[16] Wilson Phraner, D.D., "The Evangelization of Our Own Land the
Key to the Evangelization of the World," *The Assembly Herald*, X, n. 1,
(January, 1904), pp. 27-30.

[17] Charles L. Thompson, D.D., "Opportunity and Responsibility Today," *The Assembly Herald*, X, n. 1, (January, 1904), p. 26.

[18] John Dixon, D.D., "Problem of the Immigrant," *The Assembly
Herald*, XIII, n. 3, (March, 1907), pp. 5-6.

With these Slavs and Italians we are getting in our State the continental idea of the Sabbath, the socialist's idea of government, and the communist's idea of property, and the pagan's idea of religion. These ideas are antagonistic to those embodied in our civilization and free institutions — our American ideals being largely the out-growth of our Protestant faith. Hence we believe that the urgent need is that the Gospel be preached to this new immigration.[19]

Missionary work could not be delayed any longer. Personnel and money were invested in this direction.[20] The separateness of the immigrants was deprecated.

"Living their own lives ... practicing their own superstitions and beliefs, breeding anarchists, communists, socialists, Sabbath breakers, blashemers," [21] the immigrants were not following the expected pattern of assimilation.

------

[19] ———, "Synodical Home Mission in Pennsylvania," *The Assembly Herald*, XIII, n. 3, (March, 1907), p. 117. The Pennsylvania Presbyterian Synod had spent in 1906 the sum of $40,000.00 for work among immigrants and $5,000.00 more were needed for 1907.

[20] John Dixon, D.D., "Our Foreigners," *The Assembly Herald*, XII, n. 8, (August, 1906), p. 388. "Italians! A million and one-half of Italians in our Land! Those coming from Northern Italy are more intelligent than their southern brethren and are very receptive to Protestant teaching. Our over thirty churches have about 900 members. Our work could be very easily increased ten-fold if there were only more equipped Italian ministers." In 1904 the New York Presbytery had begun a new approach toward immigrants. D.J. McMillan, "Work among Foreigners in New York," Ibid., p. 389. "The Home Board and the Women's Board," wrote Dixon, "care for the European races to the extent of thirty-three thousand dollars each year: ten thousand for Italians; sixty-five hundred for Germans; fifty-nine hundred for Hungarians; forty-seven hundred for Bohemians; seventeen hundred for Ruthenians; and the balance in smaller sums for Greeks, Jews, Portuguese, Russians, Syrians and Poles .... It may safely be estimated that the self-supporting synods and presbyteries spend no less than seventy-five thousand dollars every year. Thus fully one hundred thousand dollars is spent annually by our Church for our European immigrants." John Dixon, D.D., "Our Church and the Foreigners," *The Assembly Herald*, XIV, n. 1, (January, 1908), p. 30. The work, however, was not moving in any significant way. The Presbyterian Italians of Newark were already decreasing. Between 150-240 were showing up at the meetings, when they were 260 in 1901. Davis S. Lusk, "Forming Friendly Centers," *The Assembly Herald*, (April, 1913), p. 203. In Detroit, after six years of work, the church services averaged from sixty to seventy men. Rev. Alfred H. Barr, "Work Among South Italians and Sicilians in Detroit," *The Assembly Herald*, XV, n. 1, (January, 1909), pp. 29-30.

[21] Wm. P. Fulton, D.D., "Redeeming the Cities," *The Assembly Herald*, (April, 1913), pp. 191-194.

The Protestant attitude seemed to be that God had brought these people to America and if America could now save herself, she would save the world: no need to "put up the bars."

> No greater opportunity ever came to the Christian people of America to do mission work than to evangelize, Christianize, Americanize and assimilate these multitudes of immigrants in our midst into one composite people, united liberty-loving, flag-honoring, God-fearing, Christ-following, Christian.[22]

What will be the end product of Americanization?

> Within the next decade this army of strangers will be assimilated. *They will be Americans of some sort.* The battle is begun, our only hope is in the immediate action. The unscrupulous politician, the murderous saloon, and the Roman Catholic Church, un-American and unscriptural, are after these strangers. Will our Protestantism bear the test? [23]

Norman Thomas, who heard the call to socialism while pastor in Italian Harlem, shared the convictions of the Protestant establishment on this subject. The social work of the Church and its Extension Committee and Home Missions was "in the interest of both religion and Americanism." His work in East Harlem, the work at the Jan Hus Settlement House and at Labor Temple was "Americanization work of the best type." [24] Italian-American Protestant ministers and church workers generally accepted a concept of Americanization in accord with the official position of the Protestant establishment. This became another cause of their isolation from the mainstream of the life and institutions of Little Italy. In their view, "the Italian needs to be Americanized as well as Christianized." [25]

The Protestant ethic of economic and social success as the guarantee of God's favor found, in its encounter with the Italian immigrants, a confirmation of its long standing judg-

---

[22] *Ibid.*, p. 193.

[23] Austin H. Folly, D.D., "Who is My Neighbor?" *The Assembly Herald*, (April, 1913), p. 196.

[24] Letter dated April 3, 1918, Norman Thomas to Rev. Wm. Adams Brown, New York Public Library, Norman Thomas Papers (NTP).

[25] Rev. Stefano L. Testa, "For the Italian: A Ministry of Christian and Patriotic Appeal," *The Assembly Herald*, XCII, (January, 1911), p. 11. Antonio Mangano, *Training Men for Foreign Work in America*, pamphlet, n.d., n.p., 1917c. For a different view of Americanization in relation to missionary work among Italian immigrants, see the booklet of the Baptist Church, Italian Baptist Missionary Association; *Report of the Committee on Americanization*, (New York, 1918), pp. 22.

ment that Latin and Slavic peoples were inferior as persons and as nations.

The Immigrants Spoke for Themselves

The mass of Italian immigrants was slow to move in any direction. They had brought with them the suspicious caution of their poverty-stricken villages, their mistrust of almost everybody, and a total lack of confidence in the institutions of the State and the Church. If the Americanizers were tempted to consider the immigrants bad, unintelligent, criminally disposed and superstitious, the immigrants found demands made on them by outsiders a threat to their ways, while their concern was with survival rather than with ideologies. Once their social and political conservatism had given them some security within their group, the immigrants began to move geographically and socially out of Little Italy.

The Irish and Anglo-Saxon interpretations of Italian immigration are but two views of a phenomenon still under study. Historical perspectives and sociological hypotheses often yield to the need for rationalization, which in turn tends to influence the subjects chosen for research, the selection of data, the recording of observations, the theoretical and practical inferences drawn as well as the manner of presenting conclusions. Among the questions raised by the presence of Italians in the United States and the way they related to the broader American society, the role of religious institutions has received scanty attention and even that has been from defensive or peripheral perspectives, incapable or unwilling to discover the key function of these religious institutions.

Today, a central fact of the American political system is the persistence of ethnic groups identifiable in voting, denominational lines and occupational stratification. Stokely Carmichael and Charles V. Hamilton remarked very much *a propos* that in America: "No other group would submit to being led by others. Italians do not run the Anti-Defamation League of B'nai B'rith. Irish do not chair Christopher Columbus Societies." [26]

---

[26] Stokely Carmichael and Charles V. Hamilton, *Black Power. The Politics of Liberation in America.* (New York, 1967), p. 49. For the persistence of ethnicity in America, see Andrew M. Greeley, *Why Can't They Be Like Us? Facts and Fallacies About Ethnic Differences and Group Conflicts in America.* (New York, 1969), pp. 76.

The various elements in the American pot have not really melted together over the years, but there seems to be no question of the "Americanness" of the ethnic groups now included in the American system. Italian immigrants have followed the pattern of inclusion. They committed themselves to the values underlying the assumption that being an American was a desirable goal. Even the foreign-language press, which could have been a main carrier of ethnicity, was instead a means of assimilation, as Park observed: "Under the terms of its existence, the (ethnic) press is apt to aid rather than prevent the drift toward the American community." [27]

The faith of ethnic people in the American creed was supplemented by the experience of full membership in a national community which did not destroy the smaller sub-communities. Thus, successful inclusion resulted from asserting the accepted values and at the same time mobilizing power and economic interests. Power, structurally conceptualized, relates to the ability of a group to be self-determining, while involved in the larger social system and manipulative of it by means of an institutional nexus which the group has at its disposal. [28] The focus is no longer on anomic individuals, but on the alienated, insulated and isolated groups. Since the mass of immigrants were silent and not much given to literary expression, what has to be said about them has to be inferred. [29] The established hierarchies of the Catholic and Protestant Churches have often spoken about and for the immigrants; and so did the socialist-anarchist newspapers. The Italian immigrant mass, however, spoke for itself, in its own way, by deciding to accept the American creed and move into the mainstream of American society. The ethnic Church's place in this process of inclusion was determined by the patterns of social and insti-

---

[27] Robert E. Park, *The Immigrant Press and Its Control*, (New York, 1922), p. 79.

[28] Madeline H. Engel, "Powerlessness as an Element of Delinquent Behavior," Fordham University, Department of Sociology, 1969 (mimeo). Talcott Parsons, "Full Citizenship for the Negro American? A Sociological Problem," in Talcott Parsons and Kenneth B. Clark, *The Negro American*, (Boston, 1966), pp. 709-754.

[29] Grazia Dore, *La democrazia italiana e l'emigrazione in America* (Brescia, 964), pp. 26-27. Oscar Handlin, "*Immigration as a Feature of American History*" (Oswego State University College, 196) p. 15 (mimeo).

tutional interaction, of which it has been the symbol and the unifying system.[30]

The Growth of Italian Parishes

The historical growth of Italian ethnic parishes seems to follow three stages of development: a first attempt to incorporate Italian immigrants within the Irish parishes; then, a clear separation and a consequent building period; finally, a fusion of Italian and Irish, among others, into a new type of social group, the Catholic segment of the American population.

First attempts

On February 17, 1864, the church of Our Lady of Grace was incorporated in Hoboken. In what was missionary (for Catholics) territory in the State of New Jersey, the few hundred Catholics comprising the parish were proud of the organization they had achieved. Their priests were even happier. The pastor, Father Anthony Cauvin, had arrived in New York in 1847 and, after serving the Italian and French populations around Canal Street, he was sent by Bishop Hughes in 1851 to minister to the same ethnic groups in Hoboken. He had been a tutor in the family of Count Cavour. In fact, Victor Emmanuel, king of Sardinia, presented him with a silver ostensorium, and the Cavour family gave him some liturgical vestments, "in recompense for the services rendered by him for so many years to the Italians of New York, especially to the Genoese, whom he attended in their sickness and instructed, and many of whom continued to come to him for confession." [31]

Grazia Dore, "Some Social and Historical Aspects of Italian Emigration to America," *Journal of Social History*, (Winter, 1968), p. 115.

[30] For a recent re-interpretation of the relation between the Italian immigrants and the Catholic Church, see Rudolph J. Vecoli, "Prelates and Peasants: Italian Immigrants and the Catholic Church," *Journal of Social History*, (Spring, 1969), pp. 217-268.

[31] Joseph M. Flynn, *The Catholic Church in New Jersey* (Morristown, N.J., 1904), pp. 65-166. Edwin Vose Sullivan, ed., *An Annotated Copy*

Father Gennaro de Concilio, a brilliant Neapolitan, disciple of the philosopher San Serverino, had come to America in the Spring of 1860 to assist Father Cauvin at the request of Bishop James Roosevelt Bayley of the newly erected diocese of Newark. Northern and Southern Italians did not yet constitute a large colony. De Concilio could act, then, as chaplain at nearby Seton Hall University, where he became a professor of logic (1860-62), outstanding for his scholarship. He founded the church of St. Michael and the Italian Church of the Holy Rosary in Jersey City. He became the treasurer of St. Raphael's Society in 1889 and wrote the famous Baltimore Catechism used for fifty years, without revision, by the children of immigrants and their native co-religionists as well in all Catholic schools and religious classes in the United States.[32]

The organization of churches for Italian immigrants, however, did not start in New Jersey. St. Mary Magdalene de' Pazzi in Philadelphia had been established in 1852.[33] Great Italian missionaries like Rosati, Mazzucchelli, Cataldo and a score of others had already implanted the Church in the West and the South of the United States. On the Eastern seaboard, the start of Italian immigration was marking the beginning of what came to be catalogued by historians as the "Italian problem."[34]

---

of the Diary of Bishop James Roosevelt Bayley, First Bishop of Newark, New Jersey, 1853-1872. Ph. D. Thesis, Department of History, University of Ottawa, 1956. Vol. II, p. 42-43. Fr. Cauvin returned to Nice and died there in 1902.

[32] Edwin Vose Sullivan, ed., op. cit., vol. II, pp. 156-157; vol. I, entry for April 10, 1860. St. Raphael's Society Papers, Center for Migration Studies, Staten Island, New York.

[33] Giovanni Schiavo, Italian-American History, vol. II, The Italian Contribution to the Catholic Church in America (New York, 1949), p. 354. — Historical Sketches of the Catholic Churches and Institutions of Philadelphia (Philadelphia, 1895), pp. 99-100.

[34] Andrew F. Rolle, The Immigrant Upraised. Italian Adventurers and Colonists in an Expanding America, (Norman, 1968). Amalia Capello, Notizie storiche e descrittive delle Missioni della Provincia Torinese della Compagnia di Gesù nell'America del Nord (Torino, 1898); Rev. Henry J. Browne, "The 'Italian Problem' in the Catholic Church of the United States, 1880-1900," Historical Records and Studies, vol. 35, 1946, pp. 46-75.

In 1860 foreign-born Italians in the United States numbered 11,677, and a decade later they had increased to 17,157.[35] These immigrants, anticlerical but Catholic, aroused the concern of diplomats and bishops. Six months after the Italian colony of Hoboken saw the incorporation of its church, the Italian ambassador to Washington, Commendatore Bertinatti, expressed a desire to visit the new Archbishop of New York, John McCloskey. Father Pamfilo da Magliano, who had led the settlement of Franciscans in New York State in 1855,[36] wrote to Archbishop McCloskey that Bertinatti was

> said to have received an order, with promises of funds from his Government, to adopt some plan for the amelioration and education of the Italians residing in New York. "I may advert," he adds, "that both he and the Consul General, apart from their political differences, are very zealous for the Catholic religion and seem very anxious to save, by some means, their countrymen from the baneful influence of Protestantizing societies. The plan that he would submit to Your Grace is to have an Italian church and an Italian school under the care of Italian Ecclesiastics." [37]

In the Spring of 1866 the parish of St. Anthony of Padua was created for both the Italians and the Irish of Manhattan's Lower West Side.[38] Philadelphia, New York, Newark, and Boston had organized Italian congregations by 1875. Between 1870 and 1880 over 43,000 new immigrants arrived and from 1880 to 1890 the tide swelled to almost 268,000.[39] The percentage of returnees was extremely high, however, and the U.S. census of 1890 registered only 182,580 foreign-born Italians. Thus, the Italian migration movement had an almost temporary character. In any case, Italian colonies were springing up rapidly in California, New England, Louisiana and New York and their religious care had entered a critical phase.

---

[35] U.S. Department of Commerce, Bureau of the Census, *Fourteenth Census of the United States, 1920* (Washington, D.C., 1922), II, p. 695.

[36] Giovanni Schiavo, *op. cit.*, pp. 322-331.

[37] Letter dated August 27, 1864, Fr. Pamfilo da Magliano to Archbishop J. McCloskey, AANY.

[38] St. Anthony of Padua School. *Souvenir of the Golden Jubilee, 1874-1924.* (New York, 1924).

[39] U.S. Department of Labor, Bureau of Immigration, *Annual Report of the Commissioner General of Immigration, 1920.* (Washington, D.C., 1920), pp. 181-182.

The "Italian Problem"

In July 1883 the Passionist priest Gaudentius Rossi forwarded an urgent letter from Baltimore to the Auxiliary Archbishop of New York, Michael A. Corrigan:

> Having learned from various organs of the public press that Your Grace is one of the members of the American hierarchy honored by our Holy Father, Leo XIII, with a special invitaton to Rome, I have several times felt interiorly moved to write to you on behalf of many thousand spiritually destitute Italian Catholics in this vast Republic, many of whom are in the State and diocese of New York. On various occasions I witnessed the spiritual wants of these poor, though industrious and well disposed people, in Pittsburgh, Pa., Louisville, Ky., Chicago, Ill., and, more recently, in Baltimore, Philadelphia and New York, preaching for them and administering the sacraments to them. But during the short period of a mission or retreat the spiritual good effected cannot be of a lasting duration without a sufficient number of zealous Pastors, able and willing to take care of the flock. In New York City, His Eminence the Cardinal Archbishop has in his great zeal entrusted the care of Italian Catholics to several Franciscan Fathers, who have for some years labored much for them. But these of late have so rapidly increased in number by immigration, that more spiritual help becomes a pressing necessity. This want is almost daily augmenting by new arrivals from Italy in different parts of these United States, and more especially in New York . . . ." [40]

Rossi suggested to Corrigan that he obtain a missionary band from Don Bosco in Turin and informed him that he would also urge Bishop O'Hara of Scranton, who was about to leave for Rome with Corrigan, to do the same.

On October 10, 1883, Archbishop Corrigan left for Rome. He had attempted in 1880 to induce some Italian priests to join his diocese but without complete success. As soon as he arrived in Italy, he approached Don Giovanni Bosco for help, which, at the moment, could not be given. Corrigan raised the issue of Italian immigration at the Vatican and possibly with other churchmen in Italy. He certainly discussed the problem with the American archbishops who were in Rome with him for a series of meetings in preparation for the Third Plenary Council of Baltimore. The assembled members of the

---

[40] Letter dated July 31, 1883, Fr. Gaudentius Rossi to Archbishop M. A. Corrigan, AANY.

American hierarchy concluded that there was no reason why the Italians should not be urged to attend existing churches if Italian-speaking priests were provided for them. The Council itself in 1884 even avoided the issue of Italian immigration. However, a new situation was emerging and missionary bands and mixed congregations were not an adequate response. A new system had to be adopted, along the lines of ethnic parishes already tried for German Americans.

Pressures were mounting. The new wave of immigration from Italy was creating strains and demands in the Irish parishes where Italians were settling. In 1866, St. Patrick's Old Cathedral parish, on Manhattan's Lower East Side, had been composed almost entirely of men and women of Irish birth or descent. In the parish school there were four boys of German parentage, two or three whose parents were French, and one whose father was a Negro. By 1882, the influx of Italians forced the church to make special arrangements, such as services conducted in Italian in the church basement on holy days and the feasts of patron saints. From 1882 to 1890 over a thousand marriages and five thousand baptisms were performed for Italians in that basement.

In his report to the bishop, the pastor reassured him that Italian children were admitted into the parish school without question.

> "We are anxious to receive them," he wrote. "We request the Italian priests to urge their people to send their children to the school. We have now in the school two hundred and fifty bright, intelligent Italian children, and we are now trying to arrange with the Brothers of the Christian Schools to provide Italian Brothers. When these are obtained, we shall open classes where Italian will be taught." [41]

By 1909 the parish school had 2,800 childen receiving free education.

> "Nine tenths of these children," Hannigan reported, "are of the Italian race, and bright, clever little pupils they are, destined one day to play an important part in the affairs of our country. One may see here, in miniature, the country assimilating the immense immigration it receives, and see it, too, without fears for the future welfare of the nation." [42]

---

[41] ——, "A Report of the Italian Work." in Stephen J. Hannigan, ed., *Souvenir of the Centennial Celebration of St. Patrick's (Old Cathedral). New York. 1809-1909.* n.p.

[42] Thomas F. Meehan, "The First Pastors of St. Patrick's," in Stephen J. Hannigan, *op. cit.*

But beneath the initial peaceful encounter between the Irish and the Italians, cultural and ethnic differences were simmering toward an acute expression of their conflicting interests. The clash was all the more acute because of the close contacts which accentuated their language and class differences. All of the cities with large Irish populations — New York, Boston, Philadelphia, Chicago, Baltimore, Detroit — had considerable Italian colonies by 1920. Almost eighty-five percent of the Italians lived in the eight states where seventy-five percent of the Irish had settled.[43] The latter resented the intrusion of a new group and began to move out.[44] Thomas F. Lynch, pastor of Transfiguration Church in the Lower East Side of New York, describes the growing conflicts in a typical letter that portrays what was repeated in church after church throughout the 1880's. The letter is addressed to the Vicar General of the Archdiocese.

> I write to make a formal application for the money, which has been collected in the Basement Chapel of this church, from the Italian congregation, which has worshipped there for nearly *nine years*. This money has been deposited in a Savings Bank, by the Franciscan Fathers of 106 Sullivan Street, in the name of the late Cardinal McCloskey, and the books are in the hands of the Franciscan Fathers. The amount of the fund is about $5,000.00 (five thousand dollars.) This sum is the accumulated money of the ordinary voluntary offerings (on the plate and for seats) of the Italian worshiping in the Basement. During this period of nine years' occupation of the Basement of this church by the Italians, the Rectors of this church have received no money in compensation for the *use of the Basement*, the *keeping* of the same *in a good state* of repairs, the *cleaning* of the same, the use of the vestments, and all other things necessary for the celebration of Mass. During the incumbency of Rev. Fr. McGean, the Italians paid for a new Sanctuary *railing* to replace one which they had thrown down, in a rush for palms on a Palm Sunday... The larger portion of the aforesaid fund has been accumulated during the last five years, and mainly through my effort in securing two Masses on Sunday instead of one (as formerly) for the accommodation of the Italians, and by insisting that they should be exhorted to support the church and charging five

---

[43] John B. Duff, "The Italians," in Joseph P. O'Grady, ed., *The Immigrant's Influence on Wilson's Peace Policies* (Lexington, Ky., 1967), p. 112. U.S. Bureau of the Census, *Fourteenth Census of the United States: 1920, Population*, II, 904.

[44] Rev. Daniel A. Quinn, "St. Patrick's Lyceum", in Stephen J. Hannigan, ed., op. cit.

cents for a few reserved seats in the middle aisles. When the Italians first began to worship in the Basement not more than two or three dollars was received on Sunday through them. Now, the usual amount of receipts from them on a Sunday is twenty dollars ($20.00).... The Italians do not constitute a separate congregation, but are a part of the congregation of this church and should therefore contribute their share toward the expenses.... Besides this special class for Italians, many Italian children frequent the Parochial School....

I respectfully submit that the accumulated fund would barely suffice to cover these different items of expense borne by the Rectors of this church. [45]

When in 1902 the suggestion was made to turn this church over to the Italians, one of the trustees "expressed himself in rather strong language on the Italians." [46]

Not only was the ecclesiastical financial system of urban America, based on the principle of voluntary participation and support, new to the immigrants' experience, but the cultural expressions of the faith common to Italians and Irishmen were at opposing poles. The Jansenistic, legal orientation of the Hibernian was confronted with the Mediterranean, ritual orientation of the Southern Italian. By the summer of 1892 some protests must have reached the Archbishop of New York. To Corrigan's inquiry, Father Lynch replied with a first hand account of a colorful aspect of Little Italy:

In answer to your favor of the 4th inst., in reference to public processions of Italians, carrying statues of Saints through the streets, I would say that no such procession has ever gone forth from this chruch. The procession of St. Donatus (which you forbade) was held on last Monday with all the noise of brass band and fireworks in the streets of the 6th and 14th wards of this city. This procession passed the church of the Transfiguration about ten o'clock. A priest (in cassock and surplice) and four altar boys came after the brass band. Then came the statue of St. Donatus carried on the shoulders of four men. Women and small girls followed with large and small candles and the men of the society brought up the rear. In order to find out whether the procession came from the church of the Most

---

[45] Letter dated September 20, 1886, Rev. Thomas F. Lynch to Rt. Rev. Msgr. Preston, V.G., AANY.

[46] Letter dated February 28, 1902, Rev. F. McLaughlin to Archbishop M. A. Corrigan, AANY. Also, Petition dated January 8, 1894, Giovanni Cantino et alii to Archbishop M. A. Corrigan, AANY, protesting that Transfiguration Church was kept closed during the most important holydays and asking the archbishop "to comply with the desires of the entire Catholic population."

Precious Blood I visited the church after the noon hour, and found that the procession had just disbanded, and the statue had been replaced in the usual place before the altar in that church. One of the Piacenza priests walked in the procession. The whole church was decorated with tinsel. The Italian girl selling pictures at the door of the church gave me all the necessary information to prove that these priests had disobeyed your orders.[47]

The feelings of the immigrants, on the other hand, can be surmised from a letter a Manhattan Italian sent in 1915 to the Bishop:

A short time ago in the church of St. Matthew, West 69th Street, an Italian mission was given by the Rev. Fathers Biasotti and Greco. This was a splendid success, a real awakening of the Italian colony in this part of the city.... Given an Italian Church with services in the Italian language, our people would not be so negligent in the observance of their religious duties. They are for the most part very poor and feel ashamed to attend the American Church, which they cannot even understand and which does not appeal to them in any way, and seems altogether a different thing from the Church so highly revered and respected in their own country. Here, in my humble opinion lies the reason that the parents are so indifferent to the church, and their children even more so....[48]

The religious fraternal societies never gave in to the orders of the bishops and processions disappeared only with the disappearence of the first generation, when a new sacred cosmos was absorbed by the children of the immigrants, patterned after the needs of the absorbing society. While Americans regarded the processions of the saints as evidence that the Catholic church was a lower class, foreign conglomerate, the patriotic attitudes of Italian priests were viewed as rebellion against the Papacy.[49] A typical view of an Irish pastor is in a letter to Corrigan in 1891:

---

[47] Letter dated August 10, 1892, Rev. Thomas F. Lynch to Archbishop M. A. Corrigan, AANY.

[48] Letter dated November 30, 1915, Mario Terenzio to Cardinal Farley, AANY.

[49] In 1905 John Talbott Smith summed up well the official ecclesiastical view of the Italian immigrants, unorthodox in their religious practice, ignorant, with pastors who didn't care for them, although progress was seen after 1902. As for political ideas, "Nothing more hateful to American Catholics could be named than the 20th of September, which the Italian colony celebrated as the consummation of national glory, the date of Victor Emmanuel's occupation of Rome and of the downfall of the temporal power. For very slight cause the Irish would

In reference to the conduct of the Piacenzan priests in this city on the occasion of the 20th of September.... The Piacenzan Fathers *never* speak in defense of the rights of the Holy Father either in or out of the pulpit and made no allusion to the celebration on the previous Sunday. They think it would be "bad policy"...and would estrange the people from them. Father Rampini gave an excellent discourse on the rights of the Holy Father on the Sunday before the 20th of September and several Italians came to him and told him he had a "hot head" on the subject and that he ought to be silent like the Piacenzan priests.[50]

In 1889, a complaint was sent to Rome charging that a priest sent by Scalabrini marched between two flags — the Italian and the American — which were born in a procession in New York for the unveiling of the statue of Garibaldi.[51]

The latent conflicts became increasingly open and often vehement. The patience of the immigrants was running short. They knew that they were abused, but they did not know how to fight back. Priests arriving from Italy were regarded as troublemakers and apostates and the burden of proof was with them if they wanted to be considered differently.[52] Father Gambera's insights, derived from forty years of work in the Italian colonies of New Orleans, Pittsburgh, New York, Philadelphia, Boston and Chicago, as reported in his *Diary*, further illumine the situation.

The hundreds of thousands of immigrants, from the beginning, were in need of churches, schools, old age homes, and being at that time poor and unaccustomed to support the church, many abandoned her rather than submit to

---

any moment have attacked the annual procession, eager to drive the Garibaldians off the face of the earth, as in the case of the Orangemen; and for considering them Catholics and aiding them to keep their faith alive, that was out of the question."

[50] Letter dated October 12, 1891, Rev. Thomas F. Lynch to Archbishop Corrigan, AANY.

[51] Letter dated December 21, 1889, Giovanni Cardinal Simeoni to Archbishop M. A. Corrigan, AANY. Simeoni was Prefect of the S. Congregation for the Propagation of the Faith.

[52] Letter dated August 24, 1917, R.E. Diffendorfer to Norman Thomas, NTP. In a statement Thomas prepared concerning the dispute that ensued from the publication of Mangano's book *Sons of Italy*, he recalls his six years of work with Italian newcomers in Harlem and expresses himself against creating divisions among them. Regarding Mangano's book, Thomas remarks that there are some errors, but not big ones; that what is said about ex-priests is not exact; that the 35 ex-priests of Italian origin do valuable work. But Mangano's position against the use of ex-priests was reinforced by Pannunzio in an article, that was unchallenged, for *Zion's Herald* of Boston. See NTP, Letters 1917.

that sacrifice and many were saying: the little Padre makes us lose our faith; he wants money. One has to pay as in a theater. The American bishops and the clergy of all nationalities, with rare exceptions, did not care for the Italians, and they excluded them from the churches, because they were slow to give and sometimes also misbehaved; and not rarely their Irish churches resounded with humiliating accusations against Italy and its citizens. This very grave condition demanded an assistance that was *ours*....[53]

Italian churchmen were looked upon with suspicion by a good part of the American clergy because they were introduced and recommended by Papal letters, and

"we were suspected," Gambera continues, "as secret agents and therefore, instead of receiving us with courteous, fraternal trust, they avoided us with unjust diffidence." [54]

It is interesting to recall here the findings of Bishop Clancy's inquiry on Irish immigrants in 1900 and the impact of emigration on their religious practice. The drinking habit was not helping religion and indifference to the sacraments was summed up by an elderly Irishman writing to the old country, when he said: "This is the greatest country in the world, fresh meat three times a day and you needn't give a damn for the priests." Then, to the question: Are many of the Irish people lost to the faith? the reply was: "While there is a leakage owing to the reasons given above, still I would say there is no wholesale loss. While a good many became indifferent, few apostatize or lose their faith." [55]

The Italian immigrant mass, on the other hand, was handicapped by ignorance of English, the frauds to which they were constantly exposed and the insults of prejudice.[56] The worsen-

---

Yet, the percentage of censured ex-priests or scandalous priests was probably no higher in the Italian than in the Irish, Polish or other ethnic-groups. In 1917, after more than thirty years of polemics, Norman Thomas stated that the Italian Ministers' Association had informed him that 35 Italian ex-priests were doing valuable work in the Protestant field. At that time, there were in the States probably more than the 823 Italian priests mentioned by the Catholic Directory. *Official Catholic Directory* (New York, 1918).

[53] Giacomo Gambera, *Diary*, p. 34. ACSC.

[54] Giacomo Gambera, *op. cit.*, p. 35.

[55] Letter dated October 13, 1900, Fr. J. Henry to Bishop J. Clancy of Elphin, Ireland, AANY.

[56] Letter dated April 2, 1884, E. P. Bergamini to Archbishop M. A. Corrigan, AANY. "Yours of the 1st at hand," Bergamini writes, "and would say, we would judge that we have forwarded to Italy about one million and a half Francs as I said in my previous letter for support

ing situation prompted further action in both Italy and the United States. In 1884 Cardinal Sanfelice of Naples circulated a letter to several Italian and American archbishops announcing the Constitution of committees for the protection of Italian immigrants in America.[57] At the request of Archbishop Corrigan of New York, the Congregation for the Propagation of the Faith in Rome began to scout around for pious, zealous and educated priests to be sent to assist the immigrants in America. In 1887 Bishop Scalabrini of Piacenza began an intense, intelligent campaign on behalf of the immigrants and founded the Congregation of the Missionaries of St. Charles for this purpose.[58] The Salesians began to send their priests from Turin.[59] The priests of the Catholic Apostolate, who ar-

---

of their families and to prepay passages. As a general rule the Italians get along fairly. They are willing to attempt any kind of rough labor work and when positions are obtained they live as cheap as possible, but again there are a lot of intruders who for a sum of money provide them situations and then maybe discharge in a day or so. I will call your attention to a day or two ago, when counterfeit rail-road tickets to Pittsburgh, Pa., were sold for $3.00 eash and was proved to be worthless sold by Italians but under the name of Mahoney & Co." (sic)

[57] Letter dated July 15, 1884, Giovanni Cardinal Simeoni to Archbishop M. A. Corrigan, AANY.

[58] Letters dated August 18, 1887; January 7, 1888; February 27, 1888, Bishop Giovanni Battista Scalabrini to Archbishop M. A. Corrigan, AANY.

Letters dated December 16, 1887; April 13, 1888; May 28, 1888; August 10, 1888; October 4, 1888, Archbishop M. A. Corrigan to Bishop G. B. Scalabrini, General Archives of the Congregation of St. Charles, Rome. In these and other letters exchanged between the Archbishop of New York and the Bishop of Piacenza we can trace the beginning of a sudden development of Italian churches in New York, the zeal of the priests and the response of the immigrants. Scalabrini (1839-1905) has been the key figure in calling the attention of Church and Government in Italy and in North and South America to the problem of mass emigration and in organizing religious and social assistance to the migrants. See, M. Caliaro - M. Francesconi, *L'Apostolo degli Emigranti: Giovanni Battista Scalabrini.* (Milano, 1968), pp. 238-344.

A listing of the writings of Scalabrini and a bibliography are also given in this volume, pp. 603-624. Also, "Missioni di San Carlo dell'Istituto Cristoforo Colombo instituite negli Stati del Nord America," *Bollettino dell'Emigrazione*, Anno 1903, n. 1, pp. 59-60.

[59] Ernst Coppo, "Salesians of Don Bosco," in *The Catholic Church in the United States of America.* Vol. 1, Religious Communities of Men. (New York, 1912) pp. 388-390.

rived in 1882, intensified their activity,[60] and so did the Franciscans and various diocesan priests.

Italian parishes

The Italians of East Harlem in New York wanted a decent place of worship away from the courtyard where the Society of Our Lady of Mt. Carmel was forced to have its celebration. They obtained their parish in 1884, when the parish of the Holy Rosary was also erected for another segment of the same colony. In 1882 the Italian colony of Hamilton Ferry in Brooklyn organized its parish exclusively on ethnic lines. In 1886 the Italian parish of St. Raphael's was erected on 41st St. in Manhattan, and the following year the second parish of Our Lady of Mt. Carmel was established in Brooklyn. The first Italian parish on New York's Lower East Side, St. Joachim, was founded by the priests of Bishop Scalabrini in 1888. In 1889, the first Italian parish in the Bronx, St. Rocco's, was opened for that colony. During the 1880's, Italian parishes were established in Boston, New Haven, Philadelphia, Newark and several other cities. A network was emerging that would have included all Italian colonies all over the States. Either fraternal societies under the name of a patron saint[61] started the procedure for their own church or little groups of immigrants applied directly to the Bishops. A letter typical of the latter approach was sent in 1908 to Archbishop Farley of New York.

> As Catholic faithful, we feel the duty to call to the attention of your Excellency that in this country of Van Nest — West Farm — there exists an Italian colony numbering almost 2,000, that lives completely forgetful of its Christian obligations.
> The cause is that in this part of the city, there are no Italian churches or chapels where a priest of the same nationality, preaching the word of God, could keep alive in the hearts of all the sentiment of true Catholics. The people, anxious for this duty, ignorant of the English language, are forced to walk five or six miles to go to an

---

[60] Domenico Pistella, *La Madonna del Carmine e gli Italiani d'America* (New York, 1954), pp. 167. Nicholas J. Reagan, "The Italian Custody of the Immaculate Conception," in *The Catholic Church in the United States*, vol. I, *op. cit.*, pp. 236-239.

[61] Domenico Pistella, *op. cit.*, p. 45. G. Gambera, *Diary, op. cit.*, passim. Lawrence Pisani and Paul Falcigno, "The History of St. Michael's of New Haven," in *75th Anniversary-St. Michael's Church* (New Haven, 1965).

Italian Church; this, as your Excellency will understand, is not for all, nor is it always possible.

It is for this reason that the Italians of this area would be happy to have *their own Chapel with a good Italian priest* and with this letter, through us, they make an appeal for it to your Excellency, certain that you will meet their ardent desire.[62]

Other groups, tired of using the basement of Irish churches, wanted their own and succeeded in their appeal in obtaining one.[63]

The cultural, financial and job interests of the Irish group that dominated the hierarchy of the Church could not be reconciled to the Italian "invasion" into their territories — the gray areas of the cities and the low paid, unskilled jobs. Thus, Italian immigrants separated themselves from Protestants and even other Catholics and within the territory previously conquered by the Irish, they carved out their own neighborhoods and their own churches. The ethnic parish system, to be sure, was not closed to the significant segment of the Americanizing population that wanted to identify with English speaking parishes, nor did it succeed in drawing back into the fold all the people of the first generation who had become indifferent or the tiny minority (between 0.5 and 1 percent) that had converted to Protestantism.[64] It became, however, the most relevant institutional organization supporting the immigrants in their encounter with the surrounding groups and the dominant society.

The presence within American society of a huge mass of immigrants with a different language and value orientation constituted a special type of integration. The ethnic parish can be viewed both as an instrument of power for the immigrant group and as a subsystem in the stratification of the larger society. The strength of the ethnic community was the guarantee of successful integration. Its power was derived from its social solidarity, which shielded the immigrant from

---

[62] Letter dated May 17, 1908, Angelo Rezzano et alii to Cardinal Farley, AANY.

[63] Letter dated December 9, 1914, G. Valentino et alii to Cardinal Farley, AANY.

[64] Henry D. Jones, *The Evangelical Movement Among the Italians in New York City. A Study* (New York, 1934), pp. 39. This research was done for the Comity Committee of the Federation of Churches of Greater New York and the Brooklyn Church and Mission Federation. Rev.

anomic conditions and established a basis for bargaining with the larger society. "The church structure of an ethnic group threatened with loss of identity serves more than any other structure to organize the group as a community system." [65] The network of Italian parishes functioned to maintain the ethnic personality by organizing the group around the familiar religious and cultural symbols and the behavioral modes of the fatherland. In the peasant communities of Southern Italy, the potential immigrants conceived of their ethnic identity in terms of concrete and particular symbols and for them religion was fused with all institutions and roles. It was more a way of life than a prescribed set of beliefs and practices. In America, the peasant way of life had to be *consciously reconstituted as well as readjusted* to the conditions of urban life.[66] Thus, the immigrants most successfully transplanted

---

Frederick H. Wright, D. D. "How to Reach the Italians in America. Shall They Be Segregated, Missioned, Neglected or Welcomed?" *The Missionary Review of the World*, N. S. XXX (August, 1917), pp. 589-594: "There are over three million Italians in this country, and the work of evangelization, although thirty or more years old, has only touched the outer fringe of the problem." Minnie J. Reynolds, "The Religious Renaissance in Italy," *The Missionary Review of the World*, N.S. XXIV (August, 1911), pp. 597-603: "There are today 220 Italian Protestant churches in the United States. In over 100 of them the first nucleus was a group of Italians who had been Waldensians in Italy." Rev. Chas. E. Edwards, "Our Latin and Slavonic Population," *The Assembly Herald* (August, 1901), pp. 300-302. Rev. G. P. Williams, "Italian Work in Chicago," *ibid.*, p. 303. "Italian Work in and near Newark, N. J.," *ibid.*, p. 306-307. The Montclair Italian Evangelical Missionary Society, *First Annual Report*, combined with an address by Mr. Alberto Pecorini on the Italian Immigrant Problem, delivered at the Annual Meeting, November 30, 1903, pp. 16. Rev. William Wynkoop McNair, "The Evangelization of Our Italians," *The Assembly Herald*, XI, (August, 1905), pp. 404-409. Rev. Robert Bonner Jack, "Italians in Lehigh Presbytery," *Ibid.*, pp. 414. Rev. Samuel McLanahan, "New Jersey and her Foreigners," *Ibid.*, pp. 414-415. Antonio Mangano, *Sons of Italy: A Social and Religious Study of the Italians in America* (New York, 1917), pp. 163-166. John Bisceglia, Th. D., *Italian Evangelical Pioneers* (Kansas City, Mo., 1948), pp. 14-17.

[65] W. Loyd Warner and Leo Srole, *The Social System of American Ethnic Groups* (New Haven, 1949), p. 218.

[66] Vladimir C. Nahirny and Joshua A. Fishman, "Ukrainian Language Maintenance Efforts in the United States," in Joshua A. Fishman, ed., *Language Loyalty in the United States. The Maintenance and Perpetuation of Non-English Mother Tongues by American Ethnic and Religious Groups* (The Hague, 1966), pp. 318-357.

their religion, that aspect of their old way of life which had been institutionally sustained in the old country. The immigrant celebrated his festivals, interacted in the church societies, interpreted his family and his world in the symbolic matrix of the ethnic parish. The Italian immigrant did not care for the legal structure of religion as long as he had its reassuring symbolic presence in his midst, something that he could take for granted. The ethnic parish was not only an efficient instrument of social control, but it sanctioned, to a degree, cultural change in the ethnic community, an indispensable condition for its proper functioning as a subsystem of the national society. If ethnic stratification is viewed as an on-going process rather than as a structure, then we may say that the ethnic parish presided over the change from a communal to an associational society, a transition necessary for the social mobility of the immigrants and for their integration.[67]

When the process of building ethnic parishes was concluded, New York City, for example, had seventy-four Italian churches, distributed as follows:

Italian Ethnic Parishes and Chapels in New York City

Years	Manhattan	Brooklyn	Bronx	Queens	Staten Island
1866-1900	8	5	1	—	—
1900-1924	21	9	7	1	6
1924-1961	1	9	4	2	—

Source: Thomas B. Kenedy, ed. *Official Catholic Directory*. New York: Kenedy & Sons, 1967.

Official statistics on national churches report smaller figures than actually existed.[68] Yet, the Catholic Directory for 1918 reports the existence of 580 Italian churches and chapels

---

[67] Tomotsu Shibutani and Kian M. Kwan, *Ethnic Stratification*. A Comparative Approach (New York, 1968), p. 131.
[68] François Houtart, *Aspects Sociologiques du Catholicisme Américain, Vie Urbaine et Institutions Réligicuses* (Paris, 1957), p. 51.

for an Italian population of 3,028,000.[69] Churches were built as symbols of the ethnic community, not only in the cities where Italians lived in congested, over-crowded neighborhoods but also in rural areas and small towns. Luigi Villari, in a 1908 consular report for the district of Philadelphia — covering Pennsylvania, Delaware, Maryland, Virginia, West Virginia, Georgia, North Carolina and South Carolina — noted that there was an Italian population of less than 300,000 which was served by forty Italian Churches. He adds a description of the social environment of these ethnic churches:

> Among the manifestations of colonial life the religious processions, the so-called "parades" of the Societies, are to be noted, and above all, the banquets; they are tendered on all occasions, opportune and inopportune, for marriages, baptisms, to celebrate the feast of the patron saints, for the departure of a barber who goes to spend a couple of months in Italy and then to celebrate his return, to console a countryman on the eve of his departure for prison for some crime or other and then to congratulate him when he has finished serving his time. For funerals one spends fabulous sums; one has even seen processions of forty carriages for

---

[69] A. Palmieri, *Il grave problema religioso italiano negli Stati Uniti.* (Firenze, 1921), p. 46. In this valuable pamphlet and in his other writings Palmieri strongly advocated an efficient ethnic church to remedy evident ethnic conflicts. Without ambiguity, however, he points out that "the Catholic faith was solidly rooted in the hearts of the immigrants," and was transmitted to the second generation; that some Irish Bishops took the initiative in erecting Italian parishes and schools; that ethnic religious organizations were functional and temporary; that the future trend would be toward an American Catholic group made up of people of different ethnic backgrounds. The debate between mostly Irish and Italian priests on the pastoral needs of Italian immigrants had begun at the time of mass emigration. Gennaro De Concilio began writing on this problem in 1886 and was slowly followed by several articles and pamphlets describing the religious conditions of the Italian immigrants, the lack of clergy and the lack of religious instruction. Bernard J. Lynch, "The Italians in New York," *op. cit.* John T. McNicholas, "The Need of American Priests for the Italian Missions," *The Ecclesiastical Review*, XXXIX (December, 1908) 681-682; D. Lynch. "The Religious Conditions of Italians in New York," *America*, X, (March 21, 1914), pp. 558-559. "Catholic Italian Losses," *The Literary Digest*, XLVII, (October 11, 1913), p. 636; H. J. Desmond, *The Neglected Italians. A Memorial to the Italian Hierarchy* (Milwaukee, 1900 c.), pp. 11; "Our Italians," *The Catholic Messenger*, (December 3, 1914), p. 6; Rev. J. Gambera, "Our Italian Immigrants." *The New World*, (February 25, 1911), p. 2 . Gambera's article is a rejoinder to an article on Italian immigrants by Rev. J. J. Loughram, *Catholic Citizen* of Milwaukee (February 4, 1911); Rev. Dr. Salvatore Cianci, *Il lavoro sociale in mezzo*

the funeral of a new-born baby. Sometimes lectures, theatrical representations, or concerts are given, but almost always without success, because there is an absolute intellectual apathy even in the affluent class.[70]

In the South, the most exceptional case was the parish of Tontitown, Arkansas. Here Father Bandini was pastor and mayor of a town, composed exclusively of Italian settlers. Aside from this unique case, Italian churches were also erected in Alabama and Louisiana. Reporting on his trip in 1903 through the southern states, the Italian Ambassador, Mayor Des Planches, mentioned several Italian churches. Despite the fact that the official policy of the Italian Government at the time was anticlerical, the Ambassador repeatedly comments upon the ways in which the church was serving the immigrants. A curious example is offered by the experience of the Italian Sylvestrine Benedictines in Kansas. In 1910 the two priests who came to work among the miners were met by rocks and rotten vegetables thrown at them by those they came to serve. Then slowly, in the following seventeen years, seven Italian churches were built and the Italian priests moved away only after the mines had closed and the miners re-emigrated.[71]

---

agli Italiani (Milwaukee, 1913), pp. 20; P. Francesco Beccherini, *Il fenomeno dell'emigrazione negli Stati Uniti d'America*, (Sansepolcro, 1906), pp. 35; Rev. J. Zarrilli, D. D., Ph. D., *A Prayerful Appeal to the American Hierarchy In Behalf of the Italian Catholic Cause in the United States* (Two Harbors, Minn., 1924), pp. 26. Gioacchino Maffei, *L'Italia nell'America del Nord* (Valle di Pompei, 1924), pp. 164.

[70] Luigi Villari, "L'emigrazione italiana nel distretto consolare di Filadelfia," *Bollettino dell'Emigrazione*, Anno 1908, n. 16, pp. 26-50. F. Prat, "Gli Italiani negli Stati Uniti e specialmente nello Stato di New York," *Bollettino dell'Emigrazione*, Anno 1902, n. 2, pp. 14-41. Although the *Bollettino* was an official publication of the Italian Government, Prat does not hesitate to write: "In the United States there exists a good number of Italian Catholic priests. In New York and Brooklyn there are seventeen Italian parishes or churches with about fifty Italian priests. We can testify that, generally speaking, their work is efficacious not only for the religious assistance of the immigrants, but also for the preservation of our language...." He adds that the visit of Bishop Scalabrini will certainly renew the spirit of "italianità" in the Italian colonies; that there are very few Italians of Protestant faith; and that Italian migrants are not prone to change religion.

[71] P. Pietro Bandini, "Origine della colonia italiana di Tontitown nell'Arkansas," *Bollettino dell'Emigrazione*, Anno 1903, n. 1, pp. 61-62. Giovanni Schiavo, *op. cit.*, p. 495. *The Springdale News*, (Springdale, Washington County, Arkansas, May 15, 1908) Souvenir number, Section

In North Michigan and North Minnesota, as we learn from the *Bollettino dell'Emigrazione*, there were Italian churches in Calumet, Iron Mountain, Vulcan, Hibbing, Duluth, Eveleth.[72] In the Northeast of the United States there was no colony of some importance without its church, especially in Massachusetts, Connecticut, New Jersey and Pennsylvania. In New York, Italian churches were erected all across the state up to Lake Ontario.[73]

The separation of church and state offered free ground for competition with the Irish and then for progressive accommodation. Today, the third generation of Italians go to the same colleges as those of other ethnic origin and marry outside their own ethnic group, mostly with the Irish. A new group, in fact, is foreseen by some sociologists which would merge Irish, Italian Polish and others, based on religion rather than national origin.[74] Although some unique social identity persists, the Italians' cultural expression of Catholicism has undergone strong Irish influence and their value system has become very much that of the American middle class.

Two. E. Mayor des Planches, *Attraverso gli Stati Uniti. Per l'emigrazione Italiana.* (Torino, 1913), pp. 321. Roger Baudier, *The Catholic Church in Louisiana* (New Orleans, 1939).

[72] Attilio Castigliano, "Origine, sviluppo, importanza ed avvenire delle colonie italiane del Nord Michigan e del Nord Minnesota," *Bollettino dell'Emigrazione*, Anno 1913, n. 7, pp. 3-22.

[73] Msgr. Gherardo Ferrante, "Chiese e scuole parrocchiali italiane," in *Gli Italiani negli Stati Uniti d'America* (New York, 1906), pp. 89-94. William Pizzoglio, D. D., *St. Mary of Mt. Carmel Church, Utica, N.Y. Its History and Progress from the Beginning to the Present* (1896-1936), pp. 64. Pio Parolin, *Diario*, at the Center for Migration Studies of New York, Giovanni Sofia, *Missioni Scalabriniane in America* (Rome, 1939) pp. 223. Pio Parolin, *Ricordo del venticinquesimo anno della fondazione della Chiesa di San Pietro in Syracuse, N.Y.* (Syracuse, 1920), pp. 58. P. Costantino Sasso, *Parrocchia della Madonna di Pompei in New York (1892-1942)*, pp. 102.

[74] Will Herberg, *Protestant - Catholic - Jew*, (New York, 1955); Milton Gordon, *Assimilation in American Life* (New York, 1964); Daniel P. Moynihan and Nathan Glazer, *Beyond the Melting Pot: The Negroes, Puerto Ricans, Jews, Italians and Irish of New York City* (Cambridge, Mass., 1963). "Religion and Race seem to define the major groups into which American society is evolving as the specifically national aspect of ethnicity declines .... We can discern that the next stage of the evolution of the immigrant groups will involve a Catholic group ..." (p. 314). Monroe W. Karmin, "Ethnic Power: Nationality Groups Aim to Vie with Negroes for Government Aid," *The Wall Street Journal* (April 24, 1969). Nicholas J. Russo, "Three Generations of Italians in New York

Conclusion

The role of the ethnic parishes must be studied in the social context within which they operated and evaluated in terms of the function performed for the people they served, not from the viewpoint of the handful of displaced intellectuals and radicals who ran the ethnic press. But present research in this field barely scratches the surface. Manuscripts and letters, newspaper files and occasional publications should be patiently analyzed to reconstruct the whole saga of the immigrant communities and their churches across the United States.

In the 1880's when the immigrants felt the need for separateness, ethnic Vicariates were proposed as well as duplex parishes. Both organizational forms were incompatible with the aspirations of the immigrants and their priests. The Vicariates would have established a permanent separation; the duplex parish would have sanctioned a permanent inferiority.[75] The ethnic parish, instead, functioned as the intermediate institution which the immigrants needed and worked to obtain and in which they benefited from the meeting of old and new. In the case of the Italian parishes, whose beginning can be doc-

---

City: Their Religious Acculturation," *The International Migration Review*, III, n. 2, (Spring, 1969), pp. 3-17.

[75] Letters dated May 21, 1888; May 24, 1888; June 1, 1888, Rev. Marcellino Moroni to Archbishop M. A. Corrigan, AANY. Moroni discusses the idea of special vicariates for Italians allegedly attributed to Msgr. de Concilio and of his meeting with de Concilio regarding the pamphlet he had written, *Sullo stato religioso degl'italiani negli Stati Uniti d'America* (Newark, 1886) See, Raffaele Ballerini, "Delle Condizioni religiose degli emigrati italiani negli Stati Uniti," *Civiltà Cattolica*, XIII, II, 1888, pp. 641-653. The system of duplex parishes was already in use in 1880 in New York. "While all that we have spoken of refers to the upper church, let it not be forgotten that we have three Masses in the basement for the Italians of the parish, and that Father Ferretti, under Father McLoughlin's direction does very efficient work for that portion of his flock. Nearly twelve hundred of the sons of sunny Italy attend these services, besides which they have vespers and evening services without end. Father McLoughlin did his best to make the two races coalesce, by compelling the Italians to attend services in the upper church, but found that far better results could be obtained by having the two people worshiping separately. There are quite a number, however, of the better class who prefer to worship in the upper church...." *Souvenir History of Transfiguration Parish — Mott Strett, New York 1827-1897* (New York, 1897), pp. 44.

umented, the decision to form a separate church usually came from the immigrants themselves, rather than from the priests or the *prominenti*.[76] The parish role was essential for the reconstruction of the southern Italian villages in urban America because, as Suttles recently observed, "churches (for the ethnic groups) provide a common establishment, where a continuing group of people waive their individuality in favor of their common welfare." [77] The church was virtually the only body of social control which acknowledged the ethnic factor, which Italians could potentially make their own and whose services they could feel were simply what was due to them. The few Italian labor unions lacked the total appeal of the ethnic church while Protestant missionaries and socialist and anarchist groups were so peripheral to the immigrant mass that they produced a handful of exceptional figures and nothing else.[78]

If we keep in mind the distinction between being "moral," or practicing, and being "religious," we can conclude that the ethnic parishes with their saints and festivals, novenas and processions, and their "indifferent" congregations, held together the Italians in America, for they embodied the ideals in which the people believed and united them structurally through strong group ritual and social functions. The network of ethnic parishes became the basis of "religious success." Thomas Meehan, in the turmoil of the 1903 immigration movement, summed up the achievements of the Italians in the boroughs of Manhattan, Bronx, Staten Island and the suburban countries under the jurisdiction of the New York diocese: 18 parishes; 2 chapels; 7 churches used in part by Italians; 52 priests; 133,100 parish members; 8,670 baptisms; 1,902 mar-

---

[76] Giacomo Gambera, *Diary*, ACSC. Francesco Leveroni, et al., *Venticinque anni di missione fra gli Italiani immigrati di Boston, Mass.* (Milano, 1913), pp. 359.

[77] Gerald D. Suttles, *The Social Order of the Slum. Ethnicity and Territory in the Inner City* (Chicago, 1968), p. 42.

[78] g.b., "La nostra organizzazione," *Il Proletario*, Anno X, n. 32 (August 12, 1906), p. 1: "In America in a city that numbers 650 thousand Italians (New York) there are a couple of hundred socialists registered with the party. In a city that numbers 140 thousand Italians (Philadelphia) those registered are one hundred. I won't speak of other localities, the proportion does not change at all. If one thinks that two thirds at least of these comrades come to America already socialists, tell, tell me, comrades, to what has been reduced our work? The naked and crude truth is this: we are not doing our duty, because if

riages; 6 schools; 3,316 pupils; 5,770 in Sunday School.[79]   Along with the parishes, there were societies, orphanages, newspapers, hospitals and mission bands.   As an example of the latter, *L'Apostolato Italiano* had worked over a period of nine months in 42 parishes, in 15 Eastern dioceses where there were an estimated 150,000 Italians.   Of these as many as 19,970 attended the mission sermons and 14,980 took advantage of the occasion to receive the sacraments, in great part after many years of indifference.[80]

The apparently highly organized, separate community, which the ethnic Catholic Church provided, made the Italians another functioning group in the American mosaic, a position for which the immigrants opted as soon as they realized they had their best opportunity in staying rather than going back.

---

the immigrants escape our section it's because we have isolated our-selves from all, despising and offending those who do not think like us, secluding ourselves in our halls and discussing theories and comrades, when we are not quarreling, while outside the priest and the *prominenti* infiltrate everywhere and turn the water, that is the immigration, to their own mill."   Melvin Dubofsky, "Success and Failure of Socialism in New York City, 1900-1918: A Case Study," *Labor History*, IX, n. 3 (Fall, 1968), pp. 361-375.   Of all the nationalities in New York, the Italians "are relatively and proportionately the weakest in the Socialist organization."

[79] Thomas E. Meehan, "Evangelizing the Italians," *The Messenger*, III, Fifth Series, 1903, pp. 16-32.   "Our Duty to Our Fellow Catholic Italians," *ibid.*, pp. 89-92: "Experience shows that there is little difficulty in getting Italian parents to send their children to Catholic schools." (p. 91).

[80] *L'Apostolato Italiano*, Report of July 7, 1913, published in *L'Italiano in America*.

Three Generations of Italians in New York City: their Religious Acculturation

by Nicholas John Russo *

American sociologists have long been absorbed by the processes of assimilation and acculturation which successive waves of American immigrants have undergone. Due to the variety of methodologies, theories, and concepts applied to study in this area, there are many divergent findings. With regard to the religious practices and attitudes of the immigrants and their descendants, it is not certain, for example, whether Italian-Americans of the second and third generations neglected the religious practices of their parents, or maintained a pattern of increased religious activity associated with increased Americanization.

The purpose of this study, therefore, was to reconcile apparently incompatible sociological findings with regard to immigrants and their children, by: 1) isolating the religious factor in the assimilation process of the Italian-Americans; 2) evaluating the role of the Catholic Church in their acculturation to American life, and 3) delineating a before-and-after situation of the religious practices and attitudes of the Italian-Americans, who were contrasted with the Irish, as the dominant Catholic group in New York City.

To understand fully the process of cultural and social assimilation which the Italian immigrant and his descendants underwent, we analyzed the cultural forces which helped to shape him. Lack of political unity, government by foreign nations, and a rigid provincialism made the Southern Italian peasant quite unique. A strong sense of family-centered unity prevailed, as well as a loyalty to the community, which had its own class structure, and where few men and hardly any women received a formal education.

---

* Rev. Nicholas John Russo is Professor of Sociology at Cathedral College, Douglaston, New York.

The Italians manifested a casual attitude toward religion, which was often interspersed with what seemed to some Americans to be "magic and superstition." Creedal tenets were not taken very seriously. Instead, there was an intense devotion to the warm personages of Mary and the saints. Southern Italian Catholicism was a personal, parochial type of religion. The clergy as well as the people were poorly instructed. Formal religious instruction was absent, and adherence to Catholicism ranged from indifference to great devotion. To the southern Italian, the government, and everyone else outside his little village, was suspect; no national spirit existed and there was no cooperation with anyone outside the family circle (amoral familism).[1]

Once in New York City, he gravitated towards the ethnic slum or ghetto, living on the same block as his fellow townsmen from Italy. He remained aloof from all others, and this provincialism, used as a defense against "feeling out of place" in the new environment, reinforced his traditional bonds and enabled him to resist the influence of the outside world.

At that time (1885-1915) Americans, knowing little of cultural pluralism, feared that the Italians would never become assimilated and that the immigrant culture would perpetuate itself. However, the preservation of the ethnic community was the immigrant's means of gaining a sense of security and a feeling of belonging within a new world, which he found strange and hostile. Only his "paesani" could understand his feelings of alienation and could provide him with compensatory social and psychological satisfaction. In fact, the immigrant's loyalty to relatives and friends extended to financial matters. In time of need, the immigrant was able to secure assistance from them and seldom had to seek aid from welfare groups. Unfortunately, this regionalism was the deterrent which prevented Italians from forming large mutual-aid and philanthropic associations that could have been of greater assistance in the areas of health, welfare, and education.

The dilemma of providing for the spiritual needs of the constant waves of Italian immigrants caused "the Italian problem" in the American Catholic Church. This problem stemmed from the following factors: (1) a large Italian immigrant

---

[1] Edward C. Banfield, *The Moral Basis of a Backward Society.* Illinois: Free Press of Glencoe, 1958.

population which was poorly instructed in matters of religion; (2) variant political-religious conceptions brought from Italy; (3) few Italian priests in America; (4) inadequate churches; (5) ethnic antipathies; (6) Protestant proselytizing. Italians were often treated with prejudice and contempt, even by fellow Catholics, and because of the animosity which existed between the Church and the Kingdom of Italy, Italian men, in particular, were frequently anticlerical, although they still considered themselves Catholics.[2]

Some claimed that the Irish clergy and hierarchy did little to welcome the Italians into the ecclesial community or to reinforce them in their religious status. Therefore, some Italians joined small Protestant churches and sects, which represented a protest against the religious and social exclusion by American Catholics. American bishops established Italian-language or national parishes, and recruited priests and nuns from Italy, particularly from religious orders.

The national parish helped to maintain ethnic solidarity and thus checked rapid assimilation. It, therefore, prevented widespread social disorganization but prepared the immigrants and their children for gradual assimilation into American life. The national parish enabled newcomers to retain their ethnic ties while becoming Americanized, thereby acting as a bridge between the old world and the new.[3]

To the Italian, the American-Catholic Church was predominantly an American-Irish Church and it was characterized as: (1) English-speaking; (2) Jansenistic; (3) overly reverential for and loyal to the clergy; (4) activistic; (5) conservative; (6) too concerned with fund-raising; (7) pervaded with a supernationalistic spirit, identified with all things Irish. The Italians resented the Irish domination of the American Church, as did other Catholic immigrant groups. Some churchmen feared

---

[2] Henry J. Browne, "The Italian Problem and the Catholic Church of the United States, 1880-1900," *United States Catholic Historical Society: Historical Records and Studies*, XXXV (1946) pp. 46-72.

Aurelio Palmieri, *Il grave problema religioso italiano negli Stati Uniti*. Florence: Libreria Editrice Fiorentina, 1921.

Antonio Grumelli, "Religious Behavior of Migrants," *International Migration Digest*, Vol. II (Fall, 1965), pp. 158-64.

Hervé Carrier, *The Sociology of Religious Belonging*. New York: Herder and Herder, 1965, pp. 89-90.

[3] John L. Thomas, "The New Immigration and Cultural Pluralism," *American Catholic Sociological Review*, XV (December, 1954) pp. 310-22.

that this antagonism posed a serious threat to the future of the Church. However, most immigrants remained nominally loyal to the Church, albeit in their own way.[4]

Italians reacted to American-Irish Catholicism in three ways: (1) by conforming and internalizing Irish-American religious norms; (2) by challenging them either from within the Church, or from without by embracing Protestantism; (3) by withdrawing and becoming indifferent. Our research supports Feminella's theory: most Italians either conformed or became indifferent to American-Irish customs, but with each succeeding generation, more Italians tended to conform to the Irish norms.[5]

Since World War II, the children and grandchildren of the immigrants have left the Italian national parishes and have moved to more residential areas within the city, as well as to the suburbs. Thus, they have encountered many Irish-American priests and teaching nuns and have been subjected to "Hibernization."

The Research Design: Hypothesis, Sample and Methodology

Since all signs indicate that in religious matters, increased Americanization of the Italian brought about a gradual resemblance to Irish norms, we would hypothesize that in religious

---

[4] John J. Kane, "Catholic Separatism," *Catholicism in America*. New York: Harcourt and Brace and Co., 1953, p. 54.

Desmond Fennell, "Continental and Oceanic Catholicism," *America* (March 26, 1955), p. 670.

Robert Ernst, *Immigrant Life in New York City, 1828-1863*. New York: King's Crown Press, 1949, p. 105.

Maldwyn A. Jones, *American Immigration*. Chicago: University of Chicago Press, 1960, p. 225.

Humbert S. Nelli, "Italians in Urban America: A Study in Ethnic Adjustment," *International Migration Review*, I (Summer, 1967), pp. 48-49.

Thomas F. O'Dea, *American Catholic Dilemma*. New York: Mentor-Omega Books, 1962, pp. 121-22.

Carolyn Zeleny, "Irish-American," in *One America*, eds. Brown and Roucek. New York: Prentice-Hall Inc., 1952, p. 61.

Jessie Bernard, "Biculturality: A Study of Social Schizophrenia," *Jews in a Gentile World*, eds. Graeber and Britt. New York: The Macmillan Co., 1942, pp. 289-91.

[5] Francis X. Feminella, "The Impact of Italian Migration and American Catholicism," *The American Catholic Sociological Review*, Vol. XXII, (Fall, 1961), pp. 233-41.

attitudes and practices, the longer the Italians are in America, the more they tend to resemble the Irish.

To evaluate the results of the encounter between the Italian immigrant and American Catholicism, the following sources, both historical and sociological were used:

1. Theoretical and research materials on assimilation, acculturation, and generational differences in religious practices.

2. Books and articles from the field of history, relating to Italian immigration, and similar materials from ecclesiastical records and periodicals.

3. Interviews conducted in the Italian language with priests, nuns and laity, who emigrated to America.

4. A questionnaire, which constituted the foundation of our study, was administered to three generations of Italians and to all generations of the Irish. More than 2,000 questionnaires were randomly distributed by priests in 21 parishes in New York City. The total Catholic population of these parishes was 330,000. The parishes were both Italian national parishes and "American" parishes. To accommodate the elderly, first-generation Italians, five hundred copies of the questionnaire were printed in Italian. About sixty percent of all questionnaires were returned.

5. The results were analyzed by means of the Chi-square tests, enabling us to judge whether the three generations of Italians differed significantly from each other and from the Irish in religious practices and attitudes.

The Findings:

This study's questionnaire was administered to a population drawn from New York City in order to test the theories and findings on cultural and social assimilation, as they develop through the generations. Would there be a second generation "dip" and a return to the ancestral faith in the third generation (Hansen - Herberg),[6] or would the results show a gradual increase in church attendance with American-

---

[6] Marcus Lee Hansen, "The Third Generation in America," *Commentary*, XIV (November, 1952), pp. 492-500.

Will Herberg, *Protestant, Catholic, Jew.* Garden City, N. Y.: Doubleday and Co., 1955.

ization (Lenski)? [7] What has happened to those religious practices which were "peculiar" to the Southern Italian? Have
the Irish influenced the Italians in matters of religious practices and attitudes because of their position of "intermediacy"
in immigration history (Barron)? [8] If so, did the Italians
"take on the ways of the dominant group of the host society
in religious matters from the first through the third and subsequent generations"? Has there been a "Hibernization" of
the Italians and their descendants (Greeley)? [9] Has the third
generation been incorporated into American Catholicism (Glazer and Moynihan)? [10]

The following is a summary of our findings:

The sense of community was strong among Italians and
this helped them become integrated into American life. To
the Italian immigrant, his family, his peer group and his neighborhood were more important than institutions such as the
church, the school or the place of occupation, because the
first three elements provided him with security and a feeling
of solidarity.

TABLE 1
Mass Attendance
Item 39. Do you attend Mass?

Response	First Generation (Per Cent)	Second Generation (Per Cent)	Third Generation (Per Cent)	Irish Catholic (Per Cent)
Daily	21.1	8.8	9.4	28.1
Weekly	58.8	74.2	68.8	67.6
Monthly	8.8	5.8	3.9	.6
A few times a year . .	6.8	4.4	7.3	.6
Hardly ever	4.5	6.8	5.9	3.2
Invalid responses . . .	.0	.0	4.7	.0
Total	100	100	100	100
N	294	295	234	321

[7] Gerhard Lenski, *The Religious Factor*, Garden City, N. Y.: Doubleday and Co., 1961.

[8] Milton L. Barron, Intermediacy: Conceptualization of Irish Status in America," *Social Forces*, XXVII (1948-49), pp. 256-63.

Meyer F. Nimkoff and Arthur L. Wood, "Effect of Majority Patterns
on the Religious Behavior of a Minority Group," *Sociology and Social
Research*, XXVII (May, 1958), pp. 283-89.

Caroline F. Ware, *Greenwich Village, 1920-30.* Boston: Houghton
Mifflin Company, 1943, pp. 113-14.

[9] Andrew M. Greeley, "Quali sono le prospettive della parrocchia na-
zionale negli Stati Uniti," *Studi Emigrazione*, II, No. 5 (February, 1966)
pp. 99-109.

[10] Nathan Glazer and Daniel P. Moynihan, *Beyond the Melting Pot*,
Cambridge, Mass.: Harvard University Press, 1963.

However, the Catholic Church, the parochial school and the public school have contributed to the cultural assimilation of the Italians in New York City. There is also supporting evidence that the intermingling of American-Italians in the Catholic schools and Catholic religious and social organizations, fostered out-group marriages and is bringing about their social assimilation. The establishment of national parishes paved the way for the gradual integration of the Italians into American life, including their adjustment to the American-Irish parish.

As regards religious practices among Italian-Americans, the evidence presented supports that of Lenski's Detroit study, which shows that increasing church attendance is associated with increasing Americanization. Our research also agrees with Lazerwitz and Rowitz's [11] hypothesis that upon arrival in the United States, non-Irish Catholics adjust to the American Catholic norm of even higher church attendance derived from Irish-Catholicism. Moreover, as illustrated in Table 1, our research shows that the Irish are extremely loyal in fulfilling the precept of Sunday Mass attendance, for 95.7 percent said that they go to Mass every Sunday. Of the first generation Italians, 79.9 percent replied that they attend Mass weekly. There was a statistically significant increase to 83 percent in the second generation and a slight dip to 78.2 percent in the third generation. When one considers that the third genera-

TABLE 2
Reception of Holy Communion
Item 38. Do you receive Holy Communion?

Response	First Generation (Percent)	Second Generation (Percent)	Third Generation (Percent)	Irish Catholic (Percent)
Daily	17.3	5.5	6.5	24.0
Weekly	16.0	26.4	24.3	44.9
Monthly	15.6	25.4	19.6	17.4
A few times a year	38.4	26.4	26.5	9.0
Hardly ever	12.3	15.6	18.8	4.7
Invalid responses	.4	.7	4.3	.0
Total	100	100	100	100
N	294	295	234	321

[11] Bernard Lazerwitz and Louis Rowitz, "The Three-Generations Hypothesis," *The American Journal of Sociology*, LXIX (March, 1964), pp. 529-38.

B. Lazerwitz and L. Rowitz, "Some Factors Associated with Variations in Church Attendance," *Social Forces*, XXXIX (May, 1961), pp. 301-09.

tion also had 4.7 percent invalid responses, we submit that the dip is insignificant.

The custom of frequent Holy Communion (See Table 2) is strong among the Irish, 86.3 percent of whom replied that they receive Holy Communion at least once a month. Among the Italians 48.9 percent of the first generation replied that they go to Communion at least once a month, while 57.3 percent of the second generation and 50.4 percent of the third generation receive at least once a month. The difference of all three generations of Italians is significant when compared to the Irish norm, as is the difference from the first to the second generation. The fluctuation in the third generation may be due to the fact that the respondents represent the youngest group (ages 20-39), some of whom are unmarried and possibly are less fervent during the earlier, turbulent years of life; while the married, who are still young enough to conceive children, might have the problem of birth control, which keeps many Catholic couples from the reception of Holy Communion if the traditional teaching is violated. The Italians of the second and third generation closely approximate the Irish in their spirit of cooperation, friendliness and loyalty to the parish priests, as well as in their participation in parish activities. According to the priests interviewed during this study, the average contribution of church-going Catholics is about a dollar or less a week. More that $100 a year is considered by them to be a generous contribution. The data in Table 3 indicate that the pattern of generous and loyal church

TABLE 3

Financial Support of the Parish

Item 14. How much do you contribute to your parish church each year?

Response	First Generation (Percent)	Second Generation (Percent)	Third Generation (Percent)	Irish Generation (Percent)
$10-$29	21.5	6.4	10.7	8.4
$30-$49	24.5	5.2	10.2	5.1
$50-$100	30.9	35.2	33.8	25.2
More than $100	21.8	52.9	37.2	60.7
Invalid responses	1.3	.3	8.1	.6
Total	100	100	100	100
N	294	295	234	321

support, characteristic of the Irish, is still prevalent. Unaccustomed to church donations and collections in Italy where the church was state-supported, the first-generation Italians still maintain their original pattern.

Only half of this group answered that they give more than $50 a year. However, the second generation seems to have adopted the Irish custom of generous support, another sign of cultural assimilation, for 52.9 percent reported that they give more than $100 annually, and 35.2 percent more than $50. The third generation is also generous in its donations, but since many are in college, or not yet working, it is not as generous as the second generation.

When we turn to non-financial church support, we see that both the Irish and Italian groups show a decreasing interest in certain private religious devotions, such as retreats, novenas, stations of the cross and grace before meals. Praying for the dead is a universal Catholic practice. Having Masses said for deceased relatives and friends is especially strong among Italians and an indication of family love and loyalty, even after death. However, our results (See Table 4) indicate that there is a statistically significant generational decline among the Italians.

The Italian custom of having Masses, prayers, novenas and feasts celebrated in honor of local patron saints has persisted among the immigrants. This custom is not part of the Irish cultural pattern. Table 5 shows a very significant drop in the second generation, for 72.1 percent do not have even one Mass celebrated, nor does three-quarters of the third generation Italians. An almost complete acceptance of the Irish-American custom in this area, as contrasted with Italian customs, is seen in the results of the Chi-square test, for there is no significance in the difference between the second and third generations, nor between the third generation and the Irish. Once again, our data indicate the speed and extent of the cultural assimilation process.

TABLE 4
Requests for Masses

Response	First Generation (Percent)	Second Generation (Percent)	Third Generation (Percent)	Irish Catholic (Percent)
Item 16. How many times a year do you have Masses said for your deceased relatives and friends?				
1-5	57.8	63.1	47.0	47.6
6-10	13.3	7.1	3.9	12.8
More than 10	12.2	10.5	9.4	19.3
None	16.7	19.0	31.2	20.0
Invalid responses	.0	.3	8.5	.3
Total	100	100	100	100
N	294	295	234	321
Item 17. How many Masses a year do you have said in honor of some saint?				
1-5	48.6	23.0	13.7	11.8
6-10	2.8	1.4	.4	1.7
More than 10	3.7	1.1	.9	1.2
None	41.8	72.1	75.6	84.1
Invalid responses	3.1	2.4	9.4	1.2
Total	100	100	100	100
N	294	295	234	321

A great cult of the Blessed Virgin Mary exists in Italy, where she is called "Madonna" (My Lady), and where she is considered "Mother of All." In a way, she typifies the Italian mother, towards whom there is a strong emotional attachment in all Italian families. Italy's history, under various local and foreign rulers, has taught the southerner the value of an intermediary. Most Italian immigrants find it easier to pray to Mary or to a patron saint, who seem so human to them.

TABLE 5
Direct Prayer to God in Contrast with Prayer to an Intermediary

Response	First Generation (Percent)	Second Generation (Percent)	Third Generation (Percent)	Irish Catholic (Percent)
Item 30. I pray more to the Blessed Mother and the saints than I do to God.				
Yes	57.8	28.8	22.6	29.6
No	39.8	69.5	73.1	69.8
Invalid responses	2.4	1.7	4.3	.6
Total	100	100	100	100
N	294	295	234	321

The Irish family, in turn, is more reserved, patriarchal and strict, thus inclining the members to pray more to God than to the saints. The data of Table 5 substantiate this fact, for only 29.6 percent of the Irish replied that they prayed more to the Blessed Mother and to the saints than to God, whereas 57.8 percent of the Italian immigrants prayed to the Blessed Mother and the saints. The difference is highly significant.

Once again the influence of American-Irish norms has helped bring about another noticeable generational difference for only 28.8 percent of the second-generation Italians and 22.6 percent of the third generation pray more to Mary and to the saints. Cultural assimilation has taken place by the third generation. Both the Italian and Irish groups manifest similar patterns of sustained interest in the practice of saying morning and evening prayers, lighting votive candles, wearing religious medals and keeping statues in the home. However, the Italian practice of erecting outdoor statues is significantly ignored by the third generation.

For centuries the Sacrament of the Anointing of the Sick was called "Extreme Unction," or more popularly, "the last rites." The Irish, who were better trained in the use of the sacraments, tend to send for a priest as soon as there is any serious illness. Naturally, it is better to prepare a sick person for possible death if he is fully conscious. The Southern Italians, however, poorly trained, were afraid that calling a

TABLE 6
Use of the Sacrament of the Anointing of the Sick and Reactions at Wakes and Funerals

Response	First Generation (Percent)	Second Generation (Percent)	Third Generation (Percent)	Irish Generation (Percent)
Item 31. When somebody is sick, do you call a priest, only if there is a danger of death?				
Yes	61.9	40.0	29.1	34.4
No	35.4	58.3	64.1	67.0
Invalid responses	2.7	1.7	6.8	1.6
Total	100	100	100	100
N	294	295	234	321
Item 32. At wakes and funerals of relatives and friends, do you cry or react emotionally?				
Yes	68.4	59.0	37.3	31.5
No	29.2	39.0	56.8	67.3
Invalid responses	2.4	2.0	5.9	1.2
Total	100	100	100	100
N	294	295	234	321

priest might "frighten the patient." As a result, the priest was often called when the sick person was semi-conscious, unconscious or dead.

Our findings in Table 6 confirm the supposition that this attitude still persists among the first-generation Italians, because 61.9 percent of them replied that the priest should not be called until death was likely. We noted a statistically significant generational change, for 40 percent of the second generation and 29 percent of the third, responded that they would wait until death was likely before calling a priest. Therefore, in three generations, a complete change to American-Irish norms has taken place.

Religious practices effect behavior broader in scope than that which takes place within the Church building itself. The data summarized in Tables 7 and 8 indicate that Italian families have been getting smaller in size over the last five generations, while the Irish still tend to have large families. Both groups almost unanimously were married in the presence of a Catholic priest. Although out-group marriage is taking place among the members of both groups, third generation Italians, whose out-group percentage is 23.5, tend to marry an Irish partner when marrying a non-Italian. The presence of a large Irish population in New York City, and the influence of the Catholic religion and the Catholic school may be factors in

TABLE 7
Comparison of Responses to Items 1, 2, 3, 6, 13

| | Sex | | Age | | | Marital Status | | | | | Yearly Income | | | | | In-group and Out-group Marriage | | |
	Male	Female	60-79	40-59	20-39	Married	Single	Separated	Divorced	Widowed	3,999 or less	4,000-6,999	7,000-9,999	10,000-14,999	15,000 or over	Italian extraction	Irish extraction	Neither
First Generation N. 294	35.7	64.3	52.4	26.5	21.1	63.6	9.5	.7	1.4	24.8	65.3	18.7	7.1	7.5	.7	82.6	1.7	6.2
Second Generation N. 295	44.2	55.9	10.6	55.9	33.2	77.6	16.3	1.1	.3	4.7	15.9	25.8	26.4	22.0	5.5	69.1	5.8	8.8
Third Generation N. 234	44.0	56.0	2.6	22.6	74.8	58.5	38.5	.4	.9	1.7	16.2	28.2	27.4	15.0	8.5	47.0	11.6	2.9
Irish Catholic N. 321	42.0	58.0	28.0	41.8	30.2	62.3	23.7	.6	.0	13.4	25.2	24.3	26.5	16.5	6.6	4.7	58.6	12.1

this development. The increasing rate of out-group marriage in the Italian-American group is an index of their increasing social assimilation.

TABLE 8
Generational Variation in Size of Family

Response	First Generation (Percent)	Second Generation (Percent)	Third Generation (Percent)	Irish Catholic (Percent)
Item 4. How many children did your parents have?				
2 or less	18.4	21.3	44.4	23.7
3-4	26.9	29.9	37.7	26.2
5 or more	54.7	48.8	17.9	50.1
Total	100	100	100	100
N	294	295	234	321
Item 5. How many children do you have?				
1-2	29.9	36.3	42.2	27.1
3-4	31.3	23.3	11.1	24.3
5 or more	18.7	8.5	5.6	15.6
None	10.5	15.6	2.6	9.3
Answer doesn't apply	9.6	16.3	38.5	23.7
Total	100	100	100	100
N	294	295	234	321

Italians tend to be more family centered. They are inclined to express their feeling, external and vociferously, while the Irish are more reserved and often hide or mask their emotions, even when they are deep-seated. Most Mediterranean peoples are known to vent their feelings dramatically.

Of the Irish respondents, 31.5 percent answered that they cried or reacted emotionally at the wakes and funerals of relations and friends as contrasted with 68.4 percent of the first-generation Italians. Again there is a highly significant generational change (See Table 6) as the Italians become more culturally assimilated and adopt Anglo-Saxon and American-Irish norms of expressing grief with reserve in times of crises and bereavement, for there was a drop to 59 percent in the responses of the second generation and a decline to 37.3 percent in the third generation Italians, who claimed that they reacted emotionally at wakes and funerals.

Table 9 clearly demonstrates that increasing Americanization brings about an increase in the amount of schooling, since so much emphasis is placed on education as the chief means of social mobility in American culture.

TABLE 9

Response	First Generation (Percent)	Second Generation (Percent)	Third Generation (Percent)	Irish Catholic (Percent)
Item 7. How many years did you go to school?				
No schooling	9.5	.0	.0	1.6
Less than 8th grade . .	52.4	3.7	.0	3.1
Up to 8th grade . . .	16.7	13.9	4.8	12.1
Some high school . .	9.5	26.8	11.1	21.5
High school graduate .	6.5	28.5	36.8	25.2
Some college	2.0	16.6	17.9	18.4
College graduate or more	3.4	10.5	28.6	18.1
Total	100	100	100	100
N	294	295	234	321
Item 8. For how many years did you attend Catholic school?				
Some grade school . .	14.9	11.9	7.8	10.6
All of grade school . .	11.9	13.8	21.4	34.0
Some high school . .	2.3	1.4	2.2	8.1
All of high school . .	1.4	4.4	11.9	13.1
Some college	1.4	3.1	5.9	2.5
All of college	1.4	2.4	4.7	3.1
All of the above . . .	3.2	3.4	11.5	12.1
None of the above . .	61.2	59.6	34.6	15.6
Invalid responses . . .	2.3	.0	.0	.9
Total	100	100	100	100
N	294	295	234	321

The responses of the Irish indicated that they received more years of education than the Italians, up to the college level. (46.7 percent had some or all of a high school education.) However, only 18.4 percent had some college education and 18.1 percent had completed their college education or more. It is significant that by the third generation 17.9 percent of the Italians replied that they had some college education and 28.6 percent completed their college education and more.

As noted in Table 9 only 15.6 percent of the Irish never attended Catholic school, while 61.2 percent of the first-generation Italians, 59.6 percent of the second generation, and 34.6 percent of the third-generation Italians did not attend Catholic school.

The great increase in Catholic school enrollment among the Italians is found in the third generation and in this, they compare favorably with the Irish. Our research demonstrated that ethnic traditions have a very powerful effect on Catholic school attendance; the Irish are most likely to have gone to Catholic school while the Italians are less likely. Furthermore, there is a consistent association between generation and Catholic school attendance. Our results in New York confirm those of Greeley and Rossi in the Midwest.[12]

Our findings are also another indication that cultural assimilation is progressing rapidly through the Catholic Schools. The large pecentage of Italians in the Catholic colleges and universities might also be a means of social assimilation, for the Italians and the Irish in New York, usually in equal numbers, form the two largest groups attending Catholic schools and private academies. They are classmates and often belong to the same societies, clubs and cliques. In coeducational institutions, the two groups date and often intermarry. Of the twenty-three Italian-Irish couples interviewed during this study, fifteen of them said they met in college. When all-male or all-female colleges were attended, the students dated a partner from nearby Catholic colleges. For example, the men from Fordham, St. John's, St. Francis, and Manhattan College, dated and often married women from Marymount, New Rochelle, Manhattanville and St. Joseph's College.

Conclusion:

The findings of this study have indicated that three generations of American-Italians have gone through the process of absorbing the cultural patterns of American-Irish society, while retaining some of their own *social identity*.

By observation and significant statistical procedures (most beyond the .001 level) this study demonstrated that in almost all religious practices and attitudes, the longer the Italians have remained in the United States, the more they tended to resemble other American Catholics, especially the Irish-Americans. These findings are in conformity with those of Glazer and Moynihan, who in 1963, noted that the third-generation Italian-Americans were being integrated into the American forms of Catholicism.

More significantly, our research has indicated that social assimilation of Italian-Americans into primary Catholic groups is well under way.

---

[12] Andrew M. Greeley and Peter Rossi, *The Education of Catholic Americans.* Chicago: Aldine Publishing Company, 1966.

Selected Bibliography

Various facets of the Italian experience in the United States are slowly discovered now or have been dealt with in part in filiopietistic or plainly prejudiced ways.

But as basic, competent research proceeds, we should not put aside even the strictly ethnocentric commemorative booklets and occasional publications that together with ethnic press constitute a unique documentary guidance.

In regard to the role of Italians in the labor movement, the references on the padrone system noted in the selected bibliography at the end of the previous section of this book should be consulted. Very informative remains Edwin Fenton's "Immigrants and Unions, A Case Study: Italians and American Labor, 170-1920" (Ph. D. Thesis, Harvard University, 1957) and I.A. Hourowich, *Immigration and Labor* (New York, 1912). For Italian labor in New York City, see Raffaele Rende, *XXV Anniversario della Unione dei Cloakmakers Italiani* — Locale 48, I.L.G.W.U. 1916-1941 (New York, 1941) pp. 224. and *Ultra*, Strenna Commemorativa del XV Anniversario della fondazione della Italian Dressmakers Union, Locale 89, I.L.G.W.U. 1919-1934 (New York, 1934) pp. 126. Luigi Antonini, *Dynamic Democracy* (New York, 1944), pp. XX, 463. The socialist newspaper *Il Proletario* underneath much rhetoric carries also valuable information on Italian immigrant workers.

Regarding the comparative aspect of Italian immigrants and labor, Baily's footnotes include many of the important works relating to working class Italian immigration to Buenos Aires and New York during the period 1880-1910. In addition, the following bibliographical references supplied by Professor Baily shed further light on the relationship between labor and immigration in Argentina.

The best statistical information can be found in the Argentine national censuses, the Buenos Aires municipal censuses, the Argentine Department of Labor *Boletin*, the United States Censuses, the United States Immigration Commission Report, and in the *Statistiche sul mezzogiorno d'Italia*. The works of Fenton, Germani, Marotta and Ochs are also of importance for an understanding of the subject. In addition to these, one might profitably consult the following:

Barzini, Luigi. *L'Argentina vista come è*. Milano, Corriere della Sera, 1902. This is a collection of perspective and at times critical articles about the life of Italians in Argentina written by an editor of the Milan newspaper, *Il Corriere della Sera.*

Beyhart G.; R. Cortés Conde; N. Gorostegui and S. Torrado. "Los inmigrantes en el sistema ocupacional argentino." In Torcuato S. di Tella, Gino Germani, Jorge Garciarena y colaboradores. *Argentina, sociedad de masas*. Buenos Aires: Universidad de Buenos Aires, 1966.

3rd. ed., pp. 85-123. A first rate study of immigrants and economic development in Argentina from the 1850's to World War I.

Cúneo, Dardo; Julio Mafud; Amalia Sánchez Sívori and Lázaro Schallman. Inmigración y nacionalidad. Buenos Aires: Editorial Paidós, 1966. This is an important collection of articles on immigration and society, immigration and national character, immigration and literature and agrarian colonization.

Dore, Grazia. La democrazia italiana e l'emigrazione in America. Brescia: Morcelliana, 1964. This is a major work on Italian immigration to the New World with 168 pages on Argentina, 23 pages on Brazil, and 70 pages on the United States. The 112 page bibliography is excellent.

Fantozzi, M. "La colonia italiana en la Argentina." Revista de Derecho Historia y Letras (Buenos Aires), XXIV (1906), 561-567. Some interesting observations about the Italian community in Buenos Aires at the turn of the century.

Franceschini, Antonio. L'emigrazione italiana nell'America del Sud. Studi sull'espansione coloniale transoceanica. Roma: Forzani, 1908. An important source for details of the personal struggles and triumphs of Italian immigrants in Argentina, Uruguay and Brazil.

Germani, Gino. Estructura social de la Argentina. Análisis estadístico. Buenos Aires: Editorial Raigal, 1955. A statistical analysis of the social structure of Argentina which includes much important information about the assimilation of immigrants.

Korn, Francis. "Algunos aspectos de la asimilacion de inmigrantes en Buenos Aires." América Latina. An interesting attempt to develop an assimilation model based on nationality, social class, etc.

Lombroso Ferrero, Gino. Nell'America Meridionale. Brasile, Uruguay, Argentina. Milano: Hoepli, 1908. The same kind of book as that by Franceschini listed above which is valuable because of the details it includes about the Italian immigration in different countries of South America.

Oddone, Juan Antonio. La emigración europea al Rio de la Plata: motivaciones y proceso de incorporación. Montevideo, 1966. A scholarly analysis of the factors contributing to and opposing the assimilation of immigrants in the Rio de la Plata area.

Panettieri, José. Los trabajadores en tiempos de la inmigración masiva en Argentina, 1870-1910. La Plata: Universidad Nacional de la Plata, 1965. An interesting beginning of the study of the working class during the period of mass migration in Argentina.

Scobie, James R. "Changing Urban Patterns: The Porteno Case, 1880-1910." Unpublished paper. An important and provocative study of the evolving urban patterns of Buenos Aires with significant implications for many of the issues relating to immigration.

Solberg Carl E. "The Response to Immigration in Argentina and Chile, 1890-1914." Ph.D. Thesis, Stanford University, 1966. A well documented account of the reaction, particularly of the upper class, to immigration in Argentina and Chile. The author relies primarily on literature and magazine to build his case.

Still very much unexplored remains the area of the role and type of religion Italian immigrants transplanted in urban, industrialized America. The Archives of the R.C. Archdiocese of New York contains invaluable primary sources, many in Italian. The Archives of the

Congregation of St. Charles in Rome constitute another indispensable source. The ecclesiastical archives for the Catholic dioceses of Brooklyn, Boston, Providence, Newark, Chicago, Philadelphia, and Hartford, among others, are equally valuable. The Catholic, Protestant, and secular press at the turn of the century and well into the 1920's carry articles and editorials on the question of Italians and religion. See, among others, Bernard J. Lynch, "The Italians in New York," *Catholic World*, XLVII (April, 1888), 67-73; Laurence Franklin, "The Italian in America; What He Has Been, What He Shall Be." *Catholic World* LXXI (April, 1900), 67-80; Kate Prindeville, "Italy in Chicago," *Catholic World*, LXXVI (July, 1903), 452-461; Edmund M. Dunne, "Memoirs of 'Zi pre'," *American Ecclesiastical Review*, XLIX (August, 1913), 192-203; Albert R. Bandini, "Concerning the Italian Problem" *American Ecclesiastical Review*, LXII (March, 1920) 278-285.

For a view of the problem from the Italian side, one must consult the volumes of the periodicals *L'Emigrato Italiano, Italica Gens* (1910 on) and *Il Carroccio* (1914 on).

The impact of Protestant activities among Italians is regularly reported in *The Assembly Herald* and to a lesser extent in *The Missionary Review of the World*. Also, Aurelio Palmieri, "Italian Protestantism in the United States" *Catholic World*, CVII (May, 1918) 177-189.

An important commentary on the early period of immigration is given by Henry T. Browne, "The 'Italian Problem' in the Catholic Church of the United States, 1800-1900" *United States Catholic Historical Society. Historical Records and Studies*, XXV (1946), pp. 46-72. The lack of use of some important primary and most Italian language sources and the emphasis on the point of view of the Catholic hierarchy, however, create serious limitations for this early study. Rudolph Vecoli's attempt at reexamination of this same period was equally hampered by the limited access to primary and Italian language sources.

Important books reflecting Protestant work with Italians are: Antonio Mangano, *Sons of Italy. A Social and Religious Study of Italians in America*, (New York, 1917); William Payne Shriver, *At Work with the Italians*, (New York, 1917) and Enrico C. Sartorio *Social and Religious Life of Italians in America*, (Boston, 1918), and they contain further references pertinent to this topic. Also useful for the study of Protestant activities are: John Bisceglia, *Italian Evangelical Pioneers* (Kansas City, Mo., 1948) and F. Guglielmi, *Italian Methodist Missions in the Little Italy of Baltimore, Md.* (New Castle, Md. 1913).

From the Catholic side the best book to date is the Italian language study of Bishop Scalabrini, B. Caliaro-M. Francesconi, *Giovanni Battista Scalabrini*, (Milan, 1969) (being translated). Also indispensable is *La società italiana di fronte alle migrazioni di massa*, a 511 page special issue of *Studi Emigrazione*, vol. V, n. 11-12 (February-June, 1968). For a tentative sociological hypothesis of Italian and American Catholicism, see: Francis X. Femminella, "The Impact of Italian Immigration and American Catholicism," *American Catholic Sociological Review*, 22 (1966), 233-41.

Among the many works concerning crime and Italian-Americans, see: John H. Mariano, *The Italian Immigrant and Our Courts* (Boston, 1925); Arthur Train, *Courts, Criminals and the Camorra* (New York, 1912); John Landesco, *Organized Crime in Chicago, Part III of the Illinois Crime Survey* (Chicago, 1929); Frederic Sondern, Jr., *Brotherhood of Evil: The Mafia* (New York, 1959); Giovanni E. Schiavo, *The Truth about the Mafia and Organized Crime in America* (New York, 1962); The Italian "White Hand" Society in Chicago, Illinois, *Studies, Action and Results* (Chicago, 1908); Gaetano D'Amato, "The 'Black Hand' Myth." *North American Review*, CLXXXII (April, 1908), 543-549; Tomaso Sassone, "Italy's Criminals in the United States," *Current History*, XV (October, 1921), 23-31; Humbert S. Nelli, "Italians and Crime in Chicago: The Formative Years, 1890-1920," *American Journal of Sociology*, LXXIV (January, 1969), 373-391, which lists additional titles.

Political activities of immigrants and their children are described in the following: Fiorello H. LaGuardia, *The Making of an Insurgent: An Autobiography, 1882-1919* (Philadelphia, 1948); Arthur Mann, *La Guardia: A Fighter Against His Times: 1882-1933* (Philadelphia, 1959) and *LaGuardia Comes to Power: 1933* (Philadelphia, 1965); John Palmer Gavit, *American by Choice* (New York, 1922); Samuel Lubell, *The Future of American Politics* (3rd ed., rev.; New York, 1965), ch. iv; and Humbert S. Nelli, "John Powers and the Italians; Politics in a Chicago Ward, 1896-1921," *Journal of American History*, in press. Salvatore John LaGumina, *Vito Marcantonio, The People's Politician*, (Dubuque, 1969) is an excellent presentation of ethnic politics in New York City.

For analyses of health problems in the Italian colony: Rocco Brindisi, "The Italian and Public Health," *Charities*, XII (May 7, 1904), 483-486; Antonio Stella, "Tuberculosis and the Italians in the United States," *Charities*, XII (May 7, 1904), 486-489.

Education among Italians is examined by Jane Addams, "Foreign-born Children in the Primary Grades; Italian Families in Chicago," *National Education Association. Journal of Proceedings and Addresses*, XXXVI (1897), 104-112; Grace Irwin, "Michelangelo in Newark," *Harper's Magazine*, CXLIII (September, 1921), 446-454; Ellen May, "Italian education and Immigration," *Education*, No. 28 (March, 1908), pp. 450-453; Leonard Covello, *The Social Background of the Italo-American School Child*, (Leiden, 1967). *The Heart is the Teacher* (New York, 1958); and Leonard P. Ayres, *Laggards in Our Schools* (New York, Russell Sage Foundation, 1909).

Societies are discussed in Antonio Mangano, "The Associated Life of the Italians in New York City," *Charities* 12 (May 7, 1904), 476-82; and Ernst L. Biagi, *The Purple Aster: A History of the Order Sons of Italy in America,* (N.P., 1961).

THE RETURN TO ITALY

In general, the United States provided immigrants with a chance to be politically and religiously free, as well as with an opportunity to succeed economically. However, some immigrants, including some Italians, could not, or would not, take advantage of the American way of life. These people found it necessary and/or desirable to return to their native land. Who were the returnees? How did they differ from those who stayed in the States? For what reasons did they return to Italy? What did they experience upon their return? Did they affect Italian society by their return? Were they happy that they had returned? These questions have long been overlooked by scholars interested in migration, who tend to focus on adaptation and assimilation into the new land to the exclusion of any consideration of the migrant's orientation toward the old. The following paper seeks to provide preliminary answers to such questions and seeks to be a first step toward filling a current void in migration research.

Nostalgia or Disenchantment: Considerations on Return Migration

by Francesco Cerase *

From the many studies on migration, one or two predominant themes can usually be singled out: namely, a preoccupation with analysis of the process of the immigrant's adaptation to the society of arrival or of the process of acculturation through which the immigrant becomes a member of the new society. The adult emigrant, especially if he emigrates with his family, carries with him cultural traits foreign to the new society. Whether these are family customs, religious beliefs or whatever, they continue to direct and determine his general behavior. With a tenacity and persistence which varies from case to case, the immigrant will try to reconstruct for himself an environment in which these cultural traits preserve their original meaning. But whether one studies how the immigrant attempts this kind of adaptation — that is, whether he forces himself to reproduce conditions within which he can continue to attribute the original significance to his customs, habits and needs — or whether, instead, one studies how these cultural traits become modified, enriched, changed by the new conditions in order to be "accepted" by the culture of the new society, the point of departure of both these research perspectives is the new milieu and how the immigrant orientates his actions toward it.

It is not uncommon, however, to find in these studies references to the possibility of a return to the country of origin. They are usually passing remarks, without any attempt to enlarge upon them. One might ask if this cursory treatment [1]

---

[1] If we exclude the not unfrequent discussions on returned emigrants in the literature of the first decades of this century (see, for example, the works of P. Villari, F. Coletti, F.S. Nitti), to my knowledge, there are only a few studies dealing specifically with returned migrants, and

---

* Francesco Cerase, University of Rome, Istituto di Statistica, Centro di Ricerche di Sociologia Empirica.

stems from an unwillingness on the part of researchers to take an interest in a phenomenon which not only completely alters the direction of the research but demands in particular a careful re-examination of where and how to locate returnees in the process of immigrant integration into the new society.[2]

The main assumption of the typical approach to the study of return migration is that the experience of the emigrant revolves around his absorption into the new society. Whatever the motives or needs which induced him to leave his native country, the emigrant experiences, to some extent at least, a deep and sudden break with his old society. More or less consciously, his efforts are now directed to resolving problems new to him, to understanding needs completely foreign to his life in the old community, and these constitute the salient facts in his new experience. The corollary to this assumption is that a return may thus be regarded simply as a solution to failure to integrate.

But is it legitimate to attribute the same meaning to all cases of return? Do they all indicate the same consequences? It is this point, indeed, that has been neglected for too long in studies of the migratory phenomenon. In fact, it is much more probable that returnees can be differentiated in some

---

the problems of their reabsorption in the society of their home country, such as Theodore Saloutos, *They Remember America: The Story of Repatriated Greek-Americans*. (Berkeley: University of California Press, 1956), and William H. Form and Julius Rivera, "The Place of Returning Migrants in a Stratification System," *Rural Sociology*, 23 (1958). See also N. H. Frijda, "Emigrants Overseas" in G. Beijer et al., *Characteristics of Overseas Migrants*, (The Hague, Government Printing and Publishing Office, 1961), esp. pp. 298-300; and *Studi Emigrazione*, IV (1967) pp. 173-181, which contains an up-to-date statement on research concerning return migration. More recently return migration has aroused the interest of international organizations, such as the O.C.D.E., which has organized a seminar on the problems of returned migrants; see *Les travailleurs émigrés retournant dans leurs pays* (Paris, 1967). Finally, a short article, tackling the problem of prospective return migrants, is that of George C. Myers and George Masnick, "The Migration Experience of New York Puerto Ricans: A Perspective on Return," *The International Migration Review*, II (1968).

[2] In the article, "L'emigrazione di ritorno nel processo di integrazione dell'immigrato: una prima formulazione" in *Genus*, XXIII (1967), I have tried, referring in particular to the case of Italian migration to the United States, to locate return migration in the process of integration of the immigrant. I developed this further in, "Su di una tipologia di emigrati ritornati" in *Studi Emigrazione*, IV (1967).

way, and according to the preceding assumption the main cri-
terion for differentiation should be the different points they
had reached in the process of integration in the new society
when they decided to return to the old one.

To this end, I have first tried to extract, from the substantial amount of literature on the subject,[3] from observation of
present migratory patterns and from statements by returned
emigrants, the phases in the general process of integration.
I have then attempted to describe the important stages in this
process, introducing the new assumption that each stage is
selective in the sense that it can either be overcome, allowing
passage to the next stage under optimum conditions, or not
overcome, in which case the entire process in the following
stages is subject to disturbances and such confusion that it
could result in a return. The model which follows, however
brief, is held to be operatively valid in relation to the return
of emigrants to the extent that it clarifies and explains the
motives as well as the consequences of their return.

*The Process of Integration of the Immigrant and Types of
Returned Migrants.*

Only a few writers, like Oscar Handlin,[4] have been able
to describe the emotions and the sufferings of the immigrant
in the first months, the first years, in which everything —
human contacts, work, language, living quarters, climate, food
— is so incomprehensibly new and strange that it constitutes
a problem to resolve, a difficulty to overcome. It is like
realizing suddenly that one knows nothing any more, that one

---

[3] A review of the many problems related to the study of integration
is contained in Francesco Alberoni and Guido Baglioni, *L'integrazione
dell'immigrato nella società industriale* (Bologna: Il Mulino, 1965) in
particular, Ch. I and II. The latter is very useful for its bibliographical notes. It is also useful to recall the studies of the International
Union for the Scientific Study of Population, in particular the papers
presented by Henry Bunle, Georges Mauco, Roberto Bachi, Benjamin
Gil, Giorgio Mortara, Julius Isaac and others, published in the appendix
of *Population Studies*, Vol. III, 1949-1950. In particular I wish to emphasize the formulation of S. N. Eisenstadt in his *The Absorption of
Immigrants* (Glencoe: The Free Press, 1955), which has served as a
constant frame of reference.

[4] Oscar Handlin, *The Uprooted* (New York: Grosset and Dunlap
Publishers, 1951).

must begin to learn again, from the very beginning. It is a shock, a traumatic experience to be no longer in one's own village, one's own country, to have become an "immigrant," a term whose full significance and implication one does not yet understand. Will it be possible to overcome the obstacles of this first period?

It is true that the majority of immigrants succeed in finding, in one way or another, a sense of social participation, which, however different from that of the native country, provides a sense of comfort and security in belonging to a group. It is also true that some succumb and that, if they have a home to return to, a family waiting, they begin to turn their thoughts sadly to a return which is often hopeless. What remains of their experience in the new society is that sensation of suffering, fear, and abandonment, intermingled with the memory of "marvels," incomprehensible, "great things," seen through amazed eyes.[5] This type of return is a *return of failure.*

The factor which determines whether or not the immigrant surmounts the difficulties of this phase is his work. Whatever his particular desires and motivations, what he is really seeking is greater economic stability, the possibility of earning enough to improve his living conditions and satisfy his culturally rooted needs and aspirations. In the beginning, when lack of everything makes the simple need to survive imperative, he may be willing to accept any kind of work, but later on he obstinately seeks a job which pays as much as possible.[6] In any case, when he does find work it is usually a completely new type of job for him, sometimes a very hard one, and it occupies the greater part of his day, leaving him little time to reflect on his new condition.

If he finds work it is very probable that the immigrant will overcome the first obstacle, the shock of being in the new society. From that moment it can be said that the process of integration is underway. Even if the reactions and ultimate

---

[5] I have in mind, here, the case of the returned migrants from the United States. The discussion carried out in the text, as I shall state later, draws mainly from the experiences and results provided by a study on these migrants begun a couple of years ago and still in progress.

[6] The research referred to here shows that slightly less than half the returned migrants who changed jobs for the first time while in the United States did so in search of better pay, and this percentage tends to increase in the case of those who continued to change jobs.

intentions may differ from one case to the next, that building, that street corner, become "his" house, "his" corner; that district, even if it is a ghetto or slum, also becomes "his". Although he may try to reestablish old customs or recreate the atmosphere of his village, new habits are continually tempting him, new ways of thinking and behaving confuse his understanding of things and his values. Moreover, if his work allows him to earn well, his savings accumulate after a few years. This economic success, however small it may be, has a unique significance for him. Probably for the first time, in such a tangible way at any rate, economic success thrusts him with a jolt into the production-consumption-production process, providing him with the means to become a consumer of shoes, cigarettes, meat, and many other prized items.

This is the first turning point in his experience as an immigrant. Here he either yields to the desire to spend his earnings on a series of acquisitions which separate him further and further from the conditions of life and aspirations he had when he left, or he saves his money so that, once returned home, he can obtain those very "instruments" which would open the way to upward social mobility. Obviously, in the latter case, the immigrant continues to consider the earnings he accumulates, as well as the means of investing them, in terms of the traditional scheme proper to his own country; this scheme will be reinforced upon his return. This return is *a return of conservatism.*[7]

The reverse is true in the case where the immigrant, by acquiring more consumer habits, becomes more a part of the process of production-consumption-production and tends to define his own position in its social stratification system. He occupies the lowest position, a position he wants to leave. But at the moment at which this happens, he ceases to refer himself and his success to his society of origin and begins to refer everything instead to the new society. This can be considered the culminating point in his experience. Due chiefly to exposure to the American ideal of equal opportunity for all and to the value of individual achievement, he becomes convinced that the new society is ready to accept him as a member irrespective of his ethnic origins. It does not matter that he occupies

---

[7] It is this return which comes close to Alberoni and Baglioni's conception of *emigrazione di rapina,* based on the prospect of going

such a low position in the social ladder because if he is capable of emerging, climbing, and affirming himself, the society will accept him in a new position.

Generally speaking it can be said that at this point particularly the immigrant becomes conscious of the fact that in order to advance he must become like others and must be treated like others. But despite his desires and naturalization, he continues to be differentiated from the "natives" by his family and community patterns, [8] his particular orientation toward religion and his inability to speak the new language without the often despised accent. He becomes aware that he cannot go past a certain point. It is the critical point in his experience and as such can be considered the second fundamental stage in the process of integration.

It is a fact supported by numerous studies that there is little social mobility for the first generation immigrants. [9] At this point, the immigrant, aware of his status as "naturalized immigrant" — from which certain roles are precluded, certain memberships barred, certain types of social advancement impossible — must make a decision. He can accept the reality that this is the status which characterized most of his relations with the rest of society and, understanding the consequences, decide to adapt himself to it and continue to participate in social life in that position.

Alternatively, he can be dissatisfied and/or unable to accept this reality. He may then turn his thoughts to his country of origin and begin to consider a return to the old society a possible new alternative.

---

abroad to make a fortune as quickly as possible and then returning home. (See Alberoni and Baglioni, op. cit., pp. 279-81 and 297-302).

[8] How much these elements have been determinant in characterizing Italian colonies abroad is generally known; so much so that Nathan Glazer, in the chapter dedicated to the Italians in his and Daniel Patrick Moynihan's Beyond the Melting Pot (Cambridge, Mass., The M.I.T. Press, 1963) writes "... But still today, three generations after the founding of the first big Italian settlements in New York, the traditional bounds of neighborhood and family determine in large measure the accomplishments of American Italians." p. 186.

[9] It is interesting to note in this regard the data reported by E. P. Hutchinson in his Immigrants and their Children 1850-1950 (New York: John Wiley and Sons, 1956).

The return of the emigrant at this point is quite different from the "return of conservatism." With respect to the new society he has reached quite an advanced stage in what Eisenstadt calls the process of "absorption." [10] Both the process of acculturation and that of individual adjustment [11] have reached an advanced stage. With his experience in the new society, he is now prepared and willing to take his new values and new means back with him to the old society. This type of return is *a return of innovation*.

The thought of return can manifest itself slowly or much later when, as old age approaches, a feeling of dissatisfaction becomes real suffering and a process of "disintegration" occurs. With the nostalgic memories of an old man for his native country he begins to recall the original aspirations which induced him to leave it. That desire, renewed now, to buy a piece of land and to live out his old age peacefully and without worries becomes more and more attractive. The fruits of his own hard work are certainly sufficient to realize this, so if the occasion presents itself, and the desire is strong enough, he ends up by returning to his home country. This type of return is *a return of retirement*. And with it we come to an end of our types of returnees.

Discussion of the Typology of Returned Migrants.

The model discussed above thus presents a typology of returnees which not only clarifies the phenomenon but also indicates general lines for further inquiry. The present discussion of the typology is based on the evidence collected for a study on migrants to the United States who returned to Italy.

TABLE 1
Returned Migrants according to the Length of Stay in the United States

	Up to 5 years	From 6 to 10 years	From 11 to 20 years	More than 20 years	Total
no.	38	48	47	68	201 [a]
%	18.9	23.9	23.4	33.8	100

[a] This total is different from the one of the following tables. The difference is due to the fact that some interviews were not completed.

---

[10] Eisenstadt, *op. cit.*, Ch. I.
[11] *Ibid.*, pp. 11-13.

In Table 1 data concerning the length of stay in America are reported. One peak appears at a 6-10 year period, with which a return of conservatism can be associated. A second peak is apparent after 20 years, which seems to suggest a return of retirement. Returns of failure are associated with a stay of up to 5 years, while innovative returnees can be found mainly among those who return after a period of between 10 and 20 years.

The interviewees were asked if their stay in America was continuous or interrupted by periods in Italy. Table 2 shows that for a great number the length of their stay in America was actually the sum of several shorter periods. If vacations or short trips to visit friends and relatives are not counted and only periods of more than a year are considered, Table 2 shows that 18 percent 26 percent and 29 percent of migrants who have been in America for a total of 6-10 years, 11-20 years, and more than 20 years respectively have in fact not had a continuous, progressive immigrant experience, but have probably undergone various migratory experiences of shorter periods varying in length from 5 to 10 years, repeated several times and alternated with long stays in Italy.

The data gathered allow a more precise verification of return types. In fact, when the consequences of return migration in the life of the old community are being evaluated, one of the most important elements to consider is the economic activity the migrant engages in upon his return.[12] The data in Table 3 compares this economic activity with the length of stay in America.[13] It can be seen that about three quarters of those who do work upon their return engage in a rural

---

[12] This assertion has been supported by the case study of a couple of villages, where migrants returning from the United States came back professing different religious beliefs, that is they had left Catholics and returned Protestants, and established a Protestant Church Although this was looked upon at first as a breakthrough in the "immobility" of the village community, they failed to generate new change, and later became "absorbed."

[13] Unfortunately there is no space here to describe the sampling technique used in the research. I must say though that the main difficulty I have met resided in the fact that the "universe" was not known, that is, there was no way of finding out how many these migrants were and where they were. This may have led to an over presence in the sample interviewed, of migrants returned to rural

TABLE 2

Returned Migrants according to Length of Stay in the United States and whether This Period Is Broken by Return to Italy

Length of residence in the U.S.A.	Period of residence Broken: Returned to Italy once or more for periods of a year or less		Returned to Italy once or more for periods of more than a year		Unbroken: Never returned to Italy		Others, no reply, etc.		Total	
	No.	%	No.	%	No.	%	No.	%	No.	%
Up to 5 years . . .	4	10.8	2	5.4	28	75.7	3	8.1	37	100.0
From 6 to 10 years .	14	31.1	8	17.8	22	48.9	1	2.2	45	100.0
From 11 to 20 years .	10	21.7	12	26.1	18	39.1	6	13.0	46	99.9
More than 20 years .	23	34.8	19	28.8	9	13.6	15	22.7	66	99.9
Total	51	26.3	41	21.1	77	39.7	25	12.9	194	100.0

TABLE 3

Returned Migrants according to Length of Stay in the United States and 1st Economic Activity upon Return to Italy

Years of residence in the U.S.A.	1st Economic Activity upon Return																	
	Employed								Self-employed				Never Worked		Other		Total	
	Manual				Non manual													
	Agriculture		Other industries		Agriculture		Other industries		Agriculture		Other industries							
	No.	%	No.	%	No.	%	No.	%	No.	%	No.	%	No.	%	No.	%	No.	%
Up to 5	5	13.5	4	10.8	1	2.7	1	2.7	11	29.7	8	21.6	7[b]	18.9	—	—	37	99.9
From 6 to 10	4	8.9	5	11.1	—	—	—	—	11	24.4	6	13.3	17[b]	37.8	2	4.4	45	99.9
From 11 to 20	2	4.3	1	2.2	—	—	—	—	23[a]	50.0	7	15.2	12	26.1	1	2.2	46	100.0
More than 20	—	—	2	3.0	—	—	—	—	13[a]	19.7	1	1.5	48	72.7	2	3.0	66	99.9
Total	11	5.7	12	6.2	1	.5	1	.5	58	29.9	22	11.3	84	43.3	5	2.6	194	100.0

[a] Among these are quite a few old men who upon their return have bought a house and a plot of land where they spend many hours a day cultivating vegetables and a little fruit, mainly for use in their own family or, sometimes, even for sale in the village market.

[b] Among these are respectively 4 and 5 women who joined their husbands in the United States to return to Italy shortly afterwards.

occupation.[14]   Among those who have returned after a short
period, a high percentage are employed as laborers. The reverse
is true in the case of returnees who remained in the United
States for a long period. Almost all of these are engaged in
independent occupations, which reflect the fact that they have
acquired land or begun a business of their own.

These considerations lead to another basic aspect of the
problem: the use to which the migrant puts his money.[15]
Obviously, in the cases referred to above, at least, it is invested
according to very traditional patterns, typical of "petty provincial" values. On the other hand, those who upon their
return have not gone to work (they represent just about one
half of the total) live on American social security or a veteran's
pension. These returnees tend to put their savings into post
office accounts, or else, as is the case for those who returned
quite recently, to leave their money in the United States in
savings accounts or stocks.

Table 4 helps to clarify the different patterns of economic
activity upon return, according to the length of stay in the
United States. Here the period 11-20 years has been broken
in two, 11-15 and 16-20. It is then apparent that those who,
upon return, engage in an economic activity in some industry
other than agriculture are practically all to be found among
those who have had a continuous immigrant experience. If one
accepts the suggestion that the returned migrants, who have
alternated migration periods with long periods of residence
in their homeland, have indeed undergone repeated migratory
experiences, and since pratically all of them have engaged, upon
return, in an agricultural occupation, one can reasonably argue

---

villages. In assessing the results of the research this must be kept in
mind. It is just as important to note, and this will become clear later
in the text, that for certain aspects of the problem of interest here, to
have neglected emigrants who have returned to large cities does not
undermine the validity of some of the conclusions.

[14] In particular, the "failing" nature of the return of those who come
back after a short period — within two years after departure, for example — is clearly indicated by the relatively high percentage among
them of those who returned to a manual employment, usually an
unskilled job in agriculture.

[15] The first thought the migrant has upon return it seems, is the
purchase, or better, the construction of a house or an apartment if the
return is to a city. The house of the *Americano*, sometimes surrounded
by a garden and equipped with all modern conveniences, is now characteristic of many villages of the Center-South of the country. Carlo Levi
in his *Christ Stopped at Eboli* acutely observed this many years ago.

TABLE 4

Returned Migrants according to Length of Stay in the United States, whether This Period is Interrupted by Return to Italy, and 1st Economic Activity upon Return

| Years of Residence in the U.S.A. | Period of residence in the U.S.A. uninterrupted or interrupted by return to Italy for periods of a year or less | | | | | Period of residence in the U.S.A. interrupted by returns to Italy for periods of more than a year | | | | | Others Cases | Total |
| | 1st Economic Activity Employed | | 1st Economic Activity upon the Return Self-employed | | | 1st Economic Activity Employed | | 1st Economic Activity upon the Return Self-employed | | | | |
	Agriculture	Other Industries	Agriculture	Other Industries	Never Worked	Agriculture	Other Industries	Agriculture	Other Industries	Never Worked		
Up to 5	7	4	7	7	7			2			3	37
From 6 to 10	3	3	7	5	15	1	2	3		2	3	44
From 11 to 15	1		6	4	7		1	6		1	6	32
From 16 to 20			7	1	1			3	1		1	14
More than 20		1	6		24		1	6		11	17	66
Total	11	8	33	17	54	1	4	20	1	14	30	193

that the first entries of "Agriculture" in Table 4 ought to be greater. In that case the percentage of returned migrants who engage in an economic activity in an industry other than agriculture is highest among those who have had a continuous migratory experience of about 11-15 years.

In conclusion, some of the propositions suggested by the data of Table 4, are that the longer the stay in the United States, the higher the tendency to engage in an independent economic activity upon return [16]; that the relationship between length of stay in the United States and the occupation upon return is complex, and is dependent primarily upon whether the immigrant's experience has been broken by long periods of temporary residence in his homeland or not. The ratio between returned migrants who engage in an agricultural occupation and those who have not, tends to diminish slightly as the length of stay in the United States increases (except for those who have experienced a very long period of migration).

Further considerations, however, emphasize the "conservative" nature of the returns to the land, particularly in the southern part of the country.[17] In fact, beyond revealing the persistence of a traditional cultural and economic pattern accord-

---

[16] This tendency toward self-employment is also reflected in the finding, not reported in the text, that the percentage of migrants who at the time of their last occupation in the United States were self-employed is 11 percent, compared to 2 percent at the time of their first occupation. Futhermore, it was found that this is the only kind of upward social mobility experienced by the migrants interviewed. This is a fact which has a particular relevance in connection with the "second fundamental stage" in the process of integration outlined above in the text.

[17] It should be made clear that the following considerations and conclusions refer essentially to the South. In a previous work on return migration (a paper sent to the 6th International Congress on Sociology, Evian, France, 1966) the author, discussing the thesis of the different role played by emigration in the North and South of the country, tried to state this differentiation more precisely. Although enough evidence has not emerged to allow a definitive statement, this author tends to believe that in itself return migration has not had in the North a different role from the South. The only conclusion which can be safely made is that where the returned migrant found a social environment in the process of change he adapted and was able to take advantage of it, as is the case in the North; where instead he found a social environment entrenched in its traditions and inflexible in its structure, as in the South, he had no choice but to accept this reality and adapt to it. But it is exactly with this acceptance and this adaptation and their consequences that the text deals.

ing to which the possession of land constitutes the principal, if not the only, sign of economic security, prestige and social mobility, the returnees show the continuing prevalence of the age-old feelings of powerlessness and resignation — manifest in such phrases as "What else is there to do here?" The passage of time has left these attitudes unchanged.[18] With only a very few exceptions, crops, systems of cultivation, and the returned migrant's ideas about agricultural investment differ in no way from the traditional scheme of things.   Nor does his work experience in America seem to have been of any help to him; the reply of most returned migrants, "In America I did something entirely different," makes this very clear. In fact, once again, it helps to reinforce the idea that the American experience remains for these people something in itself, apart, detached from present necessities and aspirations. [19]

On the other hand, however, a return to the land cannot help but reawaken and reanimate old feelings of bitterness. This return is politically characterized by the "reestablishment" of the returned migrant in his position of "peasant," suspicious, diffident toward the State and politics. As a logical consequence, control of the political life of the community remains in the hands of that "petty" bourgeoisie which, incapable of seeing beyond its own interests and jealous of its own position (which even if miserable is, at the community level,

---

[18] The assessment of the consequences of returned migrants on the whole seems to differ remarkably from that of Joseph Lopreato. See his *Peasants No More* (San Francisco: Chandler Publishing Company, 1967) where the author, basing his conclusions on a research monograph of a village in the South, speaks of the returned emigrants after World War II as constituting a "New middle class." For further comments on Mr. Lopreato's book, see my review of it in the *International Migration Review*, Vol. II (1968).

[19] In particular, the tendency to put money in safe investments, that is, investments which yield steady income such as the purchase of apartments as well as land, is widespread among returned migrants. This should have as a major consequence an inflow of money and a remarkable stimulus to production and consumption for the local economy. But this does not happen or happens only to a very slight degree because true modern building enterprises are completely lacking *in loco* and most construction is left to small firms at almost the artisan level, with backward methods which in the end are very expensive. Furthermore, a large part of this new income, instead of remaining in local circulation, flows out to purchase goods not produced locally. These are some of the considerations which demonstrate how the economic behavior of returned migrants has "conservative" consequences.

nevertheless prestigious), has come to identify itself with the status quo, reacting negatively to any agitation for change.

Considerations of this type are even simpler and clearer in their implications for the migrant who returns late in life, with the comfort and economic security of his pension and his savings. The return to Italy is regarded as a true act of retirement from all activity. "I am retired, you know," they repeated in reply to many questions, and some of them refused to be interviewed on the grounds that they had returned to Italy to live in absolute peace, determined that in no way and for no reason would that tranquility be disturbed. On the other hand, many of these retired migrants are ultra-cautious lest they commit some action which could somehow compromise their ties with the United States and, in particular, jeopardize the punctual arrival of their pension.[20] We would add that these returnees especially feel they are looked upon with envy, or more frequently with a kind of hostility, by the local population. Moreover their own attitude and behavior reinforce and qualify the name *Americani* which is usually attributed to them. It therefore follows that, on the whole, they live a life which in a certain sense is very marginal with respect to the rest of the community. Isolated as they seem to be, they tend to remain outside discussions of local problems and their influence on final decisions is usually negligible.

In conclusion, although many returned migrants criticized certain pecularities in the political order of the country and found certain economic and social customs unsatisfactory and inadequate, quite out of date, and so on, *their reabsorption into the life of the community has had no consequence of innovation on the economic or political patterns of behavior in the community itself.*

This conclusion becomes even more meaningful if we consider that these two types constitute the great majority of returns. This confirms empirically the validity of the premises on which the model described above is based.

---

[20] To what extent this "pension" seems sometimes to influence certain attitudes among returned migrants is illustrated by the case of two friends who had both emigrated to the United States and were called up to serve in the Italian army during the First World War. One returned to answer the call while the other joined the American Army. Now they find themselves together again in the village square, the former with his misery of an old peasant, bitter and resentful toward his country, the latter satisfied with the wisdom of his choice and the comfortable existence his American pension helps him maintain.

The factors determining the role the migrant plays upon return to his old community must be found principally in the aspirations, needs and attitudes which made him return. The milieu into which the returned migrant becomes reabsorbed seems to have the more passive function of a "recipient." His lack of innovative thrust corresponds to the absence of a stimulus to change on the part of the social environment into which he returned.

The understanding and assessment of the reciprocal influences between the attitude of returned migrant, and the social environment to which he returns — while quite clear and explicit in the case of these two types of returns — become much more problematic in the case of the return of innovation.

Return of Innovation

While some of the current literature discusses return migration, it almost always deals with cases which fit into the two types mentioned above; an analytical study of returns of innovation has yet to begin.[21]

As the preceding model indicates, this type of return occurs among individuals who broke with the society of departure, rejected some of its cultural traits and replaced them with others belonging to the new society. Thus, these returnees have their own aspirations, discover a new meaning of the value of their abilities, and finally seek new and greater rewards from their own work. They end up with a broader concept of society and a more complete sense of belonging to it.[22] In their case the search for a full sense of belonging to the new society seems to have been frustrated.

They seem to experience an increasing dissatisfaction with certain habits, certain ways of thinking, certain ways of enjoying life which they seem unable to adopt and toward which

---

[21] The awareness of this neglect has been expressed very recently in the article "Puerto Ricans: A Perspective on Return," op. cit.

[22] Some authors, including Handlin, op. cit., somehow neglect the importance of the fact that emigration, beyond the suffering and shocks it causes, provides an occasion for many emigrants to live for the first time outside of and in a reality completely different from that of their old village, freed as it were from the restrictions of century-old systems. However negative some of the consequences of this sharp, if not brutal, "liberation" may be, greater attention should be given to the positive effects which it can have, providing for some the only possibility of complete renewal of their own convictions and orientations.

they become intolerant. On the other hand they convince themselves that these elements of dissatisfaction would not persist if they returned to their country of origin. The very anticipation of the disappearance of these elements which frustrate them provides them with energy and enthusiasm, which they project outside the society of immigration toward their old society. The idea of returning becomes stronger. Conscious of the value of the new experiences and new means which their new work and life have allowed them to acquire, they look upon the return not simply as a reabsorption into something which existed before, but more as a search for a fuller affirmation of their own abilities.

However difficult the decision to return may be, once it is made it gives rise to completely new hopes. Everything learned in terms of new ways of thinking, work skills, values, is projected, when migrants think about returning, to their native country. They hope these new ideas will now serve through their actions to transform the old society in the same way that they have transformed them.

These considerations help to underscore the assertion that in the case of returnees of innovation the reciprocal influences between the attitudes of the immigrant and the milieu to which he returns are more problematic than in the other types of return. Moreover, who exactly are these returned migrants? What are the actual conditions they find upon return? What chance of success do they have? And how successful are they in realizing their goals? These are only some of the questions which urgently require thorough study. The results of the present study can only be considered preliminary, but they clarify some of the fundamental components of the problem. These are: scarcity in both absolute and relative numbers of innovating returnees, hostility or at least lack of encouragement at the local level and complete lack of interest at the national level toward them; and finally, as a direct consequence of the preceding facts, a powerlessness and lack of sufficient energy on the part of the returnees to introduce and establish, on their own, new models of behavior.

In the first place, if we agree that this type of returnee can be associated with an 11-20 year stay in the new society, or even only about ten years, the data in Table 4 show the scarcity of the type. This raises the first question: why are they so few? If the model described above is generally valid, we can assume that all those who surmount what we have called the second fundamental stage in the process of integration are potential subjects for innovative returnees. Why, then, does such a small percentage succumb to the temptation to return? Why does the return become for them a real "alternative," while the great majority obviously "resists," (except those who later on will return to retire, with quite the opposite consequence for the home country)?

The main reason, of course, can be found in the very nature of the process of integration. At this point the immigrant has reached a stage in which his attachment to the new society is very strong and a return implies another break, another separation from a community which has contributed in no small measure to his formation and has shared with him a long series of efforts and sufferings. But apart from that, what does the prospect of return offer as compared with the security of the present, even if at times this is a little bitter? This consideration prompts many to take a trip to Italy. When the migrant sees his relatives, his old friends, his village, his church, he continues to ask himself the meaning of the emotions which are aroused in him. Not only this: he tries to understand clearly what possibilities of being reabsorbed economically are open to him. Open a store, a restaurant, a hotel or simply find a job?[23] What jobs can he hope to get? Whom should he ask? Who can give him information and suggestions and who is willing to do so? How can he be sure of the good will and good intentions of those who offer their services? Where can he find at least a minimum guarantee that in case of need he can count on someone's help? Often it is the reply to these questions which prevents him from transforming his idea to return into a real alternative to his dissatisfaction with the society of immigration. The fear that the encouragement of his old friends may be dictated more by their hope to profit from his return than by a true understanding of his situation does not help to reassure him.[24]

It was stated earlier that the second basic component of the set of problems related to the reabsorption of this type of returned migrant can be found, at least in part, in the attitude

---

[23] This is above all the case of those who think of returning to a town or city. How many are there who after an unfruitful and useless trial period, choose to return to their country of immigration?

[24] And with this doubt in mind, he may return to America.

of the local ruling class,[25] that collection of economic interests which manages to maintain a surprising equilibrium among its component "forces" through a distribution of the local political power and patronage.

It is surprising how this balance seems to remain substantially intact in spite of apparent political upsets. Whatever the results of the frequent political elections, the subtle logic of compromise bids everyone come to agreement quickly. Certainly it is not external forces which can threaten this equilibrium. The source of greatest danger is in fact, a disruption of this balance from some new internal situation.

It can be stated that return migration of the "innovation" type, *if properly encouraged or even organized, can in the long run furnish a force disrupting the old balance.* No doubt this is how it is seen by large sectors of the local ruling class. The latter, quite accustomed to other types of returnees, who reinforce the old equilibrium, grow quickly suspicious of any returned migrant who shows no interest in buying a miserable little piece of land or who does not content himself with depositing his money in the post office and spending his time sitting in the local café.

It seems very important in this regard to observe who among the migrants interviewed said they had particular difficulties in their relationship with the local population. If we exclude those who have had unpleasant experiences with small businessmen and other villagers who tried to take advantage of them dishonestly on the grounds that they are "rich *Americani,*" we find that those who tried upon their return to introduce some innovation had the most bitter comments in this regard. In their case the term *Americano* assumes a very different connotation. *Americano* means above all some one who got rich, no one knows how — "as if money alone is enough to change people!" — or someone who thinks he can do who knows what — "but he'll learn and pay for it at the same time!" It is also interesting to note that these observations are expressed not so much by big landowners or party leaders as by representatives of that middle stratum which

---

[25] There exists now a rich literature on the Southern ruling class. The most effective pages perhaps are to be found in the writings of the *meridionalisti,* especially Guido Dorso. More recently Grazia Dore in her *La democrazia italiana e l'emigrazione in America* (Brescia: Morcelliana, 1964) has singled out just as effectively the interests which have determined the attitude of this ruling class toward emigration.

persists in seeing any chance for social mobility only within the limits of the difficult game of clientelism tied to the old order.

What is the returned migrant's reaction to all this? He faces the situation alone and he soon realizes that he has only one choice: accept these conditions or else move to a big city where no one realizes his presence and where it would surely be difficult for him to start something which would really bother anyone.

We met a few of those who insisted on remaining and tried to realize the projects for which they had returned.[26] What had they to say about their life experience since their return? In particular how were they received by the public authorities, on the local and national level, and what kind of contact did they have with them? What emerges, more than anything else, is the bitter recognition of the administrative abuse of authority,[27] as one of them insisted on defining it. First the building permit never arrives, then the commercial license is refused. But why, after all, persist in wanting to do things one's way? Compromise is possible. "That's how things are done here." Once one enters into the game, the same old ways repeat themselves. No alternative is offered.

It must be noted that there are really very few returned migrants of the "innovation" type to be found in the villages and small towns of the South who upon their return have the means to set up, on their own, a new type of farm that helps to implement land reform, for example, or to build a hotel with a view to exploiting the tourist possibilities of the area. And even when there are more than one, it cannot be assumed that together they constitute a strong enough force because they almost always return at different times and by the time the second or third arrives, the first has already been "absorbed."

The case of those whose means are more limited is more

---

[26] Speaking of one of these with a young technician in the small town to which this emigrant had returned, the former commented, "You should have seen him when he first arrived, full of energy and enthusiasm. But look at him now, after three years; he's tired, always with a defeated expression on his face. He couldn't make it with the local mafia and he had to accept the dubious honor of clientelism."

[27] A widespread abuse of authority, affecting all aspects of the life of the community and, the interviewee pointed out, "sometimes it is even a matter of arbitrary authority which I can't understand."

dramatic. Whatever innovations they have in mind, and however convinced they are of their superiority, the energy at their disposal is insufficient to overcome the obstacles which oppose the realization of their projects. Once their enthusiasm has dwindled, their first effort at innovation withers away. Then, depending upon age and means, they soon join the ranks of the conservative returnees who buy a piece of land and become resigned to the idea, "What else is there to do here?" The idea then becomes an inescapable reality, or else they withdraw within their new house on the outskirts of the village and retire like so many others.

As we reflect on these problems it seems obvious to ask what role the ruling class on the national level has assumed in regard to return migration. In contrast to all the discussions and publicity about encouraging or discouraging emigration, there is a complete lack of interest, if not of "policy" with respect to migrants who return.

If we are to believe in the sincerity of the many programs dedicated to encouraging the much desired entrepreneurship at the local level — and the preceding considerations have thrown sufficient light on the important contribution that a certain type of returned migrant could make — the reception reserved for the returnee ought to be quite different and his contact with public officials should not be limited to the tax collector, the local chief of police and the municipal registry office, with their annoying, insistent questions about his citizenship. It is no wonder that he resumes an attitude of persistent diffidence toward the state.

With the exception of those whose return is one of failure and, in a particular way, those who return to retire, the returned migrant is a very different person from what he was when he left 5, 10 or 20 years previously. Due to the difference stemming from the new means he possesses, the new ideas and aspirations which occupy his thoughts, or simply from the memory of a different way of living which he experienced, it is very likely that his reaction to certain events, certain stimuli is quite different from what it would have been had he never emigrated. However simple and generic this observation may seem, it should be sufficient to emphasize the necessity of according him a new kind of reception geared to the rightful acknowledgement of this difference as a valid potential for renovation of backward forms of behavior.

It suffices here to point out the concrete possibilities

inherent in an action which would serve not only to counteract the consequences of the hostility of the local ruling class but, with a much larger scope in mind, would lay the basis for a program of agrarian reform. For example, there could be action to encourage and direct the resources and energy of those who return with new ideas which could provide a real alternative to a return of conservatism. Such action could pave the way for new types of investment, a new chance to work and to advance socially, the beginning of an economic and social reality which would be really different. In the first place, it is essential to eliminate or at least restrain the squandering of savings accumulated with so much sacrifice. We might think of some kind of cooperative association, for example, to focus this limited energy on some feasible enterprise.[28] Above all, it must be repeated, there is need to provide a clear indication that the migrant's own efforts and capabilities can be oriented toward some undertaking — other than land — which, with a quite different kind of economic security, can guarantee social mobility outside the traditional scheme, the limits of which his migratory experience has enabled him to recognize.

---

[28] In this perspective, the importance of such a policy of intervention becomes even more evident if we take into account the possibility it has of absorbing the means and the energy of the mass of emigrants which is constantly on the move between Southern Italy and North-Central Europe, apparently confused by their own purposes and interests. During the conversation with the young technician referred to in note 26, we discussed the backwardness of the construction methods and modes of production in general, in spite of the fact that often workers who had worked abroad with very advanced techniques were employed. The conclusion emerged that because they lacked a theoretical and cultural preparation and were incapable of acquiring it during the emigration period, whatever specialized work experience they had abroad, once it was extracted from the economic system to which it belonged, became something apart, useless, unless a whole new system of production could be introduced into the old community. But it is also these specialized skills which a program of intervention should take into account, providing the guidelines for their utilization.

Selected Bibliography

by *Francesco Cerase*

There are very few studies which specifically deal with the problem of returned migrants and their reabsorption in the social system of their homeland. None deals solely with returning Italian migrants. Students interested in this long neglected research field will find the following sources helpful: Theodore Salutos, *They Remember America: The Story of Repatriated Greek-Americans* (Berkeley: University of California Press, 1956); William H. Form and Julius Rivers, "The Place of Returning Migrants in a Stratification System," *Rural Sociology* 23 (1958); a research on Dutch migrants by N. H. Frijda, "Emigration Overseas," in G. Beijer *et al.*, *Characteristics of Overseas Migrants*; and George C. Myers and George Masnick, "The Migration Experience of New York Puerto Ricans: A Perspective on Return," *The International Migration Review* 2 (Spring 1968), 80-90, *Studi Emigrazione* IV (1967), 173-81, George R. Gilkey, "The United States and Italy; Migration and Repatriation," in *The Journal of Developing Areas* (1967), 23-35.

More recently return migration has aroused the interest of international organizations, such as the O.C.D.E., which has organized a seminar on the problems of returned migrants; see *Les travailleurs émigrés retournant dans leurs pays* (Paris, 1967). Finally, students conversant with Italian will find very useful, Antonio Perotti, *Programmazione e rientro degli emigrati*, Centro Studi Emigrazione (Rome, 1967).

E 184 .I8 T6 1977 c.1
Tomasi, Silvano M.,
The Italian experience in
 the United States

DATE DUE

NOV 1 2 2003	
GAYLORD	PRINTED IN U.S.A.